AMERICAN POETRY SINCE 1960

—some critical perspectives—

AMERICAN POETRY SINCE 1960

–some critical perspectives–

edited by Robert B. Shaw, 1947–

A CARCANET PRESS PUBLICATION

Printed in Great Britain
by W & J Mackay Limited, Chatham

For
JOHN BERRYMAN
1914–1972

. . . flame may his glory in that other place
for he was fond of fame, devoted to it,
and every first-rate soul
has sacrifices which it puts in play,
I hope he's sitting with his peers : sit, sit,
& recover & be whole.

—Dream Song 157—

Footnotes have been placed at the ends of chapters. A reading list, following chapter order, is provided on page 209.

This is the second volume in Carcanet's Critical Series. Already published is *British Poetry Since 1960 : a critical survey*, edited by Michael Schmidt and Grevel Lindop. Forthcoming is *New Irish Writing*, edited by Douglas Dunn and Michael Schmidt.

Contents

Preface

THIS BOOK of essays offers a multi-focussed view of American poetry since 1960. While it does not aim to be an all-embracing survey, it takes account of many of the period's salient features, of reputations inflated or deservedly attained, of achievements dubious or assured. Despite the last sentence I should hasten to say that a Johnsonian balance has not been too severely maintained in the ensuing contents. The majority of these critics are favorably disposed toward the poets they are scrutinizing; and their essays, in any case, tend to be descriptive rather than prescriptive or polemical. Beyond seeing that high spots were hit my plans in commissioning these essays have been few and simple. I have enlisted critics who have an informed and intense engagement with their subjects. And I have taken pains to choose critics who are not all of the same stripe. Some of my contributors are at the beginning, some in the midst of their careers; some are themselves practising poets while others have confined their energies to criticism and the classroom. They are various in their enthusiasms. Were all of them assembled in one room to discuss contemporary poetry it is likely that there would be more sparring than spontaneous accord. I believe this book has avoided the bland uniformity of tone and outlook which characterizes many such collections. But even as I read these essays over, enjoying their heterogeneity, the mind's rage for order asserts itself; and somewhat to my dismay I discern the currents of shared assumptions below the surface diversity. It may be useful here to point to a few of this volume's recurring themes. Readers who dislike generalizations or prefer to make their own may pass on to the essays without further ado.

I note first that these essays support the prevalent view of 'sixties poetry as a poetry of revolt. Both in style and choice of subject, poets during this decade were dissenting from the modernist school of poetics derived from Eliot and Pound and still ascendant in the 'fifties. *Howl* might not have been enough to shatter the hegemony of academic formalism, but *Life Studies* certainly signalled its declining power. The basic challenge, whether it came from Ginsberg or Lowell, was directed against the Eliotic cult of impersonality. The poet no longer hedged himself about with ironic literary allusions, but presented the reader with (we were asked to believe) unvarnished portraits of himself, the more warts the better. The full complexity of confessionalism is only now beginning to be sifted by critics. Some questions: Are we to think that authenticity is a *necessary* virtue in a poem any more than impersonality was? Are Sylvia Plath's poems to be seen as "authenticated" by her suicide? What makes a poem authentic: fidelity to truths of human nature or to particular circumstances of the poet's life? Are confessional poems, however personal their content, really less "literary" than Eliot and Pound? (Think of Ginsberg's use of the Bible, Blake, Whitman and Christopher Smart.) These questions have a haziness about them which is in keeping with the amorphous quality of the confessionalist movement: it has always seemed less a movement than an ill-defined crowd.

As if the personalization of content had not complicated the discussion sufficiently, the accompanying changes in verbal and metrical style must be evaluated as well. Free verse of the William Carlos Williams variety, gaining ground during the 'fifties, carried the field in the next decade. To be sure, there remain notable poets who habitually make use of traditional forms: one could name for a start Elizabeth Bishop, Richard Wilbur, W. D. Snodgrass, Howard Nemerov, John Hollander, James Merrill and Anthony Hecht. These poets are all, however, over forty years of age, and it would be impossible to point to as many poets in the generation following theirs who write in rhyme and meter. In Massachusetts X. J. Kennedy has recently begun publishing a magazine called *Counter/Measures* which prints only metrical poems. It is to appear once a year: this modest publication schedule suggests some not very surprising facts about supply and demand. Some critics see in current verse the final triumph of the imagist movement; in a kind of McLuhanite millennium the visual quality has subdued the aural to a murmuring inconsequence. We might take this opinion more seriously if the fad for concrete poetry had been anything more than a fad. The most insistently visual poems must still employ words, and the human race has not yet developed the knack of reading a poem without listening to how it sounds, and judging it at least partially on that account. I think, more simply, that the trend toward free verse is a logical adjunct of the revolt against impersonality. Traditional metrics are seen as hindering the unique voice from achieving its full expression. While I do not hold this view myself, there is no doubt that many American poets from Whitman on have come to hold it after frustrating struggles with the fixities of meter. Lowell is not the only formalist who has unfettered his style, as the studies included here of W. S. Merwin and Adrienne Rich will show. A connection hard to define may exist between radicalism in poetic style and in politics. If so, it is ironic that the American myth of development, of the necessity of disowning the past by crossing established boundaries, should be reflected so conspicuously in the careers of poets who abhor the political consequences of that myth. To counter the oppressions of the expanding State, our poets have sought out a style that will promote an expansion of the empire of the self.

Such expansiveness is nowhere more evident than in the trend toward the longer poem, which comes in for consideration in more than one of these essays. What is important is not the fact of greater length—the refusal to be enclosed in the lyric moment—but the solipsistic character of these poems. They are not third-person narratives; they are epics of self, or, to put it less grandly, diaries (rather than novels) in verse. They present the sufferings and ambiguous triumphs of an individual consciousness moving through time and trying to come to terms with it. By the amassing of mutually reflective units (not one Dream Song but 385) each momentary perception is submerged in the flux of the whole. The only constant is the voice of the poet, or (as in the case of Berryman) that of his surrogate character.

I could examine some more minute aspects of the ego's search for a new sublimity, but I think that several of my essayists have performed that task admirably; and I should not wish to steal any thunder from them, or (what is more likely) summarize too crudely their finer perceptions. Let me close by noting a trend which appears to run counter to what I have discussed thus far. I mean the "primitivism" of such poets as Snyder, Wright and others, which Alan Williamson elucidates so sensitively in his essay. Such poetry tries to avoid egoism by posing as *tribal* speech; rather than pit himself against society the poet washes his hands of society altogether and heads off (in body or spirit, no matter which) to join the Iroquois. Can a language so easily shuck off the civilization that formed it? The title of Williamson's piece, "Language Against Itself", suggests the dilemma these poets face, and I refer the reader to his treatment of the problem. Poetry invoking a group-consciousness, of course, is nothing new to blacks. Fear of the oppressive majority fosters solidarity among the oppressed. That a kind of ghetto mentality should have developed among middle-class white poets over the past several years indicates how desperately alienated they have become from their fellow countrymen. Most Americans find current poetry obscure, and for good reason. The poetry is grounded in assumptions so distant from the solid citizen's way of thinking that it might as well be framed in a foreign tongue. Writing on the eve of a second Nixon administration, I see no reason to suppose that this gulf will be narrowed in the foreseeable future. Like the Russians, we have among us a band of internal emigrés, a few who write and a slightly larger number who read what is written—the only clean reading, perhaps, in an age grown gray with newsprint. For this audience American poets continue to fulfil their chosen duty. That duty remains what it has always been: in the words of the dead Master to whom this book is dedicated, it is "to terrify & comfort".

Robert B. Shaw

Appointments with Time:
Robert Lowell's Poetry
through the *Notebooks*
by Frances Ferguson

WHEN WALT WHITMAN organized his "Song of Myself" into 52 sections in the original 1855 edition of *Leaves of Grass*, that 52-part design was itself a manifestation of Whitman's repeated assertion of the interpenetration between himself—or his selves—and the universe of time progressing through weeks. As a unifying device, this numerology represents one mode of translating the poetic object, with all its presence, into the realm of temporal process and recurrence. The numerology symbolically unifies the poem with the idea of the temporal process out of which it was constituted; but its very obvious factitiousness constitutes an assault on the independent, internal unity of the poem. The poem-as-object falls prey to the ravages of process, becomes "subject to revision"—as Whitman himself demonstrated by changing it for the 1860 edition.

Over the last century, the poet's struggle with time has become increasingly conspicuous, if not more intense. A poet like Eliot figures a paradox implicit in the struggle: by pointedly reducing numerous poems to their fragments in order to be able to create his own poem, "The Waste Land", the poet calls into question the historical endurance of the work of other poets and, simultaneously, the endurance of every poem of his own which has come into being before the immediate present. Emerson had earlier, in a journal entry for May 28, 1839, insisted that

> There is no history. There is only biography. The attempt to perpetuate, to fix a thought or principle, fails continually. You can only live for yourself; your action is good only whilst it is alive,—whilst it is in you. The awkward imitation of it by your child or your disciple is not a repetition of it, is not the same thing, but another thing. The new individual must work out the whole problem of science, letters and theology for himself; can owe his fathers nothing. There is no history; only biography.[1]

The modern poet compounds Emerson's anti-historical subjectivity by dwelling upon the passage of biography—and autobiography—into history. From the time of Wordsworth, the poem already in print has come increasingly to seem a tombstone upon the consciousness which constituted it before the endless wave of Heraclitean flux overwhelmed it.

Poetry must take place in the present, and the modern poet sees that present as an ellipsis which must be broadened and filled to keep the ever-encroaching past from colliding with the future. When T. S. Eliot makes poetry out of self-evaluation in "East Coker" ("That was a way of putting it—not very satisfactory:/ A periphrastic study in a worn-out poetical fashion"), the pastness of his own past words is as onerous as the pastness of the "worn-out poetical fashion" of previous poets. Since "every moment is a new and shocking/ Valuation of all we have been," new patterns must end-lessly be found if the present is to be seen under the aspect of meaningfulness.

Robert Lowell's career has exemplified in every phase this perspective which I have identified as "modern"—the thrust towards ever-more-direct confrontations with time. Both *Land of Unlikeness* and its impressive sequel, *Lord Weary's Castle*, reinvigorate conventional forms while courting a future of apocalypse. Filtering his vision of contemporary America through the context of a sordid American tradition, Lowell achieves tremendous power by an almost total rejection of the present. The apocalypse follows hard upon the sins of America's past, and the poet treats the time from which he prophesies as minimal. The violence of language and tone in Lowell's early poems suggests that the poet-prophet behind them already finds himself surrounded by the sparks of the "fire next time," after which there will be no next time.

It seems to me that Lowell very rightly recognized that poems like "Dea Roma" and "Where the Rainbow Ends" were not susceptible of infinite proliferation: they very nearly deny themselves the time in which they have come into being, and they too are charred by the fire which they describe and invoke. In the early poems, Lowell attempts to outwit time by making poetry out of the open admission that time has won the contest with human consciousness. But the poetry is a poetry which can only document its own existence in terms of pyrrhicism.

There may have been silence in heaven after the final prophetic notes of *Land of Unlikeness* and *Lord Weary's Castle*, but the earth had heard such apocalypticism before, without having halted in its course or in its speech. Lowell's heavily allusive language itself pointed the paradox. Although Lowell translated the words of Thoreau, Melville, Jonathan Edwards, the Bible, and a host of others into his own prophecies of the final end, a continuity was implied in the act of translation which produced "The Quaker Graveyard in Nantucket". If Lowell was to continue to write, he had to see his own apocalypse as a temporizing gesture, a beginning rather than an ending.

Although the two earliest volumes of Lowell's poems present themselves as poetry of vision, Lowell substitutes for this a poetics of revision in subsequent work. On the most basic level, even *Lord Weary's Castle* is a revision of *Land of Unlikeness*. A passage from "Cistercians in Germany" (*Land of Unlikeness*) is rewritten to form the ending of "At the Indian Killer's Grave" (*Lord Weary's Castle*); poems like "The Quaker Graveyard in Nantucket" provide *Lord Weary's Castle* an air of completeness which *Land of Unlikeness* lacked. But the varieties of revision embedded within both early volumes come to represent, in the later work, both an embryonic subject and a means for the continuation of the poetic enterprise. When Lowell borrows—or "steals"—from Thoreau, Melville, or Milton in "The Quaker Graveyard", he has already begun to reach beyond the simplest interpretations of Pound's command, "Make it new," and has pointed to a self-conscious treatment of literary works as existing and enduring objects—objects which endure largely through their capacity to change under the pressure of the perceiving consciousness. Just as Eliot's "Animula" and "Marina" simultaneously assert the continued existence of Dante's verses[2] and Shakespeare's *Pericles* and also explore a road not taken by the earlier poets, so Lowell's "The Quaker Graveyard" establishes itself through revision, seeing again.

Imitation—seen as a repetition constituting re-vision—is not Lowell's attempt to supplant all previous literature. Rather, it represents his recognition that poetry documents the movement of consciousness—which can only be living—upon the objects of consciousness—which have an observable existence but no living consciousness. In the eyes of Lowell-as-poet, all previous literature exists initially as an aggregation of enduring objects and, eventually and significantly, as an index to a once-living consciousness which can be renewed by an altering re-vision. If Emerson and Stevens directed their attention to the consciousness acting upon the objects of the world, Lowell constructs an imaginative order in which the new poem may openly take those very acts of consciousness as objects for a new subjective creation.

What I want to maintain is that Lowell (in *Life Studies*, *Imitations*, and *For the Union Dead*) was adding a complication to the complex dualism from which Emerson insists that

> A man should know himself for a necessary actor. A link was wanted between two craving parts of nature, and he was hurled into being as a bridge over that yawning need, the mediator betwixt two else unmarriageable facts.[3]

For Lowell, poetry becomes a process of engaging the mind of an additional mediator, so that an additional personal and historical time can be recaptured from the other side of inevitable temporal disjunction. Lowell both performs his own mediation between personal time and transcendent time and also introduces the necessity for mediating between his own mediation and the mediations of other consciousnesses. The poet thus becomes both the "mediator betwixt two else unmarriageable facts" and the mediator between two else unmarriageable mediators.

Even in *Life Studies*, the book which has repeatedly been regarded as the poetic autobiography which instituted the contemporary school of "confessional poetry", Lowell was writing a very peculiar sort of confession, because the disjunction between the Robert Lowell writing in the present and the past Robert Lowells which he describes immediately introduces a disjunction between Robert Lowell and other subjectivities external to him. The effort to recapture his own past selves tends to accompany an effort to recapture other past selves.

What initially appear to be the most intensely personal, unborrowed poems in *Life Studies*, poems about Lowell's struggles against madness and the collapse of his first marriage, frequently rely upon complicated movements of the Lowellian speaker into and out of the consciousnesses of various literary characters. "Home after Three Months Away" may serve as an instance of this movement.

> Gone now the baby's nurse,
> a lioness who ruled the roost
> and made the Mother cry.
> She used to tie
> gobbets of porkrind in bowknots of gauze—
> three months they hung like soggy toast
> on our eight foot magnolia tree,
> and helped the English sparrows
> weather a Boston winter.
>
> Three months, three months!
> Is Richard now himself again?
> Dimpled with exaltation,
> my daughter holds her levee in the tub.
> Our noses rub,
> each of us pats a stringy lock of hair—
> they tell me nothing's gone.
> Though I am forty-one,
> not forty now, the time I put away
> was child's-play. After thirteen weeks
> my child still dabs her cheeks
> to start me shaving. When
> we dress her in her sky-blue corduroy,
> she changes to a boy,
> and floats my shaving brush
> and washcloth in the flush. . . .
> Dearest, I cannot loiter here
> in lather like a polar bear.
>
> Recuperating, I neither spin nor toil.
> Three stories down below,
> a choreman tends our coffin's length of soil,
> and seven horizontal tulips blow.
> Just twelve months ago,
> these flowers were pedigreed
> imported Dutchmen; now no one need
> distinguish them from weed.

> Bushed by the late spring snow,
> they cannot meet
> another year's snowballing enervation.
>
> I keep no rank nor station.
> Cured, I am frizzled, stale and small.

Here, Lowell engages poetry to cordon off the time that was wrested from him by insanity. The talismans left by a now-departed nurse ("gobbets of porkrind" left for the birds) linger to remind Lowell, who has just returned from a mental hospital, of the days before he left home, three months before. And seeing these talismans as physical reminders of lost time, he marks that lost time by repeating "Three months, three months!" before asking with irony, "Is Richard now himself again?" Although this mocking query directly echoes Collie Cibber's adaptation of *Richard III*,[4] Lowell here seems to be casting his returning, though fleeting, identity in the image of Richard II, the poet-king who also bears the marks of a man-poet continually "beside himself," torn between the nothing and the all of his sense of himself. Numbers beat through the poem like notations of broken time—numerical images of the disjointed music in which Richard II images his life.

> . . . How sour sweet music is,
> When time is broke and no proportion kept!
> So is it in the music of men's lives.
> And here have I the daintiness of ear
> To check time broke in a disordered string;
> But for the concord of my state and time
> Had not an ear to hear my true time broke.
> I wasted time, and now doth Time waste me;
> For now hath Time made me his numb'ring clock.[5]

Lowell identifies no coherent selfhood for himself in the poem as he climbs down the chain of being—going from Richard, to polar bear, to dead tulips in his imaging of himself. There is no explicit debate between Lowell's divided selves like that which one recognizes in Richard II—only the abbreviated notation of temporal disjunction in "three months away" echoing from the title. There is no progression in time through the course of the poem—only the consciously exaggerated emphasis upon blocks of time which have evaded Lowell. But Lowell creates an identifiable unity through the complicated allusion to Richard II which dominates the poem. The identification of himself with Richard provides a coherent focus for the absence or multiplicity of selves; it filters the apparently random sequence of images through the memory of Richard's cry, "My thoughts are moments." Lowell's allusiveness here represents an insistence that two disorders (Richard's and his own) make an order, that an order can be salvaged from the surrender to time.

For all its brilliance, Lowell's use of allusion in "Home after Three Months Away" represents a danger. Implicit in the identification with Richard II and in the surrealistic juxtapositions of the poem is a recognition that order must be imported, because the poem takes place so squarely in the present moment that it can find unity only in analogizing itself to images of other disorders. The radical shorthand of Lowell's link between himself and Richard II stabilizes the poem, but without any sense of limit. The personae of Lowell's autobiographical poems and the images of the poems seem constantly to find no rest within themselves and to point out giddily in all directions toward the external infinite—"no circumference anywhere,/ the center everywhere,"[6] Lowell everywhere.

In *Notebook: 1967–68* (1969) and *Notebook* (1970), the problems inherent in Lowell's allusive techniques have been multiplied, and they have, I think, been met less successfully than in *Life Studies, For the Union Dead*, and *Near the Ocean*. The two editions of *Notebook: 1967–68* gesture compulsively toward the world of experience beyond the poems, and *Notebook* compounds the self-conscious inadequacy of these gestures with an additional appeal to temporal process. Although Lowell declares in the "Afterthought" to both volumes[7] that "the time [of the whole volume] is a summer, an autumn, a winter, a spring, another summer" and that his "plot rolls with the seasons," he obviously increases the dependence of his poems on temporal schemata in *Notebook* by adding enough poems to turn each poem into a token of a calendar day. By the time one has read through "The End", one has read 366 poems, one poem for each day of a leap year; and the coda of nine poems similarly refers one to the world of time in the sequence "Half a Century Gone", in which one poem is offered up to each decade of Lowell's life. The coincidence between the numerical patterns of *Notebook* and the year implicitly postulates a kind of unity which enables Lowell to insist that "the poems in this book are written as one poem,"[8] but this is a coherence so postulated and so little felt that each individual poem in the volume tends to become indexical. Each poem is less an entity than a reminder of the existence of the others; individual poems—and individual words— undergo devaluation in the notebooks.

From *Life Studies* through *Near the Ocean*, Lowell mitigated his impatience with both words and the world of temporal process with a dogged, exacting scrutiny of specific words and objects. Poems like "My Father's Bedroom" (*Life Studies*), "Jonathan Edwards in Western Massachusetts" and "Hawthorne" (*For the Union Dead*) and "Fourth of July in Maine" (*Near the Ocean*) hang on phrases and physical objects as persistent emblems of the inner minds of the figures about and to whom Lowell writes his verse portrait letters. He accords both words and objects the dignity of endurance, extending Emerson's observation that "A man may find his words mean more than he thought when he uttered them, and be glad to employ them in a new sense"[9] to give a new sense to the words and objects of other men. In these "middle" volumes, Lowell's language takes on a subdued form of power as his confidence in the inherent freshness of each repeated use of a word appears. Setting the same word down repeatedly, so that the various instances emerge with the force of a new word each time, balances the aggravated insistence upon double meaning in the early work. This linguistic balance points to a heightened, far-ranging conception of *rime riche*, in which word-retentiveness becomes equivalent to the retentiveness of consciousness. Although this poetry recognizes its ability to recapture consciousnesses lost to time as limited (especially in a poem like "Jonathan Edwards in Western Massachusetts"), Lowell's repetition of his own words and his repetition of the words of others becomes a chant against the erosions of time.

In the notebooks, certain stylistic elements of Lowell's conception of *rime riche* remain. In the third poem of "Harriet", one of the finest sequences in the notebooks, "wood" rhymes itself repeatedly, with a slight difference at each occurrence as the consciousness of the aging process advances itself step by step. The tone of such devices has, however, shifted towards a recklessness which asserts that words and the human consciousness behind them are so fragmented by the temporal process that repetition is no longer incremental. Lowell's notebooks document the movement of a spirit untinged but tarnished by its strain. For all of the labor involved in producing their sheer bulk, they bespeak a passivity, a succumbing to process. Lowell, "learning to live in history," produces a book of poems that is history only by Lowell's interpretation of it—"What you cannot touch."[10] Lines stick in the memory—occasionally even a whole poem here and there, but the fragmentation of perspective has reached such an extreme that the notebooks finally seem to dedicate themselves to the "horrifying mortmain of ephemera."[11]

Each volume of the notebooks is, as Lowell explains, "less an almanac" than the story of his life.[12] Each is his daily life, with dailiness seen in terms of previous Lowell poems, previous poems and prose by other writers, the lives of previous writers, the lives of various historical and literary characters, the future of his daughter, and the future of the world. Although the posited relationship between each poem and the course of a year lodges the poems firmly in the present, the present also has to bear the weight of infinite time. In the poetry from *Life Studies* through *Near the Ocean*, Lowell depended upon the organizing powers of memory to rescue vanishing emblems; in the notebooks, he rushes to change before those emblems can have been admitted even as "sad,/ slight useless things to calm the mad" ("Waking Early Sunday Morning", *Near the Ocean*). The poetry of the notebooks is a poetry of restlessness. And Lowell casts his restlessness into justification and example in poems like "The Nihilist as Hero", the first poem in the sequence "We Do What We Are".

. . .

One wants words meat-hooked from the living steer,
but the cold flame of tinfoil licks the metal log,

the beautifully unchanging fire of childhood
betraying a monotony of vision.
Life by definition breeds on change,
each season we scrap new cars and wars and women.
Sometimes when I am ill or delicate,
the pinched flame of my match turns living green
the cornstalk in green tails and seeded tassel. . . .
A nihilist has to live in the world as is,
gazing the impossible summit to rubble.[13]

Image-making—and the imagination itself—burst through the bland pessi-
mism of the bulk of the poem as the "pinched flame" is transfigured into a
"living green/ the cornstalk in green tails and seeded tassel." But Lowell
allows himself only this two-line moment of insight before annihilating it
with a doctrinal pronouncement. In the earlier version of this poem, Lowell
concluded with the ambiguity of

Only a nihilist desires the world
to be as it is, or much more passable.[14]

By allowing the poetic consciousness the possibility of discovering the "more
passable" as the more tolerable for even a moment, the ambiguity of these
lines validates the image-making which precedes them. In the later version
of the poem, however, Lowell closes the poem by reduction in announcing
the dictates of the "world as is" to his poetic self. However strong the imagination may appear in its Joshuan capacity to tumble "the impossible summit,"
"rubble" seems a paltry product—a fallen Babel rather than a Jericho won.
As in the poem, "For John Berryman",[15] with its crashing, self-reflexive
punning on "working through words" (". . . you/ know what I have worked
through—these are words. . . ."), Lowell denies both his words and his
images any but the briefest possible duration. There is no ending to this kind
of poetic process, because it passes time by endless cancellations of every new
moment. The re-vision represented in the notebooks disdains the orders
which can be constructed from a new penetration of the objects of memory;
and although the poetry is occasional, it rests upon a fundamental impatience
with the occasional. Re-vision, here, is the recognition that the moment
which Lowell has just admitted into the present has already passed away, so
that Lowell can only look back over his shoulder at his rejections as he moves
towards the future.

Perhaps the most disputed boundary in poetry and criticism from the time
of Pound and Eliot to the present is the line between change and chaos.
Poetry—like that of Lowell's notebooks—which takes for subject the temporal "world as is" continually seeks that uncharted line and tries to walk it.
But a demon guards that line from too-near-approach; and the demon is
always the monotony of change—the dullness of chaos—which infects a poem
like "The Nihilist as Hero". In the midst of the ceaseless change in Lowell's

notebooks, a future must endlessly be postulated, a future in which all will be made well—and given significance. "Reading Myself", the final poem in the sequence "We Do What We Are", is perhaps the most explicit of Lowell's manifestos of this dedication to the future. Summarizing his previous poetic career, Lowell derisively describes himself:

> I memorized tricks to set the river on fire,
> somehow never wrote something to go back to.

However impossible it may be to step twice in the same river, to step a second time in a river of fire is unimaginable, and Lowell sees himself as having burned his rivers along with his bridges. The poem breaks off, shifts to describe a poetry which treats its own lack of finality as a mark of promise:

> No honeycomb is built without a bee,
> adding circle to circle, cell to cell,
> the wax and honey of a mausoleum—
> this round dome proves its maker is alive,
> the corpse of such insect lives preserved in honey,
> prays that the perishable work live long
> enough for the sweet-tooth bear to desecrate—
> this open book . . . my open coffin.

Instead of the rubble of "The Nihilist as Hero", Lowell extracts building materials in "Reading Myself". The "wax flowers" of continually satisfying, contained poems past change are converted into their essence, the wax and honey of a mausoleum never complete as long as the poet remains a continuing subjectivity. Lowell's distrust of his own past poetical moments—which is, for the most part, a radical distrust throughout the notebooks—persists in "Reading Myself", but the one poem which will include all of his poems hangs over the imagery as an emblem of future, transcendent justification.

The scarcity of Lowell's appeals—implicit or otherwise—to any sort of justification in the notebooks yields a poetry which has already provoked numerous critics to *pro forma* complaints about the obscurity of modern poetry in general and Lowell's notebooks in particular. Lowell certainly seems to court obscurity in choosing his poetic materials: "I have taken from many books, used the throwaway conversational inspirations of my friends, and much more that I idly spoke to myself."[16] Although one imagines that most poets find their materials in much the same way (as Wordsworth was certainly doing in poems like "We Are Seven"[17]), Lowell's description of his borrowing from literature and life is notable for its insistence upon the obliquity of his materials. The stuff of his poetry in the notebooks, we are told, is necessarily obscure, because Lowell is continually writing from a process of intense and random personalization.

The degree to which Lowell adheres to the personalization of his materials —the degree to which Lowell shuns the universalization and stabilization of his materials—becomes striking when one contrasts a poem like Randall

Jarrell's "Well Water" with almost any of Lowell's sonnets in the notebooks.
Jarrell opens his poem with a "throwaway conversational inspiration" that
announces itself as such ("What a girl called 'the dailiness of life'"). In
Jarrell's treatment, however, that "throwaway" inspiration has to be reasoned
through, explicated, and cast into images. "'The dailiness of life'"

> . . . is well water
> Pumped from an old well at the bottom of the world.
> The pump you pump the water from is rusty
> And hard to move and absurd, a squirrel-wheel
> A sick squirrel turns slowly, through the sunny
> Inexorable hours. And yet sometimes
> The wheel turns of its own weight, the rusty
> Pump pumps over your cold sweating face the clear
> Water, cold, so cold! you cup your hands
> And gulp from them the dailiness of life.

The monotonous repetition of the *petit quotidian* transforms itself in the last
four and a half lines into the repetitiveness of a psalm-singer. Although the
images of the poem move from pump-handle through squirrel-wheel with
an obvious nonchalance about the laws of the physical universe, "Well
Water" finds a point of rest beyond its own randomness and illogicality.
For the poem concludes with the kind of benevolent pragmatism which allows
one a moment of naive shamelessness in which to suggest hopefully that even
randomness and pain may have saving, unfathomable purposiveness.

Jarrell's "Well Water" is a useful contrast to most of the poems in Lowell's
notebooks, because it uses a "throwaway conversational inspiration" to drive
a wedge into the sense of oppressive temporality. However strong Jarrell's
distrust of words may have been at other moments (as in "*Seele im Raum*",
for example), he here appropriates the random phrase and allows the mind's
retentiveness to become a process of extension which generates its own
opposite—redemption. The disjunctive incrementalism of the poem—the
movement from "'the dailiness of life'" to well water, to pump, to squirrel-
wheel, to pump turning of its own weight—plays a curious confidence trick
upon time, the antagonist to the consciousness. "Well Water" is a modern
definition poem which bases itself on the assumption that every definition,
symbol, or analogy invariably constitutes a failed identity, because time
exercises a continually disjunctive pressure, diverting the subject from its
object and the self from its anterior self. By taking the monotony of temporal
change for subject and by worrying that temporal monotony through a necessarily failed process of definition, Jarrell manages to cancel time altogether—
so that the human consciousness appears to stand free of the temporal process
altogether.

Whereas Jarrell's poem converts a throwaway phrase into an attempt to
isolate a moment beyond the temporal process, Lowell continually uses the
throwaway to move toward a vision of temporal reductivism. The extreme

personalization of the poetry in the notebooks necessarily involves obscurity, because Lowell insists upon melting the recognizable rocks of the grounds of knowledge into ephemera. In the sequence, "Writers", for example, Lowell denies himself all access to both the work of other writers and to the enduring consciousnesses which emerge from that work. Consequently, he adopts something like the stance of a literary gossip, recounting his conversational exchanges with various writers. The written word lasts too long, Lowell seems to be saying; and his writers become talkers, being granted only their unenduring and least essential vocabularies.

In these poems, Lowell's writers talk with him in a tone ranging from triviality to incoherence; unprotected by the order of their art, they stand exposed, muddled. But most terribly, the death-rattle creeps into their voices, as in "Robert Frost", the final poem in the sequence "Writers".

> Robert Frost at midnight, the audience gone
> to vapor, the great act laid on the shelf in mothballs,
> his voice musical, raw and raw—he writes in the flyleaf:
> 'Robert Lowell from Robert Frost, his friend in the art.'
> 'Sometimes I feel too full of myself,' I say.
> And he, misunderstanding, 'When I am low,
> I stray away. My son wasn't your kind. The night
> we told him Merrill Moore would come to treat him,
> he said, "I'll kill him first." One of my daughters thought things,
> knew every male she met was out to make her;
> the way she dresses, she couldn't make a whorehouse.'
> And I, 'Sometimes I'm so happy I can't stand myself.'
> And he, 'When I am too full of joy, I think
> how little good my health did anyone near me.'

The figure of the vulnerable Frost is tremendously moving, but his interlocutor Lowell is distressing. The Lowell writing the poem recalls an earlier Lowell of youthful ebullience and callowness, but both Lowells tend to bully Frost—the later Lowell being more successful. Frost's defense against the earlier Lowell was his own ominous pronouncement upon the painful distance between one's work and one's life, the self and others; but the later Lowell takes Frost at his word—and with a vengeance. The poem catches Frost in the middle of the process of divesting himself of all the props of his art; and the art is all prop, so that Frost's poetical self seems to exist merely as a mask for the audience. Like the audience, the poetical self vanishes. Additionally, the opening phrase—"Robert Frost at midnight"—hangs over the whole poem to locate a temporal endpoint past which there can be no appeal to any saving aspects of process. The play on Coleridge's title thrusts Frost against a Faustian moment of decision while also reducing him to the unconscious, ephemeral existence of an insubstantial natural element. As a part of process, Frost must move or be moved, but that movement is limited by his moment; past midnight, there is only annihilation.

The conversational inspiration emerging through the poem is obscure, not because one needs to know Frost's or Lowell's history in order to comprehend the poem. Although one may puzzle over the mention of Merrill Moore, the poet-psychiatrist, the fundamental obscurity of the poem lies in its reductive appetite for rushing its subject out of existence. Randall Jarrell, in a comment on Lowell's poetry, maintained that Lowell "bullied" his early work but that "his own vulnerable humanity" had later been "forced in on him."[18] In the notebooks, however, Lowell often appears to bully vulnerable humanity —in himself and in others. Having recognized the inevitability of temporal process and its culmination in mortality, Lowell becomes the henchman of time as he pushes the characters and objects of his poems from the obscurity of meaninglessness into nonexistence.

Lowell's obscurity in the notebooks is the obscurity of a poetry which sets out, through a poetical recasting of a traditional Hegelian view of historical time, to make nonbeing increasingly tangible with the passage of historically poeticized time. In Hegelizing his poetry, Lowell attempts to yoke the passage of personal historical time with a growth analogous to the development of the phases of World-History, as Hegel outlines them in his preface to *The Philosophy of History*. For Hegel, the culmination of the development of World-History is the Old Age of the German world:

> The Old Age of Maturity is weakness; but that of Spirit is its perfect maturity and strength, in which it returns to unity with itself, but in its fully developed character as Spirit.[19]

For Lowell, the culmination of the development of personal history is the Old Age of "Obit", the final poem in the notebooks:

> Before the final coming to rest, comes the rest
> of all transcendence in a mode of being, stopping
> all becoming. I'm for and with myself in my otherness,
> in the eternal return of earth's fairer children. . . .

In spite of Lowell's echoes of Hegel, however, one wonders whether the notebooks actually figure forth the development which "Obit" proclaims. Through the poeticized personal history of the notebooks, Lowell clearly struggles to reconcile a language of representation—which represents the world of historical time—with a language of self-consciousness or spirit— which represents the eternity beyond duration. Poetry is his mode of confronting historical time, but poems are not properly objects of historical change, because literary works are (in some sense) intended to endure. In subjecting his poems to historical time by linking them to temporal schemata and by discarding them in progress, Lowell incorporates his own words, his own poems into a language of representation which marks duration. Although some such incorporation seems inevitable in any poetry striving for self-consciousness, Lowell's minimalization treats everything under the rubric of representation and historical time as mere rubble to be stared through. "This History, too . . . is for the most part, really unhistorical, for it is only the repetition of the same majestic ruin."[20] Lowell frequently and finally stakes the poetry of the notebooks on the possibility of wresting a spiritual autonomy from the flux of historical time. But one finishes each of the volumes, *Notebook: 1967–68* and *Notebook*, with a sense of the triviality of historical time and a Satanist's question—Can there be an eternity which is not in love with the productions of time?

NOTES

[1] Ralph Waldo Emerson, *Selections from Ralph Waldo Emerson*, edited by Stephen E. Whicher (Boston: Houghton Mifflin Company, 1960), p. 135.

[2] *Purgatorio*, Canto XVI, ll. 85–88.

[3] Emerson, *Works*, (New York and Boston: Fireside edition, 1909), I, pp. 197–198. Quoted in Charles Feidelson's *Symbolism and American Literature* (Chicago: The University of Chicago Press, 1966), p. 144.

[4] This was pointed out by Marie Borroff in a discussion, New Haven, 1971.

[5] *Richard II*, Act V, v, ll. 42–50.

[6] "1958", *Near the Ocean* (New York: Farrar, Straus and Giroux, 1967).

[7] "Afterthought", *Notebook: 1967–68* (New York: Farrar, Straus and Giroux, 1969), p. 159; *Notebook* (New York: Farrar, Straus and Giroux, 1970), p. 262.

[8] *Notebook*, p. 262.

[9] Emerson, *Journals*, edited by E. W. Emerson and W. E. Forbes (Boston, 1909–1914), IV, p. 337.

[10] "Mexico—5", *Notebook*, p. 103.

[11] "Harriet—2", *Notebook*, p. 21.

[12] "Afterthought", *Notebook*, p. 262.

[13] "The Nihilist as Hero", *Notebook*, p. 211, ll. 4–14.

[14] "The Nihilist as Hero", *Notebook: 1967–68*, p. 127, ll. 13–14.

[15] "For John Berryman", *Notebook*, p. 255.

[16] "Afterthought", *Notebook*, p. 263.

[17] See the Isabella Fenwick note on "We Are Seven" in Wordsworth and Coleridge, *Lyrical Ballads*, edited by R. L. Brett and A. R. Jones (London: Methuen and Co. Ltd., 1963), pp. 279–280.

[18] Randall Jarrell, jacket blurb, *Notebook: 1967–68*.

[19] Georg Wilhelm Friedrich Hegel, *The Philosophy of History*, edited by C. J. Friedrich (New York: Dover Publications, Inc., 1956), p. 109.

[20] Hegel, *The Philosophy of History*, p. 106.

How to Read Berryman's *Dream Songs*
by Edward Mendelson

ANYONE WHO writes about *The Dream Songs* puts himself in a dangerous position. The poem's landscape resembles in some places a minefield where an explanatory footstep triggers explosions of warning and invective, bursting in the face not only of critics but of all readers. Berryman's mildest warning to his expositors is both a simple renunciation and a complex, tragic claim:

> These Songs are not meant to be understood, you understand.
> They are only meant to terrify & comfort.

Henry (Henry Pussycat, Henry House, Mr Bones, Berryman's verbal stand-in, the poem's agonist) maintains that the "ultimate structure" of the Songs is inaccessible to critical analysis, that the Songs lack the regular articulated structure that informs "cliffhangers and old serials," that his "large work . . . will appear, / and baffle everybody." One response to bafflement seems to have little chance of success, considering its source:

> When the mind dies it exudes rich critical prose,
> especially about Henry . . .

Henry knows the etiology of lit. crit., so "back on down boys; don't express yourself," he warns. "His foes are like footnotes" ("comic relief,—absurd"). The structure of the Songs does not articulate deep inside the poem where criticism could rout it out, but is "according to his [Henry's] nature": the skeleton of the poems is "Mr Bones" himself.

Berryman's ludditisms (there are dozens of them) against the critical act amount to an elliptical statement about the poem's organization, its way of being. Unlike most of the recent verse that gets filed away in one's memory under the heading "confessional," Berryman's poem invents a form and language assertively its own, an achievement possible only because Berryman wrestled successfully the master voices of Hopkins, Auden, Cummings and Pound. He also has a strategy of his own, one which looks at first like the familiar confessional self-justification ("Miserable wicked me, / How interesting I am," Auden parodied in another context) but is in fact far more complicated. The title *The Dream Songs* asserts the subjectivity of the poem's occasions: dreams are events absolutely inaccessible to shared or common experience. But neither are they events subject to the organizing power of the dreamer himself. The poem claims to derive from mental activity at a place so deep in the poet's self that the self is no longer in control. Berryman makes an explicit disclaimer of responsibility in a forenote to the completed work:

"Many opinions and errors in the Songs are to be referred not to the character Henry, still less to the author, but to the title of the work." That is to say, the Songs are not what they appear to be, a transparently autobiographical series of dramatic monologues (trespassed by other voices now and then), but a verbal corporation whose members are uncontrolled responses to—and translations from—the world of experience, and whose rules are flexible and mostly hidden.

Yet the poems are not only dreams but "Songs", and they are always patterned and often musical. Berryman suggested the solution to the paradox of the title *The Dream Songs* in an interview: "Henry? He is a very good friend of mine. I feel entirely sympathetic to him. He doesn't enjoy my advantages of supervision; he just has vision." *Entirely sympathetic*: Berryman is too shrewd not to mean this in its fullest sense, that Berryman's feelings and Henry's are precisely the same. *My advantages of supervision*: though the statements in the poem are in Henry's voice, the Apollonian will to pattern and outline is the poet's own. The portion of the Songs which is the most regular in form and meter, most grave in language, is the Opus Posthumous series, written after Henry's "death" (in the center of the poem) when he is most subject to supervision by the living. And an arithmetical precision surrounds the Songs, though Henry keeps mum about it: seventy-seven Songs in the first volume, *77 Dream Songs* (1964); 77×5 in the completed 385 Songs; fourteen (7+7) in the Op. Posth. series that opens the second volume, *His Toy, His Dream, His Rest* (1968); seven epigraphs; seven Books in all. And the title of the second volume comes from a source no less formal and playfully sedate than the Fitzwilliam Virginal Book, where three songs may be found in sequence with the titles "A Toy", "Giles Farnaby's Dreame", and "His Rest". (The connection was noted by Professor Edith Borroff of Eastern Michigan University; to whom my thanks.)

The Songs have a formal frame, and, despite dozens of variations, each Song is built upon a regular pattern of three six-line stanzas, rhymed variously, with the number of feet in each line varying around 5–5–3–5–5–3. Berryman said that the Songs are not individual poems but "parts" of a single poem. As for the structure of that single poem, Berryman allowed in another interview that there is a "plot" to the work, but "its plot is the personality of Henry as he moves on in the world." After sixty years of *The Cantos*, readers are more or less accustomed to poems organized in the autobiographic-picaresque mode, but Berryman's Songs, unlike the Cantos, have a recognizable beginning, middle, and end. A poem may be autobiographical, and Henry's public experiences are the same as Berryman's, but before personal experience can fit into a literary form it must endure a cataclysmic transformation. Berryman wrote that one problem involved in a long poem is "the construction of a world, rather than the reliance upon one existent which is available to a small poem"—and this is an invitation to a phenomenological rather than structural reading of the Songs.

This issue deserves further definition. Everything in a poem that makes its world different from that of life is derived ultimately from the *closure* of art, its beginning and middle and end. In life no one has any clear sense of one's beginning, nor, after the fact, can one have any sense at all of one's end. (In a late Canto Pound put it simply: "No man can see his own end.") One can close one's life, as Berryman did, but one cannot look up at the clock afterwards and begin something new. In an age that worships process and fragmentation, tentativeness and aporia, even the most deliberately fragmented works of literature, even the last shavings of *The Cantos*, still imply the existence of larger closed structures which they are fragments *of*. Though Henry "moves on in the world," and, at the end of the first volume of the Songs, is explicitly "making ready to move on," the whole poem is finished and sealed. (There are, to be sure, miscellaneous Songs outside the main work, but these have the role that Wordsworth hoped to assign his minor poems in relation to his projected masterwork *The Recluse*: "little cells, oratories, and sepulchral recesses" attendant on the central edifice.) The world of *The Dream Songs*, the world that is "according to [Henry's] nature," depends *from* the kind of events that happen there, the verbal events that translate the dream.

Don Quixote met a prisoner who had written his own story, *La Vida de Ginés de Pasamonte*. "Is it finished yet?" asked Don Quixote. "How can it be finished," answered Ginés, "when my life isn't." Berryman's special kind of transformation of extended personal experience into finished forms is probably his most important achievement, a model of method, if not a model of what to do with a method. At a time when most "confessional" verse tends to the dreary anecdote told in formless chat, Berryman's enterprise towards an idiosyncratically appropriate language, in an appropriate form, is courageous and rare. He said that "we need a poetry that gives up everything—all kinds of traditional forms—and yet remains rich." To make such poetry involves a long and risky effort, and Berryman certainly did not develop his style all at once. His earliest work, written in what he dismissed as "several fumbling years," was written "in what it's convenient to call 'period style', the Anglo–American style of the 1930s, with no voice of my own, learning from middle and later Yeats and from . . . W. H. Auden." But although Berryman managed it well, the voice of the "period style" was insufficient for his purposes. In one early poem, for example, he begins by out-Audening Auden:

> The statue, tolerant through years of weather,
> Spares the untidy Sunday throng its look,
> Spares shopgirls knowledge of the fatal pallor
> Under their evening colour,
> Spares homosexuals, the crippled, the alone,
> Extravagant perception of their failure;
> Looks only, cynical, across them all
> To the delightful Avenue and its lights.

The voice is Auden's but the heart is absent. Yet Berryman does not want to maintain this clinically hard detachment, and he reaches at the end of the poem a tone quite different, a tone which is the poem's real object:

> the dark apartment where one summer
> Night an insignificant dreamer,
> Defeated occupant, will close his eyes
> Mercifully on the expensive drama
> Wherein he wasted so much skill, such faith,
> And salvaged less than the intolerable statue.

Insignificant dreamer . . . wasted so much skill, such faith. The ironic depreciation hides the twin giants, self-aggrandizement and self-pity. Berryman wants to fit himself into the poem, but the voice won't let him do it until the last lines, and even then only with a strained tone and forced bitterness. The early poems are always assured and learned, always excellently sleek examples of their kind, but they never quite land successfully in the fields of egocentricity over which they so longingly hover.

Berryman devised various strategies for making his personal statements, but during the 1940s, at least, most of these strategies were limited to dramatic indirection. Some of the best poems in his second book, *The Dispossessed* (1948, including most of his first book, 1942, titled *Poems*—of course), are the "Nervous Songs", spoken by "the demented priest," "a professor," "the captain," "the young Hawaiian," "the tortured girl," "the man forsaken and obsessed," and so forth. Each poem is a complete dramatic lyric in itself, but together they coalesce into the different aspects of a single "personality," one dissociated and tense, but still ultimately complete and whole. This unification is of course never stated, only implied: each "Nervous Song" speaks for a different kind of "nerve." In *Berryman's Sonnets*, written apparently in 1946 and published when they came of age twenty-one years later, a love affair provides the occasion for a sonnet sequence in which aggressively modern clotted syntax and eclectic diction depend heavily upon Petrarchan form and convention: through Sydney by Hopkins. Here, as in the later poems of *The Dispossessed*, Berryman began to twist received syntax in his first experiments towards the language of *The Dream Songs*, but his essentially traditional forms (for some short poems he even borrowed terza rima) still restricted the force of the idiovocal statements he was trying to learn to make.

With *Homage to Mistress Bradstreet* (1956) Berryman first successfully fused his by now perfected syntax into a thoroughly personal form and subject. This remarkable poem, probably the most consistently successful that Berryman ever wrote, has a narrative "plot" which may be described briefly. The poet imagines the body of Anne Bradstreet, and "summons" her from the centuries; she speaks her history, which, through one of Berryman's best imaginative leaps, turns out to be a grimly witty narrative of modern, almost

suburban isolation and detachment, set in Puritan New England; Berryman
and Anne, each to the other a ghostly presence, speak a dialogue, and each
almost takes the other for a lover. But Anne escapes the (to her) temptation
offered by the twentieth-century voice, and asserts her seventeenth-century
independence. Berryman's voice returns to the poem only after Anne's
death. The structural device through which Berryman first creates Anne
Bradstreet, then is thrown off by his own creation, might appear to be a con-
ventionally modernist sleight-of-hand, a familiar form of play with the status
of appearances, but Berryman summons a vast emotional universe of personal loss and assertion to the device, and succeeds in rendering it as deeply
moving as it is artificial. The tortured syntax, here as earlier borrowed from
Hopkins but rendered insistently secular, finally enjoys a wide enough range
of situations to render into its language. Berryman moves easily from the
grave to the comic, as in the arrangements for Anne's marriage, her resigned
loss of sensual "bliss" to religious severity:

> vanity & the follies of youth took hold of me;
> then the pox blasted, when the Lord returned.
> That year for my sorry face
> so-much-older Simon burned,
> so Father smiled, with love. Their will be done.
> He to me ill lingeringly, learning to shun
> a bliss, a lightning blood
> vouchsafed, what did seem life. I kissed his Mystery.

Or the astonishingly persuasive rendering of her first childbirth:

> No. No. Yes! everything down
> hardens I press with horrible joy down
> my back cracks like a wrist
> shame I am voiding oh behind it is too late
>
> hide me forever I work thrust I must free
> now I all muscles & bone concentrate
> what is living from dying?
> Simon I must leave you so untidy
> Monster you are killing me Be sure
> I'll have you later Women do endure
> I can *can* no longer
> and it passes the wretched trap whelming and I am me
>
> drencht & powerful, I did it with my body!
> One proud tug greens Heaven. Marvellous,
> unforbidding Majesty.
> Swell, imperious bells. I fly.

(There is little that is quite as intense and various as this in all of English
poetry.) And finally, Berryman's meditation after Anne's funeral:

> Headstones stagger under great draughts of time
> after heads pass out, and their world must reel
> speechless, blind in the end
> about its chilling star, thrift tuft,
> whin-cushion—nothing. Already with the wounded flying
> dark air fills, I am a closet of secrets dying . . .
>
> O all your ages at the mercy of my loves
> together lie at once, forever or
> so long as I happen.
> In the rain of pain & departure, still
> Love has no body and presides the sun,
> and elfs from silence melody. I run.
> Hover, utter, still,
> a sourcing   whom my lost candle like the firefly loves.

(The phrase "Love . . . presides the sun" recalls the final line of the *Paradiso*, "L'amor che muove il sole e il altre stelle," and suddenly deepens Berryman's conversation with the dead.)

The lost and isolated voice of the poem gains force through its reduplication in the seventeenth and twentieth centuries, but Berryman was not satisfied. *The Dream Songs* resume his quest for a single voice, but the quest is not completed or resolved until the middle of the work. In *77 Dream Songs* Henry "has a friend, never named, who addresses him as Mr Bones and variants thereof," and usually engages Henry in the midst of one of his bursts of blackface or burnt-cork monologue—another distancing pose which Berryman managed to give up before too long.

> You may be right Friend Bones.
> Indeed you is. Dey flyin ober de world,
> de pilots, ober ofays. Bit by bit
> our immemorial moans
>
> brown down to all dere moans. I flees that, sah.

What is characteristically Berryman's in this sort of passage is not the distancing dialect so much as the sudden shift to a vaguely "high" style in "our immemorial moans," which, in addition to the effect of the dialect, distances the Song doubly. Berryman is always ready to walk along the dangerous cliffs of self-indulgence ("O ho alas alas/When will indifference come, I moan & rave"), but only by taking risks can he achieve the mutual conciliation of the colloquial and the formal which the Songs propose, bend to the breaking point again and again, and finally ratify and consummate.

The risks of Berryman's style are great (rhymes on "O" or "pal" have little merit, unless some lies in their nose-thumbing insouciance towards The Tradition), but the risks of his subject are greater. Although there is no lyric or narrative stance available in literature that is more tedious than the Wild

Old Wicked Man, Berryman persists in delighting in it. Leaving aside for a moment the "plot" of the poem, one can approach it usefully according to Berryman's own suggestions. In the interview where he denied the presence of an "ulterior structure," he indicated that what is most important in the poem's organization is the *kind of event* that happens in any of its various territories: "Some of the Songs are in alphabetical order [117–122, for example, allowing an obvious inversion of the first two phrases of 118; and so much for narrative pattern]; but, mostly, they just belong to areas of hope and fear that Henry is going through at a given time." The primary event in the Songs is of course the dream, yet what ordinary language knows as dreams are imitated rarely. Abrupt endings, sudden shifts in referent and style (recalling to its source the technique named by MacNeice the "dream parataxis"), fantasies of sexual power and weakness, all refer obliquely to dreams, but Berryman uses the word "dream" in a wider sense. Disputing Freud, he writes in a late Song that "a dream is a panorama/of the whole mental life." This statement is a revision of the romantic conception of the dream—a conception elevated by Freud from poetic assertion to scientific dogma—which is premised on the belief that dreams are messages from the psychic interior. When Berryman elevates his domestic miseries and petty wrongs into the material of secondary epic—without, apparently, it ever occurring to him that the subject might not deserve so much paper and type—he adopts a standard romantic convention, but does so partly in order to invert it. Berryman's most characteristic literary *manner* is that of a Wordsworth *in extremis* ("Wordsworth, thou form almost divine, cried Henry"), aware of the real pain in the world: his poems intimations of mortality, tranquillity (at best) recollected in emotion; his great work not a preparation for future effort, but a record of loss, a Postlude, or the decay of the poet's world. But instead of listening, resolving, communing, Henry acts, and his most characteristic *action* is scrambling or stumbling up to proceed again, after one more defeat, the death of one more friend, one more hollow and temporary pleasure. Henry's dreams give no comfort. Freud suggested that dreams are the guardians of sleep. Not Henry's dreams:

> I can't go into the meaning of the dream
> except to say a sense of total LOSS
> afflicted me thereof:
> an absolute disappearance of continuity & love
> and children away at school, the weight of the cross,
> and everything is what it seems.

Everything is what it seems: the loss is real; no romance or celebration can remedy it. Berryman's stance refuses the private luxuries of the romantic vision, a privacy he finds in its most limiting form in Wallace Stevens. The Song "So Long? Stevens" brilliantly demolishes this extreme version of romantic self-consciousness:

He lifted up, among the actuaries,
a grandee crow. Ah ha & he crowed good . . .

What was it missing, then, at the man's heart
so that he does not wound? It is our kind
to wound, as well as utter

a fact of happy world. That metaphysics
he hefted up until we could not breathe
the physics.

Berryman's dreams, for all their irresponsibility, are responsive, openly conscious as well as self-conscious, or so Berryman claims. Again from an interview: "What is wrong with poetry now is that poets won't take on observation, dealing with what is sent into individuals from the universe. It would seem to be that the job of the poet, if I may speak of such a ridiculous thing, is to handle the signs, to field them as in baseball."

So much does Berryman claim for his art. But do the events in the dreams or in their Songs stand up to the claim? Berryman's notion of "what is sent into individuals from the universe" is necessarily determined by his idea of the "universe" itself. *Homage to Mistress Bradstreet* is among other things an historical narrative, yet its central statements are "about" isolation and love. Anne Bradstreet seems at times an historical convenience. She is not a Yeatsian "mask" but a *projection*. In *The Dream Songs* the poem's universe is that of a man at the extremes of noisy passion and unhappiness, but also, alas, when considered outside his world of private eros and thanatos, *l'homme moyen social*. Berryman and Lowell admire each other enthusiastically in print, but their phenomenal worlds are vastly different: where Lowell takes everything in the *polis* for his subject, Berryman's social commentary—except where the subject is at least marginally "literary," as in the trials of Soviet poets—is nearly as crazy as the later Yeats, and much less sonorous. "I'd like to write political poems, but aside from *Formal Elegy* [which hovers somewhere near John Kennedy], I've never been moved to do so." (Actually this is not quite true: *Poems* and *The Dispossessed* include some political verses reading like watered Auden. And Berryman once described the early "Winter Landscape" as a poem which indicates "what is necessary to be said—but which the poet refuses to say—about a violent world." This borders on the sophistic, but Berryman's refusal to talk about that which he cannot talk about is finally an honorable one. Graves' subject matter is no wider than Berryman's, but Graves decorously writes lyrics while Berryman raises problems for himself by exploding his discontents into epic.)

What is sent into Henry from the universe falls mostly under the vivid scarlet rubrics of death, survival, love, and fame. To the right and left of him fall so many poets; so many deaths seek him out:

I'm cross with god who has wrecked this generation.

> First he seized Ted, then Richard, Randall, and now Delmore.
> In between he gorged on Sylvia Plath.

Roethke, Blackmur, Jarrell, Schwartz, Plath—Berryman's staying power seems so much more strained, his survival so difficult, compared with the losses that surround him. Not that he is himself exempt. The very first Song in the whole work marvels at Henry's persistence after a "departure" from felicity and coherence, a departure that the line following relates elliptically to the Fall:

> All the world like a woolen lover
> once did seem on Henry's side.
> Then came a departure.
> Thereafter nothing fell out as it might or ought.
> I don't see how Henry, pried
> open for all the world to see, survived.

And throughout the first volume Henry refuses to wake, or is mutilated, blinded, or stalled:

> They sandpapered his plumpest home. (So capsize.)
> They took away his crotch.

And

> —What happen then, Mr Bones?
> —I had a most   marvellous piece of luck. I died.

(This ends Book I.) And

> I am obliged to perform in complete darkness
> operations of great delicacy
> on my self.
> —Mr Bones, you terrifies me.
> No wonder they don't pay you. Will you die?
> —My
>   friend, I succeeded. Later.

And when he isn't dying, Henry spends much of his time in hospital, immobilized.

The second volume of the Songs, *His Toy, His Dream, His Rest*, begins with Henry's "posthumous" works, when "Good nature is over" and he lies in "a *nice* pit":

> I am breaking up
> and Henry now has come to a full stop—
> vanisht his vision, if there was, & fold
> him over himself quietly.

The grave is not without its consolations, however, and when Henry's responsibilities become an issue at law, "this august court will entertain the plea/ Not Guilty by reason of death." Though Henry's trial is interrupted by the news that he "may be returing to life/adult & difficult," no one need worry. After he has been dug up, and has "muttered for a double rum/waving the mikes away," two weeks later he returns to the graveyard, desperate to get back underground:

> insomnia-plagued, with a shovel
> digging like mad, Lazarus with a plan
> to get his own back, a plan, a stratagem
> no newsman will unravel.

In the next Book, the metaphor of Henry's death translates itself, reasonably enough, into a long stay in hospital, and a more or less ordinary narrative resumes. By Book VI it is not Henry who is elegized but Delmore Schwartz who is granted a long series of elegiac Songs before Berryman sets him "free of my love," in the conventional end-of-elegy hope that he may "recover & be whole."

Henry's own elegies also end with consolation. Set against his reiterated, battological dyings are his movings-on ("recoveries" is too strong a word), which are figuratively the "movement" of the poem. The areas of hope and fear in which Henry finds himself have their geographical analogues—from India, where "his migrant heart" hurts at the thought of stability and repeated Spring, to Japan, where in the permanence of a temple he remembers that "Elsewhere occurs . . . loss," and finally, amazingly "in love with life / which has produced this wreck," to Ireland, the site of the seventh and longest Book of the Songs. Always Henry is surprised at his own resilience:

> it is a wonder that, with in each hand
> one of his own mad books and all,
> ancient fires for eyes, his head full
> & his heart full, he's making ready to move on.

Moving-on in his epic impetus. With no Ithaca or Penelope (or dozens of them, which means the same thing), no historical destiny or Roman Imperium, no Beatrice or St. Francis to draw him onwards, his straitened private energy must suffice.

Whether or not it *does* suffice for almost four hundred Songs is open to question, and one suspects, as one nears the end of the poem, that energy-scrambling-for-a-system-to-act-in is a theme pathetically at variance with the scale of the whole enterprise. Berryman suspects this also, and Henry's energy does have contexts, although they seem more and more narrow as the poem proceeds. Part way through *His Toy, His Dream, His Rest* the interlocutor and friend who addresses Henry as Mr Bones drops almost entirely from sight, and Henry is left to speak alone. Berryman finally achieves the single voice he worked towards for thirty years, but one might be dismayed by the uses to which he applies it. (Although so assertively single a voice can only, perhaps, be assertively single-minded.) Henry's chief interests, especially in the later Songs when the elegiac note has faded, are two, and the poem stutters over them almost incessantly: Henry's delight in, and difficulties with, (1) fame and (2) women. His response to publicity seems rather out of proportion, as if the occasional notice granted a very good minor poet by media that glut themselves on "celebrity" could give that poet the public currency of a Yeats, or even a Churchill. What fame he does have, and the grateful attention of his friends, fully justify a supple and active response like this one:

> he staked his claim upon obscurity:
> a prayer to be left alone
> escaped him sometimes or for a middle zone
> where he could be & become both unknown & known
> listening & not.

("Obscurity" is of course both "difficulty of interpretation" and "lack of recognition.") But a Song that begins by musing, "Fan-mail from foreign countries, is that fame?" and continues through a catalogue of awards and interviews, to end with the throwaway line, "A lone letter from a young man: that is fame"—can only sound hollow and mawkish. (It is just conceivable, though unlikely, that this is self-parody. But Berryman *likes* the subject too much for that.)

Nor does the unedifying spectacle of Henry's relations with women have much to recommend it. Early in the book Berryman manages some fine dramatic absurdity:

> Filling her compact & delicious body
> with chicken páprika, she glanced at me
> twice.
> Fainting with interest, I hungered back
> and only the fact of her husband & four other people
> kept me from springing on her . . .

And later he sounds disingenuous at finding the situation reversed:

> a Belfast man
> last night made a pass at my wife: Henry, who had passed out,
> was horrified
> to hear this news when he woke.

But usually he is much nastier than this, and seems to realize it fairly well—which does not improve the situation. The women of *The Dream Songs* are divided roughly into two familiar classes: those he went to bed with, and those he did not. The former find themselves dismissed with an epithet ("whereon he lay / the famous daughter"), the latter idealized and transfigured, their names prefixed by "Lady". In neither case does there seem to be much participation ("Women serve my turn"—*Homage to Mistress Bradstreet*). In both the relation is with another human being as object, whether debased or idolized, which is why "He was always in love with the wrong woman," and why, for all his sexual energy and success, he finds sex de-grading: "Them lady poets must not marry," and Berryman thinks one of those ladies is even "too noble-O" for sexual experience.

Death is the heaviest burden, drawing the Songs constantly to earth. Survival, moving-on, is the essential form taken by the poem's energy. The objects of that energy become the title of Berryman's next book, *Love and Fame*: and in reference both to that book and to the Songs, the first term in the title seems euphemistic, the second hyperbolic. (Berryman himself may have seen the title in an ironic light, as its possible literary source, Pope's "Eloisa to Abelard", bears a reminder of defeat: "Lost in a convent's solitary gloom . . . There dy'd the best of passions, Love and Fame.") The deepest goal of Henry's energy, its ultimate use, is the familiar lowest common de-nominator, power. "Love" in Berryman's poetry stands for the exercise of sexual power, or the worship of sexual power in idealized women. His use of fame is best described by Elias Canetti:

> Fame is not fastidious about the lips which spread it. So long as there are mouths to reiterate the one name, it does not matter whose they are. The fact that to the seeker after fame they are indistinguishable from each other and are all counted as equal shows that this passion has its origin in the experience of crowd manipulation.
>
> (*Crowds and Power*)

Berryman writes often that he prefers the praise of his friends to the baying of the crowd, but taking into consideration all his references to fame, the use of this passage does not appear unjust.

But Berryman is no naif. His power-plays are not simply subject matter for his poem, but are enacted in the poem itself. Berryman is smart enough to realize that he presents himself in the least prepossessing manner he can imagine: his personal offensiveness is not accidental but entirely deliberate, for what he wants from his readers is their critical approval despite their personal disapproval, their assent despite their awareness of what they are assenting *to*. What Berryman hopes to enjoy is not the power to delight or enchant, but the power to control those who are both conscious and unwilling.

American poets have never been able to consider themselves part of a clerisy or of any comfortably well-defined class, and for that reason have always been far more concerned with power than their European contempora-ries. Berryman's generation of poets seems to have been more obsessed with the attainment and use of power than any other in America, and its obsession proved costly. Jarrell, Shapiro, Lowell, Roethke (of whom Berryman said "He was interested in love and money; and if he had found a combination of them in something else, he would have dedicated himself to it instead of poetry"), Berryman himself—all tried or still try to exert more control than words ever made possible over people, politics, the literary pecking-order, and time which no one controls.

Yet no matter how irritating or boring or murky the Songs can be on occasion, they remain the most courageous and interesting poetic experiment of their decade. When they succeed, when they open into something rich and strange, no other poem in their historical neighborhood can equal them. Few who have written on Berryman have been able to avoid quoting one in particular of the early Songs entire, and there is no reason to buck the trend:

> There sat down, once, a thing on Henry's heart
> só heavy, if he had a hundred years
> & more, & weeping, sleepless, in all them time
> Henry could not make good.
> Starts again always in Henry's ears
> the little cough somewhere, an odour, a chime.
>
> And there is another thing he has in mind
> like a grave Sienese face a thousand years
> would fail to blur the still profiled reproach of. Ghastly,
> with open eyes, he attends, blind.
> All the bells say: too late. This is not for tears;
> thinking.
>
> But never did Henry, as he thought he did,
> end anyone and hacks her body up
> and hide the pieces, where they may be found.
> He knows: he went over everyone, & nobody's missing.
> Often he reckons, in the dawn, them up.
> Nobody is ever missing.

This song, number 29, exemplifies in an unusually clear and regular manner the paratactic method by which almost all the Songs are organized. The first sestet describes an experience in intensely private terms; the "thing" is on Henry's heart, the cough "in Henry's ears." In the second sestet he notices or remembers the world outside, and does so through a metaphor ("a grave Sienese face") whose vehicle at least is publicly accessible, although the tenor is only an unspecified guilty "reproach." Rather than locating sound "in Henry's ears," it is the bells, outside, that speak; and although blind, Henry at least "attends." Finally, in the last sestet, he acknowledges almost in defeat the social world of others, all those who persist in surviving despite his dreams of violence (the cause of the "reproach" is now identified), who remind him that the thing on his heart is only private. This neat enactment of Husserlian epistemology (awareness of self, things, others) recurs throughout *The Dream Songs*, but often in reverse order—with the awareness of others narrowing down to awareness of self—or in some other variant pattern. And this paratactic method informs the relations between Songs as well as within them. The two final Songs provide perhaps the best example. In the first Henry stands over his father's grave, initially with restrained anger, then in stagy fury:

> I spit upon this dreadful banker's grave
> who shot his heart out in a Florida dawn
> O ho alas alas
> When will indifference come, I moan & rave
> I'd like to scrabble till I got right down
> away down under the grass
>
> and ax the casket open ha . . .

The poem is bloody with death and separations. But the very last Song subsumes the death of one man into the cycle of seasons, where no endings are final:

> My daughter's heavier. Light leaves are flying.
> Everywhere in enormous numbers turkeys will be dying
> and other birds, and all their wings.
> They never greatly flew. Did they wish to?
> I should know. Off away somewhere once I knew
> such things.
>
> Or good Ralph Hodgson back then did, or does.
> The man is dead whom Eliot praised. My praise
> follows and flows too late.
> Fall is grievy, brisk. Tears behind the eyes
> almost fall. Fall comes to us as a prize
> to rouse us toward our fate.

The dead father in the previous Song balances the growing, "heavier" daughter in this one. Henry's rage against his father is transmuted into praise for the dead poet, his obsession with the past metamorphosed into concern for his daughter and her (implied) future, his destruction of his father's casket transfigured into his calm respect for the permanence of his house, also wooden:

> My house is made of wood and it's made well,
> unlike us. My house is older than Henry;
> that's fairly old.

And the Songs close heart-rendingly with a meditation and plaint on the incoherence of the world, the dualism that divides soul from flesh and so from all "things," the discontinuity that makes Henry scold his child, "heavy" and a "thing," but loved:

> If there were a middle   ground between things and the soul
> or if the sky resembled more the sea,
> I wouldn't have to scold
>   my heavy daughter.

And at the same moment that it closes, the poem thrusts itself out of its frame into the undefined future.

Love and Fame (1970), which lies outside the range of this survey, continues Berryman's development of a personal voice. He drops the Henry-doppelgänger and speaks autobiographically and directly in his own name. The title of one poem, "Regents' Professor Berryman's Crack on Race", would have been impossibly direct only a few years earlier, but with directness came a dangerous facility and self-importance. The book makes pleasant reading, but the struggles of *The Dream Songs* have diminished to chat. Berryman's last book, *Delusions, etc.*, indicates that the mad-lyric mode was Berryman's mainstay to the end, intensely personal, slightly desperate, persistent in its survivals, its paradoxes, and its celebrations.

Finally the survivals gave out. Most of this essay had been written when the news came that the body of John Berryman had been found on the bank of the Mississippi River near the campus of the University of Minnesota. Berryman had walked to the railing of a bridge, waved to a passerby, and stepped off. Whatever the pressures and necessities may have been to which Berryman finally yielded, we probably have no right to know them. But his wave of farewell, so unlikely in those circumstances, was a thoroughly public gesture: Henry's last.

The Poetry of Protest
by Robert B. Shaw

IT IS difficult, and at times it seems impossible, to dream oneself back to the first days of the 'sixties, when the Kennedys were in the White House and both the Vietnamese war and the American ghetto were holding to a low profile. Politics then seemed a festivity, and the government courted writers and artists with unprecedented favors. Robert Frost laid aside a notorious skepticism regarding the state and its intentions to celebrate the inauguration of the youngest President ever elected:

> It makes the prophet in us all presage
> The glory of a next Augustan age
> Of a power leading from its strength and pride,
> Of young ambition eager to be tried,
> Firm in our free beliefs without dismay,
> In any game the nations want to play.
> A golden age of poetry and power
> Of which this noonday's the beginning hour.

But of course the age, as it came to pass, was more Neronian than Augustan. Vietnam, civil disorder, multiple assassinations, the sudden visibility of the poor—all of these conspired to flatten the champagne. We began the 'sixties with the Peace Corps and ended them with Mylai.

The emerging pattern of stupid brutality was discernible by the middle of the decade, when Lowell refused to read his poems at the White House. Soon enough poets in large numbers were reading what they had written *against* the White House. The marathon readings (or read-ins) probably hit their peak in 1967 or '68, Johnson's last years. The anthologies followed and only now appear to be tapering off. The market may be glutted. And yet poets will no doubt continue to confront the issues as long as the issues refuse to disappear.

People who care for poetry as deeply as they do for social justice are bound to be dispirited by collections of protest verse. More than for other sorts of poetry, the ways in which *this* sort can go wrong seem clearly defined and aggravatingly predictable. Everywhere we see egos asserted, truths debased, reason abandoned and craft ignored. If the following survey is largely negative it only witnesses to the maimed and fevered condition of most of these poems—as if they were themselves casualties of war. I shall center my discussion around poems dealing with Vietnam, for these form the bulk of the decade's engagé verse. The points I make will be largely applicable to any poems which seek to criticize public policies.

I: Diatribe and Documentary

   One of the disturbing things about Vietnam poems is that they lend themselves so easily to classification. The various types may be found in any of
several anthologies; a representative collection is *Where Is Vietnam? American
Poets Respond*, edited by Walter Lowenfels. Two quotations from this book
will serve to show the genre at its least accomplished. Here is one:

> All your strength, America, is in your bombs!
> What were your eagles are now carriers of death.
> Strange loves twitch in your sermons.
>
> What fear turns you to this terror?—
> to drive people into the trenches and tunnels, to poison their land.
> What fear makes you kill the children of Vietnam so savagely?
> —pounding them to bits with your bombs.
> What shame!—to crush down the weak, to force them under the earth . . .

Here is another:

> On Thursday a Vietcong flag was noticed flying
> Above the village of Man Quang in South Vietnam.
> Therefore Skyraider fighter-bombers were sent in,
> Destroying the village school and other "structures."
> The bombing mission killed an estimated 34 schoolchildren,
> And three adults.
>
> From Man Quang survivors of the raid, not pacified,
> Tried to carry the coffins into Da Nang as a protest;
> But were held in security by Government forces,
> Who made an indemnification over the children's bodies;
> And arrested the parents.
>
> There is no information about lessons in progress
> When the school died: perhaps civics, a foreign language,
> Or the catechism; or "Practical Subjects"—pottery,
> Domestic science, woodwork, metalwork: in darkness
> Burning, dying.
>
> On Thursday a Vietcong flag was noticed flying.

The first poem is "Hecuba in Vietnam" by Thanasis Maskaleris. (I have left
Hecuba out of my quotation, but she does not really add much to the piece.)
In style this is simple invective and not much about it can be said except that
invective needs to be verbally distinguished before it is important as poetry.
The attitude of the poem is of outrage, but the heavy and exclamatory style
moves us more to annoyance with the poet than with the government. Blanket
condemnations generally sound self-righteous, and self-righteousness is the
basic flaw of many Vietnam poems.

The second poem, "Schoolday in Man Quang", by Denis Knight, stands in direct contrast, tonally, to the Maskaleris diatribe. (I have quoted this poem in its entirety.) The thinking behind it may have been: We have had enough emotional outbursts in verse about Vietnam; let the facts speak for themselves. Knight stresses the factuality of his poem by supplying it with this footnote: "This incident was reported from Saigon on March 18 and March 25, 1965, by the Special Correspondent of the London *Times*." Poems like this, which hew closely to news accounts and sometimes quote them verbatim, have had great currency of late. They undoubtedly engage our attention more seriously than the heavy rhetoric of "All your strength, America, is in your bombs!" But does a poem like Knight's succeed poetically? What distinguishes it from the news report that was its source? Knight intervenes noticeably as a poet in a few places: by putting quotation marks around "structures" he points up his parody of the neutral, dehumanized tone of officialese; by repeating his first line at the end he rounds the piece off with an implicit moral; he has made some attempts, but not very rigorous ones, to order his material in a rhythmic pattern. In the main, however, he merely hands us the facts.

Shouldn't we expect more from a poet—a *maker*—than the assembling of verifiable, datable facts? When have such facts been sought for in poetry? Nobody wants to know what particular Grecian urn Keats was writing about. Knight's footnote and the method of his poem reflect a helplessness in the face of events, an abdication of the poet's responsibility to impose form on raw experience. He does make some gesture toward meaningful form with his faint parody of official language. Most of these "documentary" poets have such a parody among their intentions. But they are confusing ends with means. It is not ultimately effective to attack the enemy in his own language when to do that limits so stringently one's freedom of expression. That the appalling details of slaughter fail to appal us as they ought to when we read them in the newspaper is something we all must acknowledge with shame. But we will not be roused from our indifference by seeing the same spiritless, bureaucratic language set down with a tired irony in verse. These oddly anonymous poets have nothing to tell us in their own right; they betray no more personality than the phantom sources whom journalists describe as "government spokesmen". I cannot read poems which employ this strategy without remembering Blake's line: "They become what they behold."

II : Autobiographies

Of course, the more thoughtful poets have appreciated the awful remoteness of the war from the consciousness of even the minority of Americans that reads poetry. Vietnam has been news for too long; just as listeners "tune out" on radio reports, readers will pass by poems which merely record facts which are common property. Some of Lowell's work of the 'sixties suggests that a political poem may gain in interest if it has an autobiographical frame. For Lowell, the political theme is subordinate; Vietnam and the social turmoil it has aroused take up positions in the endless succession of crises which one suffers if one is Robert Lowell. Public events for him lose their public character, and sometimes become very good poetry. Can it be said, then, that autobiography is a promising strategy for poems of protest? Not in general. Consider the first section of Denise Levertov's "From a Notebook: October '68—May '69":

> Revolution or death. Revolution or death.
> Wheels would sing it
> 　　　　　　　but railroads are obsolete,
> we are among the clouds, gliding, the roar
> a toneless constant.
> 　　　　　　　*Which side are you on?*
> Revolution, of course. Death is Mayor Daley.
> This revolution has no blueprints, and
> 　　　("What makes this night different
> 　　　　　from all other nights?")
> is the first that laughter and pleasure aren't shot down in.
> *Life that*
> 　　　　*wants to live.*
> 　　　　　　　　　　(*Unlived life*
> 　　　　　　　　　　*of which one can die.*)
> 　　　　　　I want the world to go on
> 　　　　unfolding. The brain
> not gray except in death, the photo I saw
> of prismatic radiance pulsing from live tissue.
> 　　　　　I see Dennis Riordon and de Courcy Squire,
> 　　　　　gentle David Worstell, intransigent Chuck Matthei
> 　　　　　blowing angel horns at the imagined corners.
> 　　　　　Jennie Orvino singing
> 　　　　　beatitudes in the cold wind
> 　　　　　　　　　　outside a Milwaukee courthouse.
> I want their world—in which they already live,
> they're not waiting for demolition and reconstruction.
> 　　　　　　　　　　　　"Begin here."
> Of course I choose
> revolution.

I do not think I will be alone in finding this passage painfully self-conscious and wasteful of Levertov's talents. Her eye and ear, which have justly earned her a reputation as one of our finest lyric poets, here seem not to be operating. The images are fuzzy and the diction and rhythms are slack. Her romantic picture of the young activists, like most of the writing done by middle-aged liberals about the younger generation, comes across as unwittingly patronizing. This in itself is embarrassing, but even more so is the histrionic posture of the poet, facing, as she asserts, a choice between life and death. If the choice is really so simple (revolution = life; Chicago's Mayor Daley = death) what is the need of all this pretentious verbiage, of echoes of Donne and the Passover liturgy? Obviously Levertov is straining to draw together an inner and an outer world, and her usual clarity of vision and speech deserts her in the attempt. As one of her young activist friends might put it, she blows her cool.

Levertov's piece points up dangers which many protestors have fallen prey to in the autobiographical mode. Even Lowell, who may be said to have the original patent on this method, has brought it off with entire success only a handful of times: in some of the *Notebook* poems, in "For the Union Dead", in "Waking Early Sunday Morning", and in perhaps a few others. In the "Waking Early" poem Lowell depicts his own spiritual dereliction side by side with a vision of the godless militarism of Johnson's America:

> When will we see Him face to face?
> Each day, He shines through darker glass.
> In this small town where everything
> is known, I see His vanishing
> emblems, His white spire and flag-
> pole sticking out above the fog,
> like old white china doorknobs, sad,
> slight useless things to calm the mad.

> Hammering military splendor,
> top-heavy Goliath in full armor—
> little redemption in the mass
> liquidations of their brass,
> elephant and phalanx moving
> with the times and still improving,
> when that kingdom hit the crash:
> a million foreskins stacked like trash . . .

Lowell brings to his writing a New Englander's historical imagination, a mind which endlessly juxtaposes past and present and marks its losses. Furthermore, he has over the years made of his own life a myth, presenting his personal sufferings as emblematic of the nation's. Levertov's uneasy jarring of focus in shifting from public to private concerns is reduced by long experience to a minimum in Lowell. Our conclusion might be that for poems with public concerns the autobiographical mode is eminently possible for Lowell, but perilous for those who lack his twenty years of practice. It takes time to develop one's potentiality as an archetype.

III: Apocalyptic and Satire

Lowell's isolated success with autobiography prompts us to look for some myth less private which poets who happen not to be Robert Lowell can use to voice their dissent. The myth which springs most readily to mind is that of the unholy city and its fall, the myth of the apocalypse. This was Ginsberg's myth in *Howl*:

> What sphinx of cement and aluminum bashed open their
>   skulls and ate up their brains and imagination?
> Moloch! Solitude! Filth! Ugliness! Ashcans and
>   unattainable dollars! Children screaming under
>   the stairways! Boys sobbing in armies! Old men
>   weeping in the parks!
> Moloch! Moloch! Nightmare of Moloch! Moloch the
>   loveless! Mental Moloch! Moloch the heavy judger
>   of men!
> Moloch the incomprehensible prison! Moloch the cross-
>   bone soulless jailhouse and Congress of sorrows.
>   Moloch whose buildings are judgment! Moloch the
>   vast stone of war! Moloch the stunned governments!
> Moloch whose mind is pure machinery! Moloch whose
>   blood is running money! Moloch whose fingers are
>   ten armies! Moloch whose breast is a cannibal
>   dynamo! Moloch whose ear is a smoking tomb! . . .

When this was first published in 1956 only a very exceptional reader would have read it as addressing a social issue. Not a concern for society but Ginsberg's excursions into madness and despair, his perception of the hell within him, provoked this outcry. Now the events of the last decade have made this esoteric vision accessible to all; Ginsberg's private nightmares are everyone's daily reading. Hindsight acclaims *Howl* as prophetic.

Present and future are superimposed in the prophet's words: to deliver his message whole he must use present facts as symbols; he must not allow himself to get bogged down in transient detail. His images must be specific without being ephemeral. Ginsberg packs a lot of the American scene, viewed from its underside, into *Howl*, lamenting "the best minds of my generation"

> who burned cigarette holes in their arms protesting
>   the narcotic tobacco haze of Capitalism,
> who distributed Supercommunist pamphlets in Union Square
>   weeping and undressing while the sirens of Los
>   Alamos wailed them down, and wailed down Wall, and
>   the Staten Island ferry also wailed . . .

but he does not catalogue in his poem the names of cabinet officers in the Eisenhower administration. He avoids tying lead to the feet of his phantasmagoria.

We have poets writing now whose language can attain to the power of prophecy but whose vision cannot. The first lines of Robert Duncan's "Up Rising" exemplify the problem:

Now Johnson would go up to join the great simulacra of men,
   Hitler and Stalin, to work his fame
   with planes roaring out from Guam over Asia,
all America become a sea of trifling men
   stirred at his will, which would be a bloated thing,
   drawing from the underbelly of the nation
   such blood and dreams as swell the idiot psyche
   out of its courses into an elemental thing
   until his name stinks with burning meat and heapt honors

And men wake to see that they are used like things
   spent in a great potlatch, this Texas barbecue
   of Asia, Africa, and all the Americas . . .

"Up Rising" in its entirety reaches unusual rhetorical heights. And yet there is something off-putting about a poem which straightway insists on an equation of Johnson with Hitler. Many of us, while holding no brief for Johnson, may still not think of him as being quite in Hitler's league. It is too bad that this should be one of Duncan's major premises, for it means that the poem will fade as its occasions do; it is less likely to escape the mid-'sixties in the way that *Howl* does the mid-'fifties. I am aware that it is not the business of a prophet to make nice political distinctions. And yet his message ought to strike us as informed with the abiding clarity of revelation, not the myopia of a past moment of passion.

Another poet who has borrowed something of Ginsberg's incantatory style is Robert Bly. It shows up especially in *The Teeth-Mother Naked At Last*, a sort of up-dated, outward-looking *Howl*, more midwestern, more lyrical. Here is one of the quieter passages:

Why are they dying? I have written this so many times.
They are dying because the President has opened a Bible again.

They are dying because gold deposits have been found among the Shoshone
   Indians.

Because money follows intellect!
and intellect is like a fan opening in the wind—

The Marines think that unless they die the rivers will not move.
They are dying so that mountain shadows can fall north in the afternoon,
so that the beetle can move along the ground near the fallen twigs.

In an apocalyptic patch Bly envisages the nation as finally polarized, young set against old, the peace movement against the increasingly authoritarian government (the "teeth-mother"):

Now the whole nation starts to whirl,
the end of the Republic breaks off,

Europe comes to take revenge,
the mad beast covered with European hair rushes through the mesa bushes in
    Mendochino County,
pigs rush toward the cliff,
the waters underneath part, in one ocean luminous globes float up (in them
    hairy and ecstatic rock musicians)—
in the other, the teeth-mother, naked at last.

This seems rather academic compared to Ginsberg's vision of Moloch.
Perhaps Bly is to be thought of as writing not apocalyptic but a sort of satire.
The Teeth-Mother contains passages like this:

The Chief Executive enters; the Press Conference begins:
First the President lies about the date the Appalachian Mountains rose

Then he lies about the population of Chicago, then about the weight of the
    adult eagle, next about the acreage of the Everglades . . .

He lies about the composition of the amniotic fluid, he insists that Luther was
    never a German, and insists that only the Protestants sold indulgences . . .

And with somewhat more compression Bly has written poems which could be
called satirical lyrics, like "Asian Peace Offers Rejected without Being Heard",
in which Secretary of State Dean Rusk's assistants

                        eat hurriedly,
        Talking of Teilhard de Chardin,
        Longing to get back to their offices
        So they can cling to the underside of the steel wings
            shuddering faintly in the high altitudes . . .

Bly is probably the best of the poets whose protests veer into satire. In
reading him (and even more in reading poets of lesser abilities) we are
reminded of how drastically the last two centuries have limited the expressive possibilities of satire in verse. The present age seems particularly to have
lost the knack for it. This may seem a queer thing to have come about in the
period which, we are told, rediscovered the uses of irony in poetry. But the
stylistic problems are obvious. We cannot write a mock-heroic poem because,
unlike the Augustans, we have no viable conception of what true heroic
style is or ought to be. As for parodies of low style, of bureaucratic language, I
have already noted that they emulate the dullness they attack. It is not only in
style but in matter that current satire lacks depth. Among all the personal
attacks on public officials written in the last decade one looks in vain for a
satiric portrait as vivid as Dryden's Achitophel, or the characters of Atticus
or Sporus in Pope. One may be tempted to say that our officials are too color-
less to inspire brilliant satires. But the satirist's function is precisely to make
insipid or negative qualities compelling as subjects (consider the *Dunciad*).

And it is not the case that our leaders have been completely lacking in color. Lyndon Johnson—what would Dryden or Pope have made of him?

The lack of a settled society, of unified codes of manners, of standards of stylistic decorum—all of these may be said to make satire difficult for us. But there is a further problem, discernible in the current crude and lifeless lampoons of public figures, and this problem may make satire impossible. The trouble is that we have lost the conception of man as a being responsible for his actions. To the Augustan satirists man still appeared as a rational creature capable of good while frequently choosing evil or folly. It is this notion of moral choice which gives humanity to characters like Corah and Achitophel in Dryden, who otherwise, in spite of the dazzling texture of the verse, would seem merely monstrous. It is this notion which provides any personal satire with its very grounds for censure. Nowadays we do not hold a man accountable for his actions. If a person behaves badly we do not blame him but (and here everyone has a favored scapegoat) the family background, the peer group, the System, the id, the schools, or the movements of the stars. Small wonder, when the atmosphere reeks of determinism, that poets should depict men as virtual puppets. But even if our government officials may at times behave like pawns of the historical process, even if some of them may sincerely believe themselves to be indestructible machines, it is the satirist's duty to remember that they are after all flesh and spirit, willing, doing and suffering, like the rest of us. Just as poets need not take their style from government communiqués, they need not base their conception of man on the behavioristic model held by the technocrats. The redemption not only of poetry but civilization hinges upon our resisting this tide of dehumanization. The following lines are Robert Bly's:

> These suggestions by Asians are not taken seriously.
> We know Rusk smiles as he passes them to someone.
> Men like Rusk are not men:
> They are bombs waiting to be loaded in a darkened hangar . . .

"Men like Rusk are not men." Even allowing for rhetorical license, isn't Bly's attitude disturbingly close to that of Calley? When Calley was charged with murdering upwards of a hundred Vietnamese, men, women and children, he had his defense ready: he was conditioned to regard these people as not human.

IV

America's poets are by and large unable to come to terms with the forces which are pulling the country apart. In its latest extreme form the American Nightmare seems as inhibiting to serious poetry as the American Dream at its rosiest ever was. The recent poems which have most impressively treated political subjects are those in which poets have confessed their feeling of impotence before disaster. I have mentioned some of Lowell's work; I might mention also some of the poems of Adrienne Rich—for instance, "Implosions":

The world's
not wanton
only wild and wavering

I wanted to choose words that even you
would have to be changed by

Take the word
of my pulse, loving and ordinary
Send out your signals, hoist
your dark scribbled flags
but take
my hand

All wars are useless to the dead

My hands are knotted in the rope
and I cannot sound the bell

My hands are frozen to the switch
and I cannot throw it

The foot is in the wheel

When it's finished and we're lying
in a stubble of blistered flowers
eyes gaping, mouths staring
dusted with crushed arterial blues

I'll have done nothing
even for you?

There is much craft here, and, just as unusual, much humility. Here the poet is telling us how she feels, not instructing us in how we ought to feel. She commands our assent all the more by refusing to court it. Our first impression when we read this is not likely to be, "Aha, protest poetry"; we will be thinking of things which resist categorization. Good poems, poems like this one, always fight free of labelling. Such individuality cannot be copied, but we can only hope that it can be emulated. The age is dominated by faceless collectivities, and in such a milieu the poet's most cogent protest lies not merely in what he has to say but in his finding an inimitable voice in which to say it.

Language Against Itself:
the Middle Generation of
Contemporary Poets
by Alan Williamson

IN THE last decade, a generation of poets has risen to prominence in America which—despite a diversity of backgrounds and coterie affiliations—is remarkably at one in its views of the poet's problems in relating to language and culture, and of the possible direction of resolution. I am thinking of poets now around forty—Gary Snyder, James Wright, Galway Kinnell, W. S. Merwin, and Robert Bly, principally, though writers as different from these, and each other, as John Ashbery, Robert Creeley, and Adrienne Rich have also responded, in their own ways, to the same concerns. For all these poets, language is at least as much the enemy as the facilitator of essential creativity. Having followed Freudian sublimation and Marxian superstructure to their ultimate conclusions, these poets not only know—as Shelley did—that language tends to simplify and conventionalize any complex inner state, but that it plays an active role in socializing and repressing us, leading us to accept external definitions of ourselves and to ignore messages from the non-verbal portions of the self, the body and the unconscious. The essential project, therefore, is to force language to transcend itself. These writers desire not a *mot juste*—however exalted by association with the Christian logos—but a word we can hear meant by the entire man who speaks it, his heart, lungs, and musculature as well as brain and voice-box. Galway Kinnell speaks of "breaking to a sacred, bloodier speech"; James Wright of "the pure clear word" and "the poetry of a grown man." Wright defines this "grown man" in terms that are characteristically bodily, proletarian, and of the dream life, as well as anti-verbal:

> The long body of his dream is the beginning of a dark
> Hair under an illiterate
> Girl's ear.

In his essay "Poetry and the Primitive: Notes on Poetry as an Ecological Survival Technique", Gary Snyder, following Charles Olson, lays great stress on the breath; but he gives it an almost mystical significance, as locating man in the physical world and in his own full self. It is "the other world coming into one's body," and "with pulse . . . the source of our inward sense of rhythm"; while "the voice, in everyone, is a mirror of his own deepest self." The

central point of Snyder's essay reverberates through much of the best poetry
of his generation:

> Poetry must sing or speak from authentic experience. Of all the streams
> of civilized tradition with roots in the paleolithic, poetry is one of the few
> that can realistically claim an unchanged function and a relevance which will
> outlast most of the activities that surround us today. Poets, as few others,
> must live close to the world that primitive men are in: the world, in its naked-
> ness, which is fundamental for all of us—birth, love, death; the sheer fact of
> being alive.

The reasons for the emergence of this shared poetic at this particular time
are, obviously, complex. Some, no doubt, are personal: all of these poets
began in the early 'fifties, at a time when accepted poetry was orderly, cere-
bral, and, through the influence of the New Criticism, rather codified; and
some (Wright and Merwin particularly) had their earliest successes with
such poetry. (Others had to wait until much later for any success.) In one
sense, these writers have learned the dangers of rational and conventionalized
utterance by fighting for their poetic lives against an extreme form of it. But
one cannot ignore the larger history, the fact that this was the first generation
to confront concentration camps and the atomic bomb, the fully revealed
destructiveness of civilized man, while still in the process of growing up.
Willingly or unwillingly, all these men have had to come to terms with the
view of their own moral history expressed by Kinnell in *The Book of Nightmares*:

> In the Twentieth Century of my trespass on earth,
> having exterminated one billion heathens,
> heretics, Jews, Moslems, witches, mystical seekers,
> black men, Asians, and Christian brothers,
> every one of them for his own good,
>
> a whole continent of red men for living in unnatural community
> and at the same time having relations with the land,
> one billion species of animals for being sub-human,
> and ready to take on the bloodthirsty creatures from the other planets,
> I, Christian man, groan out this testament of my last will.

For this generation, the search for values before and behind civilization has
become an "ecological survival technique" in deadly earnest; and (also for
the first time in recent history) there are tools other than Fancy available to
the task, in modern anthropology and depth psychology. When Snyder defies
at least fifty years of taste by calling Rousseau's Noble Savage "one of the
most remarkable intuitions in Western thought," his choice of words is worth
pondering; what once was considered a myth, whether appealing or noxious,
is now seen as an inspired scientific hypothesis, opening new areas of exploration and discovery. Almost all of these poets are concerned with the lessons

to be learned from animals, Indians, primitive or peasant cultures, the wilderness, as well as simple Wordsworthian solitary walks; and thus a whole new repertory of characteristic subjects is created. The poets less concerned with the literally primitive are often preoccupied with the evocation of a Jungian collective unconscious through free-association. But in Snyder's view, the two back countries "meet, one step even farther on, as *one*"; and "to transcend the ego is to go beyond society as well."

We may begin, therefore, with the ego, the "I" of the poet. It is interesting to compare these poets with their immediate precursors—Lowell, Berryman, Ginsberg—in this respect. The older poets intend a descriptive "I", a "voice" we recognize complexly as we do a friend's, a social ego at its richest and most individual. Their "I" seldom begins a poem; it arrives politely late, surrounded by phrases that cast back its idiosyncrasy, intelligence, tone, like so many mirrors. The "I" beginning, on the other hand, is ubiquitous in Wright ("I am bone lonely"; "I am delighted"; "I woke"), and not uncommon in any of his contemporaries. But what is more remarkable is their shared penchant for putting the "I" in the simplest of possible sentence structures, pronoun/active or linking verb, with no modifiers before or between. The "I" becomes numb, neutral, universal: a transparency through which we look directly to the state of being or feeling. (Snyder, on the other hand, prefers to omit the pronoun entirely—following in the line of Pound, Fenellosa, and the ideogram.)

The preference for simple sentence structures is not limited to first-person utterances. With these poets, no matter how wild or surrealistic the content becomes, the syntax tends to remain clear and enumerative. When Robert Bly describes the kind of free-associative poetry he desires, his metaphors are of motion from point to point, acrobatic enough, but still essentially linear: "a leaping about the psyche," "that swift motion all over the psyche . . . from a pine table to mad inward desires." This constitutes a strong break with the hitherto dominant mode of irrationalist poetry in English (that of Hart Crane, Dylan Thomas *et al.*), which, following from Rimbaud and Mallarmé, tends to suspend or confuse the normal syntactic flow, and create spaces for mystery and free-association between the words themselves. Perhaps it is the location of the mystery *in* language, or in an operation performed on language, that repels poets like Bly: better the true complexity of feeling should perish unuttered, than be confounded with the studied complexity of the intellect!

But there is a strictly literary, as well as a psychological or epistemological, aspect to the search for simplicity. These poets are Wordsworthian questioners, bent on isolating the poetry in poems from all that serves essentially mundane ends: to prepare or to seduce the reader, to shield the writer from anticipated criticisms, aesthetic or moral, to move the poem mechanically from place to place. Beginnings and endings in these poems are as abrupt and direct as the grammar is simple. There is an implicit aversion to all rhetorical

devices which set an image in an "improving"—or even an interpretive—
perspective; the image is intended to flash, like a spontaneous mental picture,
and is usually coterminous with the line. Indeed, the whole aesthetic of
"rendering" is suspect for these poets; its itemizing style of descriptive
writing seems cold and shopworn, its theory a rejection of the spontaneity
and purely inward validity of feelings. Often, these poets deliberately re-
instate the outlawed 19th Century vocabulary of feeling and awe: Wright is
devoted to the words "lovely" and "strange", Kinnell to forbidden abstrac-
tions like "infinite", "reality", "nothingness". (There is a similar forth-
rightness about human loves and loyalties, a general refusal to let the fear of
sentimentality—which after all means forced emotion—interfere with deep
commitments.) Perhaps it is all summed up in the mannerism—frequent
even with Merwin and Kinnell, poets whose natural breath-unit is as long
as Whitman's—of placing a single word alone on a line. There could be no
clearer statement that the artifice in poems is finally peripheral; the poetry
must, and can, spring from "the pure clear word," the meant word.

These generalities may acquire more substance if we look at particular
poems; I will offer two, the first James Wright's now famous, and enigmatic,
"Lying in a Hammock at William Duffy's Farm in Pine Island, Minnesota."

> Over my head, I see the bronze butterfly
> Asleep on the black trunk,
> Blowing like a leaf in green shadow.
> Down the ravine behind the empty house,
> The cowbells follow one another
> Into the distances of the afternoon.
> To my right,
> In a field of sunlight between two pines,
> The droppings of last year's horses
> Blaze up into golden stones.
> I lean back, as the evening darkens and comes on.
> A chicken hawk floats over, looking for home.
> I have wasted my life.

The relation of the "I" to this poem of almost pure sensation is self-evidently
problematic: two quite impersonal occurrences, followed by a statement of
feeling so deep as to seem nearly universal—all the more so, perhaps, because
it is a quotation from another poem, Rimbaud's "Song of the Highest Tower"
(*J'ai perdu ma vie*). The critic A. Poulin misidentifies the source as the last
line of Rilke's "Archaic Torso of Apollo" (*Du musst dein Leben ändern*), but
in a sense he is right: like Rilke's last line, Wright's forces the reader to go
back and relive the previous, the apparently objective, part of the poem in
order to come to terms with it.

One notices first the sleep of the butterfly: how entrusted, how pliable it
is, "Blowing like a leaf in green shadow," possessed of the stillness of a plant
or even of a mineral ("bronze"). It is an image of being wholly at one with

one's world; and this quality persists into the following lines through the subtle harmonizing of time and space ("the distances of the afternoon"), the sense of the cowbells as a musical measure of both. ("A field of sunlight" is another, subtler blending of categories—physical object and light—which also has the effect of making the world seem closer, more intertwined, more real.) The image of the horse-droppings offers a far more complicated, but still serene, sense of temporal process—one involving continuity ("last year's"), transmutation into mineral permanence ("golden stones"), but also beautiful consumption ("Blaze up"). In so far as one can paraphrase at all, the poem sees in a process—even a decay—that is continually productive of new beauty, the kind of visionary perfection we habitually associate with permanence alone. I suspect a Freudian undercurrent, too, in the fact that such an important position in the poem is given to dung; Wright cannot help being aware of the theories which associate our early feelings about our own fæces with the development of the categories—so crucial to our sense of being a part, or not a part, of the physical world—of subject and object, beauty and ugliness, saving and losing.

It is the evening and the chicken hawk, then, that toll Wright back to his sole self. The verb "floats", with its sense of indefinite location in time and space, itself contrasts strongly with the harmonious centrality of almost everything else in the poem; then, we are told the hawk is "looking for home." But the hawk, presumably, will find its home easily (perhaps this is why "floats" suggests buoyancy, as well as indefiniteness); whereas the human consciousness the hawk brings to mind can know the feeling of being fully at home in the physical world, fully alive, only at such brief and special moments as the poem records. Such moments seem possible, too, only when the human world is remote; the house in the poem is empty. Thus, it is the very specialness of the moment that gives birth to the sense of a surrounding waste.

If Wright's poem, though wholly novel in some respects, in others remains assimilable to prototypes (Rilke or Keats), Gary Snyder's "Trail Crew Camp at Bear Valley, 9000 Feet. Northern Sierra—White Bone and Threads of Snowmelt Water" is both harder in technique and more deeply alien to traditional Western thought:

> Cut branches back for a day—
> trail a thin line through willow
> up buckbrush meadows,
> creekbed for twenty yards
> winding in boulders
> zigzags the hill
> into timber, white pine.
>
> gooseberry bush on the turns.
> hooves clang on the riprap

> dust, brush, branches.
> a stone
>   cairn at the pass—
> strippt mountains hundreds of miles.
>
> sundown went back
>   the clean switchbacks to camp.
> bell on the gelding,
> stew in the cook tent,
> black coffee in a big tin can.

By virtue of the omitted pronoun, the poem plunges us emphatically into activity, work, rather than detached consciousness. But the succeeding lines are verbless and choppy, a delicate mimicry of the worker's extreme concentration on his task, the narrowing horizon of his senses, his almost arrested movement. The effect is so strong that, in the last line of the stanza, we get a kind of rushing sensation from a mere preposition of forward motion, or forward gaze.

And yet this day of minute labor all serves to bring Snyder slowly toward a vision that is its complete opposite, as bare, unlimited, sublime as it is detailed, focussed, concrete: "strippt mountains hundreds of miles." We are not told Snyder's emotions on encountering this sight; but if one is alert to the music of the poem, there is a quality of caught breath slowly released in the enclosing sibilants of the line. The pass marks the end of Snyder's task; he now returns in moments over the trail it has taken him all day to clear ("switchbacks" is thus a sort of pun). He returns, also, to the world of detail, but detail now irradiated—as we sense from the languorous *rallentando* of the last three lines—with exhaustion, hunger, accomplishment, the taste of the upper air.

It may have occurred to the reader that the pattern of Snyder's poem very strikingly resembles that of a religious experience. Trails are like Ways, hence Snyder's occupation strongly suggests a process of meditation or spiritual exercise, clearing the path from temporal life to the moment of Enlightenment—the sudden dropping-away of the phenomenal world in the contemplation of the infinite and eternal, All and Nothingness. The ending of the poem reflects equally age-old processes: the return to the world, the greater awareness of reality paradoxically following on the awareness of its opposite, the insight that the Way Up is the Way Down. Yet we should beware of saying, in the usual sloppy way of critics, that the events in the poem (or the poem itself) *symbolize* such an experience; they contain the experience, as a Zen koan does, even if the content is to be unlocked only by arduous subsequent meditation. Thus, from a Zen point of view, skilful and concentrated work, work which tends to fuse the categories of subject and object, being and doing, is a kind of spiritual exercise likely to lead to Enlightenment; and this Enlightenment would be no less itself for arriving through a sudden vista of mountains. (Symbolism in our usual sense presupposes a hierarchic arrangement of kinds of experience and categories of consciousness, and it is this presupposition that I think Snyder, in keeping with many non-Western traditions, would wish to exclude.)

Poems like these have been referred to, derogatorily, as "Imagist" by a well-known British critic and an American popular magazine. But this seems to me a misapplied term; for I feel in these poems no consciousness of restraint, no sense that hardness and indirection are aesthetic goods *per se*, and certainly no taboo against emotional or abstract language. The poets do choose subjects that are seemingly small and cool: rhythms of day and night, and the seasons; work, pleasure, and rest; the mind in unfixed contemplation. But they do so, clearly, because these areas of life seem stranger, more important, even more religious, to them than to earlier poets, poets committed to the ego or to one of its passionate or demonic antitheses. And meaning for all of these poets (though Snyder alone has the koan as an explicit model) would inhere in an experience and not a paraphrase, and would therefore be betrayed by a less bodily, a more explanatory, language. (I do not mean to imply, however, that all poems written in this style deal with Enlightenment; many lead into darkness or into complexity, but they have the same method, the same sense of how important spiritual events happen.) Many of the surest achievements of this generation, the poems I am most convinced would hold up by the standards of any time and any aesthetic, are in this very short, very pure genre. I would like to name a few of the most remarkable: James Wright's "The Jewel", "Twilights", "To the Evening Star", "Lifting Illegal Nets By Flashlight", "Sitting in a Small Screenhouse on a Summer Morning"; Galway Kinnell's "The Fossils", "How Many Nights", and especially "La Bagarede"; Robert Bly's "The Clear Air of October" and "Snowfall in the Afternoon", among others; Merwin's "Watchers"; and many, many poems by Snyder, but I will mention "Fire in the Hole", "Burning the Small Dead", "The Levels", "Circumambulating Arunachala", "What Do They Say". On the other hand, none of these writers is exactly indifferent to longer forms, or to what are traditionally considered the great themes. To do justice to this aspect, we must come to an individual consideration of each writer—a step no doubt long overdue, especially to the uninitiated reader who would appreciate a less vague idea of individual visions, gifts, achievements.

Gary Snyder is the most remarkable personality among these poets, and the most famous, having become, in America, a kind of patron saint of ecology. This has led to a certain amount of denigration of his thought, apparently on the theory that anything popular with the young has to be facile. Actually, Snyder, in rejecting Western culture, has prepared his peace with as eclectic and painstaking an apprenticeship as one could imagine: graduate study in Japanese and Chinese studies at Berkeley; review articles on Pacific Northwest Indian folklore at a time when the field was virtually unexplored; work in the "back country" as logger, forest ranger, and fire lookout; the greater part of six years as a Zen novice at the monastery in Kyoto. Snyder is a remarkable polemical essayist, pungent in aphorism ("A hand pushing a button may wield great power, but that hand will never learn what a hand can do"), but equally at home with the common sense, clarity, humor of a middle style. His short poems in *The Back Country* seem to me subtler in design, more intellectually suggestive than those of any of his contemporaries; I suspect this is partly due to his grounding in Zen, but I lack the knowledge to substantiate this guess further than I have done in discussing "Trail Crew Camp at Bear Valley", and so would prefer to dwell on some of Snyder's other achievements. In its total structure, *The Back Country* seems to move outward from short poems toward more ambitious poems of religious and political criticism, poems remarkable alike for their historical insight and for the canny humor and daring that spring from Snyder's essential mystic's disbelief in history. Both qualities can be seen at their best in the extended metaphor that concludes the satire "For the West":

> Ah, that's America:
> the flowery glistening oil blossom
>   spreading on water—
> it was so tiny, nothing, now it keeps expanding
> all those colors,
>   our world
>   opening inside outward toward us,
> each part swelling and turning
> who would have thought such turning;
>
> as it covers,
>   the colors fade.
> and the fantastic patterns
>   fade.
> I see down again through clear water.
>
>   it is the same
> ball bounce rhyme the
>   little girl was singing,
>   all those years.

In sound, too, Snyder is perhaps the subtlest craftsman of his generation. He derives mainly from the Pound/Williams/Projectivist line, and hence writes the most "open", the least heavily accented free verse; but his most important inheritance from Pound (and from Robert Duncan) is perhaps his use of rhyme, and of syncopated versions of traditional meters, within a free form poem to bring it nearer incantation and song. This tendency (appropriate enough to Snyder's interest in the origins of poetry) becomes increasingly dominant in his more recent books; the early *Myths & Texts* still shows some of the crabbed and pedantic side of Pound's elliptical style, while the very recent "Songs" from *Regarding Wave* have an intentional wave-pattern of intersecting consonances that becomes, at moments, almost Hopkinsian.

Galway Kinnell attained early fame with his very ambitious poem "The Avenue Bearing the Initial of Christ Into the New World", which is still arguably as good as anything he has written. It reminds one of Crane and early Lowell in its sonority, but more of "The Waste Land"—if, indeed, of anything in literature—in its ability to include a seething cauldron of urban sensations, of randomness and ugliness, yet hold its own poetic shape. What it lacks is an underlying vision or concern, beyond mere awe at the weight of humanity, the "instants of transcendence" and the "oceans of loathing and fear." At the rare points where it tries to conceal this lack through rhetoric, the poem becomes abruptly stagey. Both the strengths and the weaknesses here are prophetic for Kinnell's later work. He continues to have the most over-vaulting and Marlovian style of his contemporaries, but it is a double-edged advantage, since his share of the generational directness, and his personal fondness for metaphysical clichés, make any hamming more obvious, and less likely to be mitigated by surrounding beauties, than it would be in a poet like Crane. On the other hand, his later poems succeed in uncovering the real feeling behind the Avenue C poem and making it, itself, the subject. It is the sense of a violent, impersonal, unseemly energy behind life, stunning the ego and bringing both "transcendence"—because it makes a continuum of the personal self and the cosmos—and "loathing and fear," because it is inseparable from the threat of change and death, "the pre-trembling of a house that falls." In poem after poem, Kinnell resuffers one identical ordeal, accepting death in order to be able to accept life, and concomitantly—like his Thoreau in "The Last River"—accepting cruel appetites in order to accept his full animal being, and avoid a crueller sado-masochistic spirituality. At times the acceptance seems as negative as that, at least; but at other times it has its own special serenity, as at the end of "La Bagarede", where "the seventh / of the Sisters, she who hid herself / for shame / at having loved one who dies, is shining." Kinnell's form has not altered substantially since his second book, just as his central experience has not. It is a sequence of generally very short, always numbered free verse units; the isolations somewhat take the place of rhetoric in conferring a brooding intensity on details; and the poet is free to move quickly from himself to nature to vignettes of human life, while keeping our primary attention on the pattern that moves us into terror and out again into some form of resolution. Kinnell's poetry has a very narrow range of purely personal experiences. He can really handle only those that directly touch on his cosmic vision—passionate love, being with the dying and the newly born, political imprisonment in the South—but of these he writes extraordinarily well (offhand, at least, "Under the Maud Moon" seems as good a poem about the first year of life as I have read). But one looks in vain, in Kinnell's poetry, for the personal roots of his own vision and his repeated self-trial; though I am struck by the recurring theme of self-hatred, the special self-hatred of the large man presumed to be brutal by others, to be imprecise and blundering by himself—as it appears, for instance, in his feelings about his size at birth ("It was eight days before the doctor / Would scare my mother with me"). But I have dwelt too much on limitations, not enough on what makes the poetry convincing or overwhelming—the moments of stunned sensation in which human beings turn into force and object, and nature into embodied metaphysics, before our eyes; in which a tear is

> one of those bottom-heavy, glittering, saccadic bits
> of salt water that splash down
> the haunted ravines of a human face

and the dawn happens so:

> The song of the whippoorwill stops
> And the dimension of depth seizes everything.

If Kinnell is the most energetic of these poets, James Wright is the most lyrical and the most purely imaginative; he is also the most bent on vulnerability, on getting immediately to the essentially poetic material. He has turned to Georg Trakl, and to modern Spanish and Latin American poets, for models of such openness. He has sometimes been criticized for the foreign sound of his idioms; but (except in his earliest experiments) they seem to me as suited to his voice—and, consequently, enriching to the possibilities of English poetry—as comparable assimilations in Eliot and Auden.

Wright's themes have remained remarkably constant, from his earliest formalist work. There is the "profound poetry of the poor and of the dead"—to quote Stevens—and of the outcast (a category so comprehensively important as to include executed murderers, Swift's poetry, and Warren G. Harding). There is what I can only call a strength of misery in love; and an equally strong desire to transcend the bodily self into conditions of delicacy intuited from animals, stones, dreams. Like Goethe, Wright is drawn towards a double transcendence, pure creature and pure spirit; but oddly, his commitment to a style centered on bodily states makes his account of this tension one of the most precise and interesting in existence.

But Wright is also, unlike his contemporaries, a part of the American tradition of mythopoeic regionalism, a "sole owner and proprietor" of names and places. He names the important names in his private history with a confident insouciance that springs partly from the bardic role itself, as in the remarkable "Speak":

> And Jenny, oh my Jenny
> Whom I love, rhyme be damned,
> Has broken her spare beauty
> In a whorehouse old.
> She left her new baby

In a bus station can,
And sprightly danced away
Through Jacksontown.

Which is a place I know,
One where I got picked up
A few shrunk years ago
By a good cop.

And perhaps the key is, finally, the knowledge of place: of the northern Great Plains, which remind Wright of "the sea, that once solved the whole loneliness / Of the Midwest"; but especially of his native southeastern Ohio, where the fate and exhaustion of Eastern Europe repeats itself in towns named for the super-corporations, beside the river that is at once Indian sacred place and "Tar and chemical strangled tomb." Like Winesburg or Yoknapatawpha, Wright's places seem less the accidents of one life than scenes the American experience itself has chosen for its agons. This quality sometimes seems to me to give a necessary larger importance to Wright's poetry of emotional daring; but I am not sure one can separate the two.

The remaining two writers must be treated more briefly. Robert Bly is the most vocal theorist of his generation, and has helped other writers the most, through his magazine *The Sixties*. But his own poetry—except for the nature poems in *Silence in the Snowy Fields*, which are technically limpid, and full of a not easily expressible peace—seems too much the result of a design for irrational poetry, too little of genuinely unconscious promptings. In his recent surrealistic political poetry, I feel I hear a deep voice choking on its own anger and going shrill; I sympathize, but cannot compare the results with such miraculously heart-whole poems as Snyder's "For the West" or Merwin's "For Now".

I include W. S. Merwin as the exception that proves the rule. His sensibility is not naturally concrete or earthly; it is rather ethereal, and, like Northrop Frye's or Robert Graves', finds its music in the apprehension of orderly ritual patterns behind all temporal events. It is therefore the more remarkable how his poetry has developed toward the same tactics as his contemporaries' (the simple, quasi-narrative sentence, the isolated word, the numb "I"), toward the same loyalties, political and symbolic, and, above all, toward the same stress on the inadequacy of language:

My blind neighbor has required of me
A description of darkness
And I begin I begin but

I have deferred until now a consideration of the authors' most recent books—Snyder's *Regarding Wave*, Kinnell's *The Book of Nightmares*, Wright's *Collected Poems*, Merwin's *The Carrier of Ladders*—because I see in them a common problem, and a common temptation. They all take on more ambitious, more ideological, themes than their predecessors, but they also tend more to abstract self-explanation. And none is untouched by the kind of moral pomposity, the self-importance about the act of writing (regardless of the aesthetic value of the result), evident in Wright's

> If you do not care one way or another about
> The preceding lines,
> Please do not go on listening
> On any account of mine.
> Please leave the poem.
> Thank you.

or, more subtly, in Kinnell's bombastic peroration:

> The foregoing scribed down
> in March, of the year Seventy,
> on my sixteen-thousandth night of war and madness,
> in the Hotel of Lost Light, under the freeway

I suspect these tendencies may stem from the sense of having reached the limits of an original aesthetic project, without the clear leap into greatness which at least seems to have existed in some poetic careers. (Though, in fairness, these writers may not be so concerned with greatness. Snyder, with perhaps the best title to it, is not; he has long held the now popular radical idea that the "major poet" is a myth fostered by bourgeois competitiveness, and that future writers will be more tribal, i.e. write mainly for their friends.) But I do think all these writers have reached crises in their work, in which their poetic self-definition, being so highly moral to begin with, offers the subtlest of temptations: they can exchange a corruptible aesthetic merit for an incorruptible moral one, and then allow themselves self-repetition with the same excuse a first-grade teacher has—the lesson is not yet adequately learned. Fortunately, this is not all there is to say; for each of the new books has exploratory elements which could well be new poetic personalities *in ovo*. I would wish to mention, in Kinnell, the wonderful physical/metaphysical descriptions of infancy; in Snyder, the celebratory "Songs"; in Wright, a poem like "Katy Did", which treats for the first time a kind of Sartrean complexity in the act of self-definition, whether by names or images.

I do not wish to conclude with an evaluation. Even if the idea of greatness does remain current, it will still, I imagine, be years before anyone can intelligently measure the cost of renouncing so many of the enhancements, the structures, the tacts of earlier poetry, against the new areas of being made articulate through these poets' daring. But I do not mean to imply that these poets are a "wave of the future"; they seem to me more a clearing of the air. Most of the younger poets I know have either gone beyond into some form of Dadaism, or else made a more casual peace with language, and restricted their questioning of civilisation to content. Perhaps a poetry of such severity could only be written on the very edge, or hinge, of such a cultural crisis as we are going through. It requires a very special kind of love, and hatred, to want so much to make language do exactly what, by one's own definitions, it cannot.

Diminishing Returns:
the writings of W. S. Merwin
by James Atlas

I.

AN AGE lasts but a moment in America, where so much of what now passes
for literature is produced rather than written, and where demand is artificial.
Advanced capitalism, the prolongation of Vietnam, and a disintegrating culture have induced such psychic strains in us as to compel incautious readings
of recent events; impatient before our own unstable past, and anxious to
locate, if not restore, whatever is American, untutored critics discover themselves inventing categories where there are none, classifying what refuses to
be classified.

So it is not surprising that *Time* magazine chose in the recent past to write
about those poets alleged to dominate "Poetry Today", recording the vicissi-
tudes of "Polemical Roarers, Confessional Sufferers, Tiny Imagists, Compulsive Reporters and Cult Poets." While I suppose there is some small
measure of truth in all this, it was discouraging to learn that "today's in-
tentionally unmemorable, flatted verse seems an unnecessary and misguided
burden upon the ear and the imagination."[1] To begin with, I was not aware
that burdens were capable of being "misguided"; what is worse, that arro-
gant, unknowing journal happened on a partial truth. There has occurred a
deliberate muting of the poet's voice until it threatens to become inaudible, a
diminished ambition, a nervous capitulation to silence.

George Steiner, describing what it means to live "In a Post-Culture",
noted how "the hope of creating against time, of making language outlast
death"[2] has vanished along with "the obsessive aloneness" required for such
a chore. No longer able to manage the sheer disorder of our age, American
poets at least have shown themselves unwilling to risk a language that would
engage our imaginative energies, or dare approach a level of emotion absent
in our own experience of the world. Modern European literature, perhaps
because its concerns remain inextricable from other priorities, such as the
shoring up of culture, or providing the leisure class with significant emblems
of their difference, regards its landscape as an unchanging domain: that of
listening to those impulses of language and speech which articulate the
dilemma of existing.

If, as Christopher Caudwell believed, "poetry at every stage of its historical development reflects in its own province man's relation to his environment,"[3] then the sudden reticence of language as it appeared in the works of Kafka, Wittgenstein, and later Osip Mandelstam owed its tentative qualities to the bewildering disintegration that seized Europe during World War I. A version of Brecht's "alienation effect" was achieved in the troubled atmosphere charged with what Steiner elsewhere called "a reflex of asceticism."[4] Rather than proposing interruptions in a text, theirs was the problem of how to write at all, so that the subject of literature became literature. With Valéry, poems were to be no more than mappings of linguistic acts.

Such a condition, in which writers considered their obligation to be that of reflecting their own historical moment in all its immense confusion, extending the limits of silence until the poem threatened to become inaudible, concealed implicit dangers; what Michael Hamburger spoke of in *The Truth of Poetry* as "a private religion, a *religio poetae* irreconcilable with the exigencies of the public world,"[5] enlisted worshippers of Mallarmé's dictum that "tout, au monde, existe pour aboutir à un livre." Despite the noise of Surrealism in Paris between the Wars, and the Fascist trumpetings of Marinetti, hermeticism and a morose, laconic diction seemed the modes chosen among Eastern European poets, the French, and Austrians like August Stramm as illustrations of their surrender to silence. Brecht's "language-washings"; César Vallejo's reluctance to think of literature as having to do with life, as in these lines:

> *Un hombre pasa con un pan al hombro.*
> *Voy a escribir, después, sobre mi doble?*

and Raymond Queneau's observation that "Un poéme c'est bien peu de chose" all belonged among endeavors to reduce the poem, to regard themselves as alien.

In America, where Eliot and Pound influenced an entire generation, the late Charles Olson's Projectivism and the Black Mountain School out of which it originated deriving from Pound's Imagist experiments, the crisis of language appeared in a less immediate form. Pound's dislocation of syntax and meaning in *The Cantos*, Eliot's claim that "some rude unknown *psychic material*"[6] directs the poet's imagination: both suggested an emphasis on the writer's consulting his own experience, all the while engaged in locating a language that expresses those investigations. Discourse in the dramatic monologues of Lowell or Jarrell acted as a subtle illumination of their predicaments and maladies, where the distinctive tonalities of speech registered impulses on the verge of remaining unconscious. What mattered was the revelation of temperament, the discriminations of a mind in conflict with its own historical inheritance; Lowell's incessant chronicling of specific details in *Life Studies* was calculated to situate him amidst a various world of things that evoked a singular past, the weathered legacies of New England and, in turn, America.

II.

When Robert Bly began publishing *The Fifties*, a journal devoted to polemics and translations, from his farm in Minnesota, respected American poets appeared to be concerning themselves with a legend about their own decline. The tradition of radical antinomianism in American letters, exemplified in the philosophical rebellions of Transcendentalism and, before that, in Lowell's *Jonathan Edwards*, alive in a land where "Hope lives in doubt," obsessed those Eastern poets who dominated the pages of *Partisan Review* and borrowed the taut idioms of another age. Less austere than their Fugitive teachers, Ransom and Tate, more daring than their own earliest poems revealed (Berryman's *Homage to Mistress Bradstreet* and Lowell's *Lord Weary's Castle*, both energetic and ambitious enterprises, were still conventional), writers like Jarrell appreciated things that were "so American": old movies, television soap operas, antiques; *The Lost World* was his homage to a condition A. Alvarez described in a B.B.C. Third Programme broadcast as "the responsibility of the artist to himself, the feeling that he has to create his whole world —his moral order, his style and his tradition—for himself and from scratch."[7] There was a tradition visible to them, but no longer capable of being appropriated to their purposes.

Bly, in his poems and in the partisan articles he published above the name of Crunk, argued that American poets had been confined in their own temperaments, and that, "Part of our culture has a vested interest in the dying tradition."[8] Insisting that an opposed and urgent mode of literature was required to revive American poetry, a mode that had long been made available to Spanish, Russian, and German poets, Bly introduced them to what began as a limited audience; the various qualities of their experience, both inward and political, represented to him a means of escaping the psycho-analytic and even academic tendencies of recent American writing. His intention being "to penetrate down into an evolutionary part of the mind,"[9] Bly discerned in the leaps of association, the intense, irrational metaphors, the disturbing incoherence of those he read and translated a return to the sources of poetic inspiration.

What Bly instigated was no less than a radical critique of the American mind, and his celebrated political activism, culminating in the publication of *A Poetry Reading Against The Vietnam War*, implied that poetics and politics were inseparable. The sheer political importance of poets in other countries, the non-ideological but rebellious vigor shown in their writings, convinced him of their value to poets in America; the range of their experiments should have been instructing us about the nature of our own resistance to political events.

III.

Out of all this, the remarkable survival of an older generation (Lowell's *Notebook* and Berryman's *Dream Songs* possess immeasurable stature in our own time), Bly's influential translations, and the worsening situation in America, both political and cultural, younger poets have been conspiring to create an idiom that would be theirs alone; obliged to draw the substance of their labors, language, from an ever dwindling store, the response has been diverse and (with some exceptions) disappointing. Poets as dissimilar as James Wright and Galway Kinnell, sharing to some extent Bly's ideas, have reproduced in their poems the vivid metaphorical inventions, the inwardness characteristic of non-American poetry. Kinnell believes, "The voice is a particular recognizable voice; at the same time it mysteriously sheds personality and becomes simply the voice of a creature on earth speaking."[10] Divested of all that suggests the specific, poems like Kinnell's "The Bear" achieve a totemic significance in their identification of animal with human realms. What he thinks of as "breaking out of the closed ego of modern man" is a desire to refuse alienation, to conquer a stubborn, unyielding landscape of technological objects and, like Roethke, establish a region as his own. Rather than submit to the state of exacerbated nerves and urban terror that caused Lowell to complain about "the chafe and jar/ of nuclear war," some poets are beginning to move in the direction of "poems/ about what I was before I was born, what we were" (Neruda).

Others, having decided, perhaps, that nothing less than the minimal is capable of expressing our condition, write as if words are in danger of extinction; W. S. Merwin seems to be the most ambitious and unusual proponent of this school. Working on his own, earning a livelihood through writing and translations, Merwin has established the reputation of a leading American poet. His most recent collection, *The Carrier of Ladders*, was awarded the Pulitzer Prize in 1970, and *Selected Translations 1948–1968* won the P.E.N. Translation Prize in 1968. In England, Merwin prepared several radio scripts for the B.B.C., and since then has issued *The Miner's Pale Children*, a volume of prose.

From the beginning, Merwin has demonstrated a concern with reticence, with not speaking; *A Mask For Janus*, published in the Yale Series of Younger Poets (1952), consisted of ballads in archaic diction, songs, and mythic parables. Auden, who was then editor of the Series, noted in his introduction "The historical experience which is latent" in Merwin's poems: "By translating these feelings into mythical terms, the poet is able to avoid what a direct treatment could scarcely have avoided, the use of names and events which will probably turn out not to have been the really significant ones." What Auden meant was that these poems had been composed in a language devoid of immediate social content, abstract and imprecise. Their ornate, peculiar diction, an absence of all qualities distinguishing the modern, a derivative, self-conscious voice: this was the result of Merwin's decision to "avoid what a direct treatment could scarcely have avoided," and it has plagued his writing ever since.

Even so, an intelligence comparable to that of Wallace Stevens, though lacking Stevens' enviable grace, was at work in such lines as these, from "Dictum: For a Masque of Deluge":

> A falling frond may seem all trees. If so
> We know the tone of falling. We shall find
> Dictions for rising, words for departure;
> And time will be sufficient before that revel
> To teach an order and rehearse the days
> Till the days are accomplished: so now the dove
> Makes assignations with the olive tree,
> Slurs with her voice the gestures of time:
> The day foundering, the dropping sun
> Heavy, the wind a low portent of rain.

Harvey Gross, alluding to Merwin's as "a representative first volume," observes in his *Sound and Form in Modern Poetry* that "the poets of the late forties and fifties have shown an almost religious devotion to iambic pentameter, intricate stanzas, and close formal arrangements."[11] Rhetorical and stylized, Merwin's earliest poems conformed to the procedures of the English poetic tradition, even borrowing inversions ("The frame that was my devotion/ And my blessing was"), words ("in priestly winter bide"), and characters (huntsmen, lords, and kings); while almost no traces of this lyrical, delicate style remain in Merwin's later collections, there are undeniable resemblances between what he was writing then and a mode that owes less to some identifiable period than to the language of English literature.

The Dancing Bears, which appeared in 1954, elaborated on the techniques introduced in *A Mask For Janus*; while an extended line widened prosodic possibilities:

> And there where the spume flies and the mews echoed and beckoned
> The bowing drowned, because in her hands love and the one song
> Leap and the long faith is born gladly, there through the waters
> Of the dead . . .

still the long narrative poems, variations on old romantic tales, replete with castles and maidens, disclosed an odd self-conscious pose that should have been ironic. It was "On the Subject of Poetry" that Merwin showed a subtle control, revealing a failure of confidence in his own medium that becomes obsessive later on:

> When I speak, father, it is the world
> That I must mention. He does not move
> His feet nor so much as raise his head
> For fear he should disturb the sound he hears
> Like a pain without a cry, where he listens.

What is referred to here is that indistinct, unknown persona destined to become the speaker in Merwin's prose poems: the poet, the poet's father, or simply a man:

> I do not understand the world, father.
> By the millpond at the end of the garden
> There is a man who slouches listening
> To the wheel revolving in the stream, only
> There is no wheel to revolve.

There are two possible readings here; either the wheel revolves without the poet's intervention, or what he hears is imagined, not a thing that exists at all. Believing the world to be inaudible, conjecturing whether "the mind of heaven be a mind/ of questions", Merwin selected as a subject the tentative properties of language, and all that followed was an affirmation of silence.

Richard Howard, in *Alone with America*, proposed that Merwin's work, which then consisted of six volumes, be classified in three consecutive categories, which seems a legitimate reading of their changes; in such a scheme the middle period, embracing *Green With Beasts* (1956) and *The Drunk in the Furnace* (1960), appears to have been the most expansive and accomplished. Part I of *Green With Beasts*, subtitled "Physiologus: Chapters for a Bestiary", contained several of the poems that were selected to represent him in Donald Hall's well-known anthologies; elaborate elegiac lines, intense and varied modalities of metre and caesura, a heightened and rhetorical resonance: in these poems about "Leviathan", "Two Horses", "Dog", "White goat, white ram" Merwin explored the capacities of the sustained and complex poem, not reticent about risking the temper of elevated speech. "Fog" imitated Pound's use of Anglo-Saxon rhythms in "The Sea-Farer", compressing language, exacting from it a conscious alliteration and assonance:

> Ships were not named for haven but if we were
> There will be time for it yet. Let us turn head,
> Out oars, and pull for the open. Make we
> For mid-sea, where the winds are and stars too.

while in "Birds Waking", the repetitive insistence of Hopkins could have been detected:

> Oh let it be by this violence, then, let it be now,
> Now when in their sleep, unhearing, unknowing,
> Most faces must be closest to innocence,
> When the light moves unhesitating to fill the sky with clearness
> And no dissent could be heard above the din of its welcome,
> Let the great globe well up and dissolve like its last birds,
> With the bursting roar and uprush of song!

The sheer exuberance of orchestrated effects, emphatic and exaggerated, coupled with a loud, unashamed eloquence, claimed obvious rewards, among them the reconciliation within a single voice of traditional and modern utterance.

Idiosyncratic in his themes, concerned less with a private self than with ill-defined motifs that wavered between the pastoral and metaphysics, Merwin had mastered the techniques of writing and then amplified their truths. It was not until the publication of *The Drunk in the Furnace*, though, that his own temperament became visible, his Being-in-the-world; voyages at sea, motifs of loss, and the phenomenon of surviving death, witnessing that moment of collective disaster when "our cries were swallowed up and all hands lost," had become obsessive concerns. In several poems, such as "Bell Buoy", "Sea Monster", "Cape Dread", and "Sailor Ashore", the sea mirrors and exemplifies our own alien condition; its meanings are interpreted as allegorical; a ship leaving port "has put/ All of disaster between us: a gulf/ Beyond reckoning. It begins where we are." And the closing lines of "The Bones" recall Kafka's parable of "Infinite Hope, but not for us":

> Shells were to shut out the sea,
> The bones of birds were built for floating
> On air and water, and those of fish devised
> For their feeding depths, while a man's bones were framed
> For what? For knowing the sands are here,
> And coming to hear them a long time; for giving
> Shapes to the sprawled sea, weight to its winds,
> And wrecks to plead for its sands. These things are not
> Limitless: we know there is somewhere
> An end to them, though every way you look
> They extend farther than a man can see.

Merwin's tacit longing is to live among whatever he names, entering the world again in some other, elemental form. His is the chore of "giving/ Shapes" to things, altering their appearance, transmuting them, just as our presence in the natural world enacts a sea-change on what surrounds us.

In opposition to this eternal, devastating sea, imposing in its immense and silent depths, is urban life; this other solitude, arriving in pool halls, wretched hotels, and old men's homes, evades "the real dark" of existence, concealed in a vast, incomprehensible universe. Merwin's portrait of "The Gleaners" evokes a desolate image of the dying:

> They always gather on summer nights there
> On the corner under the buggy street-bulb,
> Chewing their dead stubs outside the peeling
>   Bar, those foreign old men,
>
> Till the last street-car has squealed and gone
> An hour since into the growing silence,
> Leaving only the bugs' sounds, and their own breathing;
>   Sometime then they hobble off.

The language of these poems is both specific and spare, cautious and intense; rejecting nostalgia, Merwin writes as if he were speaking, as if in chronicling our own decline he becomes ashamed. Terse rhythms and vague anxieties ("Do not look up. God is/ On High. He can see you. You will die.") are buried in the rubble of an abandoned home where unsalvageable machines, "crutched in their last seizures," resemble

> the framed ancestors, trapped in their collars,
> Beetling out of oval clouds from the black
> Tops of the rooms, their unappeasable jowls
> By nothing but frayed, fading cords leashed
> To the leaking walls.

The larger significance of Merwin's vision, embedded in tropes and metaphor, remained in these poems unstated but inescapable. In "Uncle Hess" and "Grandmother Watching at Her Window" the casual cadences of undisturbed, unconscious meditation created their own reflective silences, spaces in which regret was implied and imprecise; the poems were sure of themselves.

The Moving Target, which appeared three years later, announced Merwin's departure from the disciplined versification and controlled narrative style of his earlier collections. Sprawling, unrhymed lines, idiomatic speech and the notation of trivial thoughts, irrational similes ("I bring myself back from the streets that open like long/ Silent laughs"): there was in these unusual poems an oratorical "I" whose abrasive complaints echoed Eliot's dramatic monologues:

> Sunday, a fine day, with my ears wiped and my collar buttoned
> I went for a jaunt all the way out and back on
> A street car and under my hat with the dent settled
> In the right place I was thinking maybe—a thought
> Which I have noticed many times like a bold rat—
> I should have stayed making some of those good women
> Happy, for a while at least, Vera with
> The eau-de-cologne and the small dog named Joy,
> Gladys with her earrings, cooking and watery arms, the one
> With the limp and the fancy sheets, some of them
> Are still there I suppose, oh no,

Or the speaker's was a disembodied voice, addressing some unknown Other, or talking out loud; irrational comparisons, partial syllepses ("Night, I am/ As old as pain and I have/ No other story."), and puns proliferated, while the repeated use of animism ("the horizon/ Climbs down from its tree") imbued the poems with a Surrealist confusion. Cesare Pavese, discussing "Certain Poems Not Yet Written", decided against the mode of composition he called "narrating images" because "nothing can distinguish the words which evoke an image from those which evoke an object."[12] It is this, and an absence of distinction between words and things, that lies behind *The Moving Target*, where Merwin's belief is in the similitude, even synonymity, of image and object.

His departure from the discursive revelation of objects becomes more noticeable in the closing poems; interruptions of thought, intrusions of unconscious mind are more pronounced, until in "The Crossroads of the World etc." all punctuation has been omitted, except a question mark that ends the poem. After that, there is none in this volume, or in the two that have succeeded it. Line breaks appear to be random, the words themselves are arbitrary, verging on hysteria:

> These words start rising out of my wax shoes I
> Say we must tell him
> We must go up there we must go up there and You
> Are The Next we must tell him
> The persuaders say he would deafen us
> When we say No no one hears us

It is this mode that Merwin has chosen to write in since 1967, the disturbing implications of which deserve to be examined.

IV.

The compulsion to discover or invent a language capable of articulating what has happened in our time becomes essential to poets whose political experience defies expression. T. W. Adorno's claim that no poetry could be written after Auschwitz has been disproven, at least in Eastern Europe, through the most arduous linguistic efforts; there, language survives as epitaph, the discrete conclusion of an active cultural life. Even so, such poets as the Polish Zbigniew Herbert and the Yugoslavian Vasko Popa have produced a provisional literature, while the Hungarian Ferenc Juhász has participated in the tradition of his poetic ancestors, Ady and Attila József. All of these, as well as the Latin American poets, regard dislocated syntax, automatic images, unconscious associations, in effect all those properties that describe the French Surrealists, as the discourse proper to their own experience. The poems that belong to them, produced in a climate of political repression or, worse, cultural disintegration, appropriate a language reflecting their own historical moment.

In America, poems of obvious political significance, or that have as their subject politics, remain conventional in their choices of language and style; Lowell's *Notebook* contains the journal, in blank verse sonnets, of an individual whose own temperament accommodates the collective maladies of an entire age. Bly, introducing a selection of *Forty Poems Touching on Recent American History*, wants to reconcile these tensions between the personal and the political, between the spirit and the rational:

It's clear that many of the events that create our foreign relations and our domestic relations come from more or less hidden impulses in the American psyche. It's also clear that some sort of husk has grown around that psyche, so that in the Fifties we could not look into it or did not . . . But if that is so, then the poet's main job is to penetrate that husk around the American psyche, and since that psyche is inside *him* too, the writing of political poetry is like the writing of personal poetry, a sudden drive by the poet inward.[13]

What this involves, it seems, is a rejection of those poetic modes which bind the writer to surfaces, externals; in order to plunge inward, as Bly suggests, a mediation is required between two disparate sorts of discourse: the received language of literature and the language of unconscious thought.

This is where Merwin, in his later poetry, encounters an alarming contradiction; having learned the workings of what Roland Barthes describes as "a decorative and compromising instrument, a writing inherited from a previous and different History, for which he is not responsible and yet which is the only one he can use,"[14] Merwin still resists the real significance of what he practises; the disruption of language is no more than a device in *The Lice* (1967) and *The Carrier of Ladders* (1970). Monotonous, interminable, self-imitative, each poem exudes unbearable exhaustion; none supports a close analysis. Here is "The Night of the Shirts":

Oh pile of white shirts who is coming
to breathe in your shapes to carry your numbers
to appear
what hearts
are moving toward their garments here
their days
what troubles beating between arms

you look upward through
each other saying nothing has happened
and it has gone away and is sleeping
having told the same story
and we exist from within
eyes of the gods

you lie on your backs
and the wounds are not made
the blood has not heard
the boat has not turned to stone
and the dark wires to the bulb
are full of the voices of the unborn

What is the purpose of asking all these questions? Is the line "to appear" essential, or just a repetition of the previous line? What motivates the metonymous "heart"? Where is "here"? How does "their days" relate to the stanza? What is "it"? What is "the same story"? How does it happen that "we exist from within/ eyes of the gods"? What are "the wounds", what "the blood"? Where does "the boat" enter in, to what does it refer? What suggests that it should have "turned to stone"? The poem has no meaning, not even a style; it sounds like a poor translation. The *Time* article celebrated Merwin as belonging among "The Specials", a poet inaugurating "the transmutation of modern dilemmas into the no-man's-land myth, a landscape of the imagination that is universal and particular at the same time." Perhaps, but I suspect that what appealed to them was the neutral, insouciant voice at work in these poems; excessive transmutation of our "modern dilemmas" has caused us to misinterpret them; what there should be more of at this time are critiques, poems that situate us in the world, or elaborate on real conditions.

As a translator, Merwin has been able to capture the concrete and actual dilemmas of Nietzsche, Gottfried Keller, Esenin, and Mandelstam, their desperation, the disturbed and turbulent voice of exile; unlike Lowell's *Imitations*, Merwin's translations have remained close to the originals, aware of their linguistic complexities, their context, and the historical moment informing them. Even though he claims, in the Foreword to *Selected Translations*, to have forgotten most or all of the German, Italian, and Latin he learned in college, while the rest (Russian, Greek, Vietnamese, among several others) are either based on French and Spanish translations or else have relied on collaboration with various hands, these poems are secure in English. At home in the complicated origins of modern French and Spanish poetry (*The Song of Roland*, Spanish ballads, and *The Poem of the Cid*, as well as the picaresque novel *Lazarillo de Tormes*, have been issued in his translations), Merwin possesses an educated ease when called upon to translate Jean Follain's *Transparence of the World* or the late Argentinian Antonio Porchia's *Voices*; Follain, in whose poems "each detail, seen as itself, is an evocation of the processions of an immeasurable continuum,"[15] resembles Merwin in this, that the world appears absent in duration, outside of time, "au soir de l'existence". Open lines disappear like roads trailing off in the distance; and what Merwin observed in Porchia's aphorisms, an exegesis of "particular, individual experience,"[16] is here as well. It is in Merwin's own poems that, despite such profitable influences, despite his belief in translation "as a means of continually sharpening a writer's awareness of the possibilities of his own language,"[17] a concision has been lost, a rigor abandoned; his translation of Nicanor Parra's "Memories of Youth" demonstrates the dialectic of Surrealism, a coherence which includes incoherence, irrational ideas appearing in a rational relation to the world, in opposition to themselves:

> Crossing the thresholds of private houses,
> With my sharp tongue I tried to get the spectators to understand me,
> They went on reading the paper
> Or disappeared behind a taxi.
> Then where could I go!
> At that hour the shops were shut;

> I thought of a slice of onion I'd seen during dinner
> And of the abyss that separates us from the other abysses.

With Parra, emotional crises arise out of a conflict among things, objects obscure the heart's isolation, an onion slice recalls him to his own abyss. Merwin, in refusing to mean, to be responsible to what he names, sacrifices what is of crucial significance in Surrealism, the dialectical tension between language and meaning.

V.

Merwin's last volume, *The Miner's Pale Children*, exploited a genre that extends from Baudelaire through Rimbaud and Mallarmé to Francis Ponge in France, that shares affinities with Lichtenberg and imitates Kafka: the prose poem. These pieces, less fiction than parable, explore an odd region where events are unexplained, where animals talk among themselves, where hope has been "a calm lake in early spring, white because the sky above it was the color of milk." Like the fables of Donald Barthelme, or Beckett's *stories and texts for nothing*, Merwin's episodic, elusive stories exist in a dimension of the mysterious, spoken through some unidentified voice. The language is dense and detailed, but about nothing, or, to be more specific, about the problem of nothingness, as in "The Cheese Seller":

> Everything, they say, everything that ever exists even for a moment floats on the black lake, the black lake, and there at each moment what is reflected is its opposite what is reflected is. This is one of the basic truths, without which existence itself would be impossible.

What recurs is a motif of listening among the disconsolate, the mad:

> Earth has gone. We float in a small boat that was once green, at an immense height on the unlit sea. No, there is no height, for the depth of the water is infinite. Good-bye height, goodbye depth. The sea is everywhere. It has no shores. Above us the air of this sea. The black space. The stars have all moved out of sight.

Ponge, during a conversation with Philippe Sollers, described his own writings, or texts, as materialistic, in that words become "une réalité concrète, comportant toute l'évidence et l'épaisseur des choses du monde extérieur."[18] This is close to what Merwin has achieved in these prose pieces, the lessons of which could be: to write is to determine the world's actual properties.

NOTES
     [1] *Time*, July 12, 1971.
     [2] George Steiner, *Extraterritorial: Papers on Literature and the Language Revolution* (New York: Atheneum, 1971), p. 171.

3 Christopher Caudwell, *Illusion and Reality* (New York: International Publishers, 1967), p. 127.

4 "The Language Animal," *Encounter*, August, 1969.

5 Michael Hamburger, *The Truth of Poetry* (New York: Harcourt, Brace & World, 1969), p. 97.

6 T. S. Eliot, "The Three Voices of Poetry," in *On Poetry and Poets* (New York, Farrar, Straus & Giroux, 1957).

7 A. Alvarez, *Under Pressure* (Penguin Books, 1965), p. 160.

8 *The Harvard Advocate*, "A Conversation with Robert Bly," CIII, #4, February, 1970.

9 *The San Francisco Book Review*, #19 ,April, 1971.

10 "Poetry, Personality, and Death," *Field*, #4, Spring 1971.

11 *Sound and Form in Modern Poetry* (Ann Arbor: The University of Michigan Press, 1964), p. 248.

12 Cesare Pavese, *A Mania for Solitude* (London: Peter Owen, 1969), p. 27.

13 *Forty Poems Touching on Recent American History* (Boston: Beacon Press, 1970), p. 10.

14 Roland Barthes, *Writing Degree Zero* (New York: Hill & Wang, 1968), p. 86.

15 Jean Follain, *Transparence of the World*, selected and translated with a Foreword by W. S. Merwin (New York: Atheneum, 1969), vii.

16 Antonio Porchia, *Voices*, translated by W. S. Merwin (Chicago: Big Table Publishing Company, 1969).

17 W. S. Merwin, *Selected Translations 1948-1968* (New York: Atheneum, 1969), viii.

18 *Entretiens de Francis Ponge avec Philippe Sollers* (Paris: Gallimard/Seuil, 1970), p. 169.

John Ashbery:
The Charity of the Hard Moments
by Harold Bloom

OF THE American poets now in mid-career, those born in the decade 1925–1935, John Ashbery and A. R. Ammons seem to me the strongest. This essay, an overview of Ashbery's published work to date, is meant as a companion-piece to the essay on Ammons printed in my book of studies in Romantic tradition, *The Ringers in the Tower* (University of Chicago Press, 1971). Ashbery goes back through Stevens to Whitman, even as Ammons is a more direct descendant of American Romanticism in its major formulation, which remains Emerson's. Otherwise, these two superb poets have nothing in common except their authentic difficulty. Ammons belongs to no school, while Ashbery can be regarded either as the best poet by far of the "New York School" or—as I would argue—so unique a figure that only confusion is engendered by associating him with Koch, O'Hara, Schuyler and their friends and disciples.

I remember purchasing *Some Trees*, Ashbery's first commercially published volume (Yale Press, 1956, Introduction by Auden) in December, 1956, after reading the first poem ("Two Scenes") in a bookstore. The poem begins: "We see us as we truly behave" and concludes with "In the evening / Everything has a schedule, if you can find out what it is." A skeptical honesty, self-reflexive, and an odd faith in a near-inscrutable order remain characteristic of Ashbery's work after sixteen years. Also still characteristic is the abiding influence of Stevens. I remember being fascinated by the swerve away from Stevens' *Credences of Summer* in "Two Scenes":

> This is perhaps a day of general honesty
> Without example in the world's history
> Though the fumes are not of a singular authority
> And indeed are dry as poverty.

Where Stevens, in a moment of precarious satisfaction, entertained the possibility of overcoming "poverty," imaginative need, the young Ashbery identified self-knowledge with such need. Auden, hardly an admirer of Stevens, introduced Ashbery as an ephebe of Rimbaud, seer "of sacred images and ritual acts." But, actual disciple of Stevens (in his most Whitmanian aspect) and of Whitman ultimately, Ashbery necessarily began in a poetic world emptied of magical images and acts. The highly Stevensian "The Mythological Poet" opposed "a new / Music, innocent and monstrous / As the ocean's bright display of teeth" to "the toothless murmuring / Of ancient willows," sacred images for outworn seers. In the title-poem, clearly the book's best, Ashbery had found already his largest aesthetic principle, the notion that every day the world consented to be shaped into a poem. "Not every day," Stevens warns in his "Adagia", which Ashbery couldn't have read then, but Stevens' point was that on some days it could happen. The point is Emersonian or Whitmanian, and though Ashbery antithetically completes Stevens in this principle, he is ultimately, like Whitman and Stevens, a descendant of Emerson's *Nature*, though at the start a wry one:

> . . . you and I
> Are suddenly what the trees try
>
> To tell us we are:
> That their merely being there
> Means something; that soon
> We may touch, love, explain.
>
> And glad not to have invented
> Such comeliness, we are surrounded . . .

The Not-Me, as Emerson said, is nature and my body together, as well as art and all other men. Such a conviction leads Ashbery, even as it impelled Whitman and Stevens, to a desperate quest that masks as an ease with things. The poem is to be discovered in the Not-Me, out in the world that includes the poet's body. Rhetorically, this tends to mean that every proverbial cliché must be recovered, which becomes almost a rage in Ashbery's *Three Poems*. Where the middle Ashbery, the poet of the outrageously disjunctive volume, *The Tennis Court Oath*, attempted too massive a swerve away from the ruminative continuities of Stevens and Whitman, recent Ashbery goes to the dialectical extreme of what seems at first like a barrage of bland commonplaces. Emerson, in *Nature*, anticipated Ashbery with his characteristic sense that parts of a world and parts of speech are alike emblematic, so that either, however worn out, could yet be an epiphany, though the world *seemed* so post-magical:

> . . . the memorable words of history and the proverbs of nations consist usually of a natural fact, selected as a picture or parable of a moral truth. Thus: a rolling stone gathers no moss; a bird in the hand is worth two in the bush; a cripple in the right way will beat a racer in the wrong; make hay while the sun shines; 'tis hard to carry a full cup even; vinegar is the son of wine; the last ounce broke the camel's back; long-lived trees make roots first . . .

Emerson insisted each worn proverb could become *transparent*. In his rare startlements into happiness, Ashbery knows this transparency, but generally his hopes are more modest. He is, in temperament, more like Whitman than like Emerson or Stevens. Even the French poet he truly resembles is the curiously Whitmanian Apollinaire, rather than Reverdy:

Et ce serait sans doute bien plus beau
Si je pouvaise supposer que toutes ces choses dans lesquelles
    je suis partout
Pouvaient m'occuper aussi
Mais dans ce sens il n'y a rien de fait
Car si je suis partout a cette heure il n'y a cependant que
    moi qui suis en moi

Let us, swerving away from Apollinaire, call these Ashbery's two con-tradictory spiritual temptations, to believe that one's own self, like the poem, can be found in "all the things everywhere," or to believe that "there is still only I who can be in me." The first temptation will be productive of a rhetoric that puts it all in, and so must try to re-vitalize every relevant cliché. The second temptation rhetorically is gratified by ellipsis, thus leaving it all out. I suppose that Ashbery's masterpiece in this mode is the long spiel called "Europe" in *The Tennis Court Oath*, which seems to me a fearful disaster. In Stevens, this first way is the path of Whitmanian expansiveness, which partly failed the not always exuberant burgher of Hartford, while the second is the way of reductiveness, too great a temptation for him, as Stevens came to realize. The road through to poetry for Stevens was a middle path of invention that he called "discovery", the finding rather than the imposition of an order. Though there are at least three rhetorics in Stevens, matching these three modes of self-apprehension, none of the three risks Ashbery's disasters, whether of apparently joining together bland truisms or of almost total disjunctiveness. But I think that is close to the sorrow of influence in Ashbery, which is the necessary anxiety induced in him by the siren song of Stevens' rhetorics. Ashbery (who is not likely to be pleased by this observation) is at his best when he is neither re-vitalizing proverbial wisdom nor barely evading an ellipsis, but when he dares to write most directly in the idiom of Stevens. This point, and Ashbery's dazzling deflection of it, will be my concern when I arrive at *The Double Dream of Spring*.

My own melancholy, confronting Ashbery, is provoked by his second public volume, *The Tennis Court Oath* (Wesleyan University Press, 1962). Coming to this eagerly as an admirer of *Some Trees*, I remember my outrage and disbelief at what I found:

    for that we turn around
    experiencing it is not to go into
    the epileptic prank forcing bar
    to borrow out onto tide-exposed fells
    over her morsel, she chasing you
    and the revenge he'd get
    establishing the vultural over
    rural area cough protection
    murdering quintet. . . .

This is from the piece called "Leaving The Atocha Station", which (I am

told) has a certain reputation among the rabblement of poetasters who pro-
claim themselves anti-academic while preaching in the academies, and who
lack consciousness sufficient to feel the genuine (because necessary) heaviness
of the poetic past's burden of richness. *The Tennis Court Oath* has only one
good poem, "A Last World". Otherwise, its interest is now entirely retrospective; how could Ashbery collapse into such a bog by just six years after
Some Trees, and how did he climb out of it again to write *Rivers and Mountains*,
and then touch a true greatness in *The Double Dream of Spring* and *Three
Poems*?

Poets, who congenitally lie about so many matters, *never* tell the truth
about poetic influence. To address an audience sprinkled with poets, on the
subject of poetic influence, is to risk a *sparagmos* in which the unhappy critic
may be mistaken for Orpheus. Poets want to believe, with Nietzsche, that
"forgetfulness is a property of all action," and action for them is writing a
poem. Alas, no one can write a poem without remembering another poem,
even as no one loves without remembering, though dimly or subconsciously,
a former beloved, however much that came under a taboo. Every poet is
forced to say, as Hart Crane did in an early poem: "I can remember much
forgetfulness." To live as a poet, a poet needs the illusive mist about him that
shields him from the light that first kindled him. This mist is the nimbus
(however false) of what the prophets would have called his own *kabod*, the
supposed radiance of his own glory.

In *Some Trees*, Ashbery was a relatively joyous ephebe of Stevens, who
evidently proved to be too good a father. Nietzsche suggested that: "If one
has not had a good father, it is necessary to invent one." Yes, and for a poet,
if one's father was too good, it becomes necessary to re-invent one's father's
sorrows, so as to balance his glory. This necessity, which Ashbery met in all
his subsequent work, is merely evaded throughout *The Tennis Court Oath*,
where a great mass of egregious disjunctiveness is accumulated to very little
effect. Apollinaire had counselled *surprise* for the modern poet's art, but what
is surprising about a group of poems that will never yield to any reading or
sustained re-reading? Poems may be like pictures, or like music, or like what
you will, but if they *are* paintings or musical works, they will not be poems.
The Ashbery of *The Tennis Court Oath* may have been moved by De Kooning
and Kline, Webern and Cage, but he was not moved to the writing of poems.
Nor can I accept the notion that this was a necessary phase in the poet's
development, for who can hope to find any necessity in this calculated incoherence? Yet the volume matters, and still upsets me because it is Ashbery's,
the work of a man who has written poems like "Evening In The Country",
"Parergon", the astonishingly poignant and wise "Soonest Mended", and
"Fragment", probably the best longer poem by an American poet of my own
generation, and unmatched I believe by anything in the generation of Lowell.

Isolated amid the curiosities of *The Tennis Court Oath* is the beautiful "A
Last World", which in its limpidity and splendor would fit well into one of

Ashbery's later volumes. The poem prophesies the restorative aesthetic turn that Ashbery was to take, and reveals also what has become his central subject and resource, the imagination of a later self questing for accommodation not so much with an earlier glory (as in Wordsworth) but with a possible sublimity that can never be borne, if it should yet arrive. Stevens more than Whitman is again the precursor, and the greatness of Ashbery begins to emerge when the anxiety of influence is wrestled with, and at least held to a stand-off.

"A Last World", like any true poem, has the necessity of reminding us that the meaning of one poem can only be another poem, a poem not itself, and probably not even one by its own author. Ashbery emerges into a total coherence when he compels himself to know that every imagining is a mis-prision, a taking amiss or twisting askew of the poetic *given*. Mature creation, for a poet, rises directly from an error about poetry rather than an error, how-ever profound, about life. Only a wilful *misinterpretation* of a poetry already known too well, loved too well, understood too well, frees a maturing maker's mind from the compulsion to repeat, and more vitally from the fear of that compulsion. This is not what "A Last World" *thinks* it is about, but the poem so presents itself as to compel us to read it as an allegory of this poet's struggle to win free of his own evasions, and not the aesthetic evasions alone, but of everything that is elliptical in the self.

The Stevensian "he" of "A Last World" becomes a constant presence in the next two volumes, modulating from Ashbery as a self-deceiver to a per-petually late learner who is educated with the reader, so as to become a convincing "we":

> Everything is being blown away;
> A little horse trots up with a letter in its mouth,
>   which is read with eagerness
> As we gallop into the flame.

This, the poem's conclusion, is the ostensible focus of "A Last World"; the present is the flame, things vanish perpetually as we come up to them, and we are—at best—romance questers made pathetic as we read the message so charmingly delivered to us, which is hardly going to save us from joining a general state of absence. The poem seems to end dispassionately in loss, yet its tone is serene, and its atmosphere suffused with a curious radiance. This radiance is a revisionary completion of the difficult serenity of late Stevens, a completion that is also antithetical to Stevens' rockier composure, or as his "Lebensweisheitspielerei" calls it, his sense of "stellar pallor":

> Little by little, the poverty
> Of autumnal space becomes
> A look, a few words spoken.
>
> Each person completely touches us
> With what he is and as he is,
> In the stale grandeur of annihilation.

Stevens, contemplating the departure of the proud and the strong, bleakly celebrated those left as "the unaccomplished, / The finally human, / Natives of a dwindled sphere." Ashbery, counterpointing his vision against that of Stevens' *The Rock*, celebrates loss as an accomplishment, a treasure, a mint flavoring in Stevens' land of hay, which was too ripe for such enigmas:

> Once a happy old man
> One can never change the core of things, and light burns
>   you the harder for it,
> Glad of the changes already and if there are more it will
>   never be you that minds
> Since it will not be you to be changed, but in the evening
>   in the severe lamplight doubts come
> From many scattered distances, and do not come too near.
> As it falls along the house, your treasure
> Cries to the other men; the darkness will have none of you,
>   and you are folded into it like mint into the sound
>   of haying.

Loss is not gain here, and yet Ashbery takes Stevens' vision back from the last world of *The Rock* to "A Postcard from the Volcano" of 1936, where at least we leave behind us "what still is/The look of things." Absence or denudation is the common perception of the two poets, but Ashbery, though always anxious, is too gentle for bitterness, and rhetorically most himself where least ironic. Stevens' "qualified assertions" (Helen Vendler's apt phrase) become in Ashbery a series of progressively more beautiful examples of what we might call "qualified epiphanies," the qualifications coming partly from Ashbery's zeal in tacitly rejecting a poetry of privileged moments or privileged phrases. But this zeal is misplaced, and almost impossible to sustain, as will be seen in his later development.

Rivers and Mountains (1966) is a partial recovery from *The Tennis Court Oath*, though only one poem in it, "The Skaters", seems to me major Ashbery when compared to what comes after. But then, "The Skaters" is nearly half the volume, and its most luminous passages are of the same poetic ambiance as the work beyond. With *Rivers And Mountains*, Ashbery began to win back the dismayed admirers of his earliest work, myself included. The curious poem called "The Recent Past", whatever its intentions, seems to be precisely addressed to just such readers, in very high good humor:

> You were my quintuplets when I decided to leave you
> Opening a picture book the pictures were all of grass
> Slowly the book was on fire, you the reader
> Sitting with specs full of smoke exclaimed
> How it was a rhyme for "brick" or "redder".
> The next chapter told all about a brook.
>
> You were beginning to see the relation when a tidal wave

> Arrived with sinking ships that spelled out "Aladdin".
> I thought about the Arab boy in his cave
> But the thoughts came faster than advice.
> If you knew that snow was a still toboggan in space
> The print could rhyme with "fallen star".

As far as intention matters, the "you" here is another Ashbery, to whom almost the entire book is directed, as will be the recent *Three Poems*. "These Lacustrine Cities" sets the book's project:

> Much of your time has been occupied by creative games
> Until now, but we have all-inclusive plans for you . . .

"Clepsydra", the longer poem just preceding "The Skaters", is printed as the first attempt at the project's realization, and is a beautiful failure, outweighing most contemporary poetic successes. The water-clock of the title is ultimately Ashbery himself, akin to the sun-flower of Blake's frighteningly wistful lyric. A history-in-little of Ashbery's poethood, "Clepsydra" is Ashbery's gentle equivalent of Stevens' surpassingly bitter "The Comedian as the Letter C", and is as dazzling an apparent dead end. I judge it a failure not because its exuberance is so negative, in contrast to the Whitmanian "The Skaters", but because its solipsism, like the "Comedian"'s, is too perfect. Though splendidly coherent, "Clepsydra" gives the uncanny effect of being a poem that neither wants nor needs readers. It sits on the page as a forbiddingly solid wall of print, about as far from the *look* of Apollinaire as any verse could be. From its superbly opaque opening ("Hasn't the sky?") to its ominous closing ("while morning is still and before the body/Is changed by the faces of evening") the poem works at turning a Shelleyan-Stevensian self-referential quality into an absolute impasse. Perhaps here, more than in "The Skaters" even, or in his masterpiece, "Fragment", Ashbery tries to write the last poem about itself and about poetry, last by rendering the mode redundant:

> . . . Each moment
> Of utterance is the true one; likewise none are true,
> Only is the bounding from air to air, a serpentine
> Gesture which hides the truth behind a congruent
> Message, the way air hides the sky, is, in fact,
> Tearing it limb from limb this very moment: but
> The sky has pleaded already and this is about
> As graceful a kind of non-absence as either
> Has a right to expect: whether it's the form of
> Some creator who has momentarily turned away,
> Marrying detachment with respect . . .

"Detachment with respect" is Ashbery's attitude towards transcendental experience, for which he tends to use the image of transparence, as Whitman and Stevens, following Emerson, did also. Stevens, as Helen Vendler notes, tends to *sound* religious when his poems discourse upon themselves, and

"Clepsydra" like much of the *Three Poems* similarly has an oddly religious tone. All of Ashbery (I am puzzled as to why Richard Howard thinks Ashbery an "anti-psychological" poet), including "Clepsydra", is profound self-revelation. Ashbery—like Wordsworth, Whitman, Stevens, Hart Crane—writes out of so profound a subjectivity as to make "confessional" verse seem as self-defeating as that mode truly has been, from Coleridge (its inventor) down to Lowell and his disciples. "Clepsydra", so wholly self-enclosed, is an oblique lament rising "amid despair and isolation/of the chance to know you, to sing of me/Which are you." The poem's subject overtly is Ashbery's entrapped subjectivity, objectified in the pathetic emblem of the water-clock, and represented in large by the outrageously even tone that forbids any gathering of climaxes. This refusal to vary his intensities is one of Ashbery's defense mechanisms against his anxiety of poetic influences. I can think of no poet in English, earlier or now at work, who insists upon so subtly unemphatic a pervasive tone. As a revisionary ratio, this tone intends to distance Ashbery from Whitman and from Stevens, and is a kind of *kenosis*, a self-emptying that yields up any evident afflatus:

> . . . Perhaps you are being kept here
> Only so that somewhere else the peculiar light of someone's
> Purpose can blaze unexpectedly in the acute
> Angles of the rooms. It is not a question, then,
> Of having not lived in vain . . .

The *kenosis* is too complete in "Clepsydra"; the tone, however miraculously sustained, too wearying for even so intelligent a poet rightly to earn. With relief, I move on to "The Skaters", Ashbery's most energetic poem, the largest instance in him of the revisionary movement of *daemonization*, or the onset of his personalized Counter-Sublime, as against the American Sublime of Whitman and Stevens. Yet, "The Skaters" is almost outrageously Whitmanian, far more legitimately in his mode than Ginsberg manages to be:

> Old heavens, you used to tweak above us,
> Standing like rain whenever a salvo . . . Old heavens,
> You lying there above the old, but not ruined, fort,
> Can you hear, there, what I am saying?

"The Skaters" is not a parody, however involuntary, of *Song of Myself*, though sometimes it gives that impression. *Song of Myself* begins where the British Romantic quest-poem is sensible enough to end: with an internal romance, of self and soul, attaining its consummation. Whitman, having married himself, goes forth as an Emersonian liberating god, to preside over the nuptials of the universe. The daemonic parodies of this going forth stand between Whitman and Ashbery: *Paterson, the Cantos, The Bridge, Notes Toward A Supreme Fiction, Preludes To Attitude, The Far Field*. What remains for Ashbery, in "The Skaters", is a kind of Counter-Sublime that accepts a reduction of Whitmanian ecstasy, while re-affirming it nevertheless, as in the vision early in the poem, when the poet's whole soul is stirred into activity, flagellated by the decibels of the "excited call" of the skaters:

> The answer is that it is novelty
> That guides these swift blades o'er the ice
> Projects into a finer expression (but at the expense
> Of energy) the profile I cannot remember.
> Colors slip away from and chide us. The human mind
> Cannot retain anything except perhaps the dismal two-note theme
> Of some sodden "dump" or lament.

One can contrast the magnificent skating episode in Book I of *The Prelude*, where colors have not slipped away, and the mind has retained its power over outer sense. The contrast, though unfair to Ashbery, still shows that there is a substance in us that prevails, though Ashbery tends to know it only by knowing also his absence from it. His poem celebrates "the intensity of minor acts," including his self-conscious mode of making-by-ellipsis, or as he calls it: "this leaving-out business." Putting off (until *Three Poems*) "the costly stuff of explanation," he movingly offers a minimal apologia:

> . . . Except to say that the carnivorous
> Way of these lines is to devour their own nature, leaving
> Nothing but a bitter impression of absence, which as we know
>   involves presence, but still.
> Nevertheless these are fundamental absences, struggling to
>   get up and be off themselves.

"The Skaters", admitting that: "Mild effects are the result," labors still "to hold the candle up to the album," which is Ashbery's minimalist version of Stevens': "How high that highest candle lights the dark." In the poem's second part, Ashbery sets forth on a Romantic voyage, but like Crispin sees every vision-of-the-voyage fade slowly away. The long third movement, a quasi-autobiographical panorama of this poet's various exiles, needs careful examination, which I cannot give here, for nothing else in Ashbery succeeds nearly so well at the effect of the great improviser, an excellence shared by Whitman and by the Stevens of the blue guitar. With the fourth and final section, partly spoken by the persona of a Chinese scholar-administrator, the poem circles to a serene resolution, precisely prophetic of the Ashbery to come. "The whole brilliant mass comes spattering down," and an extraordinary simplicity takes its place. After so many leavings-out, the natural particulars are seen as being wonderfully sufficient:

> The apples are all getting tinted
> In the cool light of autumn.
>
> The constellations are rising
> In perfect order: Taurus, Leo, Gemini.

Everything promised by "The Skaters", Ashbery has performed, in the very different greatnesses of *The Double Dream of Spring* (1970) and *Three Poems* (1972). The first of these is so rich a book that I will confine myself to only a handful of poems, each so wonderful as to survive close comparison with Whitman and Stevens at almost their strongest: "Soonest Mended", "Evening in the Country", "Sunrise in Suburbia", "Parergon" and the long poem "Fragment". Before ruminating on these representative poems, a general meditation on Ashbery's progress seems necessary to me, as I am going on to make very large claims for his more recent work.

Though the leap in manner between *Rivers and Mountains* and *The Double Dream of Spring* is less prodigious than the gap between *The Tennis Court Oath* and *Rivers and Mountains*, there is a more crucial change in the later transition. Ashbery at last says farewell to ellipsis, a farewell confirmed by *Three Poems*, which relies upon "putting it all in," indeed upon the discursiveness of a still-demanding prose. The abandonment of Ashbery's rhetorical evasiveness is a self-curtailment on his part, a purgation that imparts simplicity through intensity, but at the price of returning him to the rhetorical world of Stevens and of the American tradition that led to Stevens. It is rather as if Browning had gone from his grotesque power backwards to the Shelleyan phase of his work. Perhaps Browning should have, since his last decades were mostly barren. As a strong poet, Ashbery has matured almost as slowly as his master Stevens did, though unlike Stevens he has matured in public. Even as Stevens provoked a critical nonsense, only now vanishing, of somehow being a French poet writing in English, so Ashbery still provokes such nonsense. Both are massive sufferers from the anxiety-of-influence, and both developed only when they directly engaged their American precursors. In Ashbery, the struggle with influence, though more open, is also more difficult, since Ashbery desperately engages also the demon of discursiveness, as Hart Crane differently did (for the last stand of Crane's mode, see the one superb volume of Alvin Feinman, *Preambles And Other Poems*, 1964). This hopeless engagement, endemic in all Western poetries in our century, is a generalized variety of the melancholy of poetic influence. It is not problematic form, nor repressed allusiveness, nor recondite matter, that makes much modern verse difficult. Nor, except rarely, is it conceptual profundity, or sustained mythical invention. Ellipsis, the art of omission, almost always a central device in poetry, has been abused into the dominant element rhetorically of our time. Yet no modern poet has employed it so effectively as Dickinson did, probably because for her it was a deep symptom of everything else that belonged to the male tradition that she was leaving out. I cannot involve myself here in the whole argument that I have set forth in a little book, *The Anxiety of Influence: A Theory of Poetry* (1972; see the discussion of Ashbery in the section called "*Apophrades*: or the Return of the Dead"), but I cite it as presenting evidence for the judgment that influence becomes progressively more of a burden for poets from the Enlightenment to this moment. Poets, defending poetry, are adept at idealizing their relation to one another, and the magical Idealists among critics have followed them in this saving self-deception. Here is Northrop Frye, greatest of the idealizers:

> Once the artist thinks in terms of influence rather than of clarity of form, the effort of the imagination becomes an effort of will, and art is perverted into tyranny, the application of the principle of magic or mysterious compulsion to society.

Against this I cite Coleridge's remark that the power of originating *is* the will, our means of escaping from nature or repetition-compulsion, and I add that no one needs to pervert art in this respect, since the Post-Enlightenment poetic imagination is necessarily quite perverse enough in the perpetual battle against influence. Wordsworth *is* a misinterpretation of Milton (as is Blake), Shelley *is* a misinterpretation of Wordsworth, Browning and Yeats *are* misinterpretations of Shelley. Or, in the native strain, Whitman perverts or twists askew Emerson, Stevens is guilty of misprision towards both, and Ashbery attempts a profound and beautiful misinterpretation of all his precursors, *in his own best poetry*. What the elliptical mode truly seeks to omit is the overt continuity with ancestors, and the mysterious compulsion operative here is a displacement of what Freud charmingly called "the family romance".

Ashbery's own family romance hovers uneasily in all-but-repressed memories of childhood; his family-romance-as-poet attains a momentarily happy resolution in *The Double Dream of Spring*, but returns darkly in *Three Poems*. Ashbery is a splendid instance of the redemptive aspect of influence-anxiety, for his best work shows how the relation to the precursor is humanized into the greater themes of all human influence-relations, which after all include lust, envy, sexual jealousy, the horror of families, friendship, and the poet's reciprocal relation to his contemporaries, ultimately to all of his readers.

I begin again, after this anxious digression, with "Soonest Mended", and begin also the litany of praise and advocacy, of what Pater called "appreciation," that the later work of Ashbery inspires in me. The promise of *Some Trees* was a long time realizing itself, but the realization came, and Ashbery is now something close to a great poet. It is inconvenient to quote all of "Soonest Mended", but I will discuss it as though my reader is staring at pages 17 through 19 of *The Double Dream of Spring*. The poem speaks for the artistic life of Ashbery's generation, but more for the general sense of awakening to the haphazardness and danger of one's marginal situation in early middle age:

> To step free at last, minuscule on the gigantic plateau—
> This was our ambition: to be small and clear and free.
> Alas, the summer's energy wanes quickly,
> A moment and it is gone. And no longer

> May we make the necessary arrangements, simple as they are.
> Our star was brighter perhaps when it had water in it.
> Now there is no question even of that, but only
> Of holding on to the hard earth so as not to get thrown off,
> With an occasional dream, a vision . . .

Dr. Johnson, still the most useful critic in the language, taught us to value highly any original expression of common or universal experience. "Has he any fresh matter to disclose?" is the question Johnson would have us ask of any new poet whose work seems to demand our deep consideration. The Ashbery of his two most recent volumes passes this test triumphantly. "Soonest Mended", from its rightly proverbial title through every line of its evenly distributed rumination, examines freshly that bafflement of the twice-born life that has been a major theme from Rousseau and Wordsworth to Flaubert and Stevens. This is the sense of awakening, past the middle of the journey, to the truth that: "*they* were the players, and we who had struggled at the game/Were merely spectators . . ." Uniquely Ashbery's contribution is the wisdom of a wiser passivity:

> . . . learning to accept
> The charity of the hard moments as they are doled out,
> For this is action, this not being sure, this careless
> Preparing, sowing the seeds crooked in the furrow,
> Making ready to forget, and always coming back
> To the mooring of starting out, that day so long ago.

Action, Wordsworth said, was momentary, only a step or blow, but suffering was permanent, obscure, dark and shared the nature of infinity, Ashbery's action is Wordsworth's suffering; the way through to it, Ashbery says, is "a kind of fence-sitting/Raised to the level of an esthetic ideal." If time indeed is an emulsion, as this poem asserts, then wisdom is to find the mercy of eternity in the charity of the hard moments. Shelley, forgiving his precursors, said that they had been washed in the blood of the redeemer and mediator, time. Ashbery domesticates this fierce idealism; "conforming to the rules and living/Around the home" mediate his vision, and redemption is the indefinite extension of the learning process, even if the extension depends upon conscious fantasy. The achievement of "Soonest Mended" is to have told a reductive truth, yet to have raised it out of reductiveness by a persistence masked as the commonal, an urgency made noble by art.

The implicit argument of "Soonest Mended" is adumbrated in "Evening in the Country", a reverie rising out of a kind of Orphic convalescence, as another spent seer consigns order to a vehicle of change. "I am still completely happy," Ashbery characteristically begins, having thrown out his "resolve to win further." Yet, this is not the "false happiness" that Stevens condemned, for it is being rather than consciousness, cat more than rabbit. The shadow of Stevens hovers overtly in this poem, the poet of the never-satisfied mind:

> . . . He wanted that,
> To face the weather and be unable to tell
> How much of it was light and how much thought,
> In these Elysia, these origins,
> This single place in which we are and stay,
> Except for the images we make of it,
> And for it, and by which we think the way,
> And, being unhappy, talk of happiness
> And, talking of happiness, know that it means
> That the mind is the end and must be satisfied.

Away from this Ashbery executes what Coleridge (in *Aids to Reflection*) calls a "*lene clinamen*, the gentle bias," for Ashbery's inclination is to yield to a realization that the mind had better be satisfied. Somewhere else, Coleridge speaks of making "a *clinamen* to the ideal," which is more in Stevens' mode, despite Stevens' qualifications. Ashbery, in his maturity, tries to be content not to originate an act or a state, though his achievement is to have done so anyway. "Evening in the Country" persuades that Ashbery has "begun to be in the context you feel," which is the context of the mind's surrender to visionary frustration. I quote at length from the poem's marvelous conclusion:

> Light falls on your shoulders, as is its way,
> And the process of purification continues happily,
> Unimpeded, but has the motion started
> That is to quiver your head, send anxious beams
> Into the dusty corners of the rooms
> Eventually shoot out over the landscape
> In stars and bursts? For other than this we know nothing
> And space is a coffin, and the sky will put out the light.
> I see you eager in your wishing it the way
> We may join it, if it passes close enough:
> This sets the seal of distinction on the success or failure
>   of your attempt.
> There is growing in that knowledge
> We may perhaps remain here, cautious yet free
> On the edge, as it rolls its unblinking chariot
> Into the vast open, the incredible violence and yielding
> Turmoil that is to be our route.

Purification here is a kind of Orphic *askesis*, another revisionary movement away from the fathers. The gods of Orphism, at least of that variety which is the natural religion of the native strain in American poetry, are Dionysus, Eros and Ananke. Ashbery's Dionysiac worship, in his recent work, is mostly directed to absence. Eros, always hovering in Ashbery, is more of a presence in "Fragment". Ananke, the Beautiful Necessity worshipped by the later Emerson and all his poetic children, is the governing deity of "Evening in the Country" as of "Soonest Mended" and the *Three Poems*. Purgation "continues happily," while the poet asks the open question as to whether the

motion of a new transcendental influx has started. Ashbery's genuine un-
certainty is no longer the choice of poetic subject, as it was in *The Tennis Court
Oath*, but concerns his relation to his own subject, which is the new birth or
fresh being he has discovered in himself, yet which sets its own timing for
manifestation.

Nothing is more difficult for me, as a reader of poetry, than to describe
why I am moved when a poem attains a certain intensity of quietness, when
it seems to wait. Keats, very early in his work, described this as power half-
slumbering on its own right arm. I find this quality in only a few contemporary poets—Ashbery, Ammons, Strand, Merwin, James Wright, among
others. Recent Ashbery has more of this deep potential, this quietness that is
neither quietism nor repression, than any American poet since the last poems
of Stevens. Webern is the nearest musical analogue I know, but analogues are
hard to find for a poem like "Evening in the Country". For, though the poem
is so chastened, it remains an Orphic celebration, as much so as Hart Crane
at his most ecstatic.

Ashbery's ambitions as a mature poet, rising out of this still Orphic convalescence, are subtly presented in "Sunrise in Suburbia". Ashbery, never
bitter, always charged by the thrill of the sun coming up, nevertheless suggests
here an initial burden too complex for the poem to bear away from him. This
burden is eloquently summed up in a line from "Parergon": "That the
continuity was fierce beyond all dream of enduring." Repetition is the
antagonist in "Sunrise in Suburbia", which quests for discontinuity or, as
the poem calls it, "nuance":

> And then some morning there is a nuance:
> Suddenly in the city dirt and varied
> Ideas of rubbish, the blue day stands and
> A sudden interest is there:
> Lying on the cot, near the tree-shadow,
> Out of the thirties having news of the true source:
> Face to kiss and the wonderful hair curling down
> Into margins that care and are swept up again like branches
> Into actual closeness
> And the little things that lighten the day
> The kindness of acts long forgotten
> Which gives us history and faith
> And parting at night, next to ocean, like the collapse of dying.

An earlier passage in the poem juxtaposes the "flatness of what remains"
to the "modelling of what fled," setting the poem in the large tradition that
goes from "Tintern Abbey" to "The Course of a Particular". The difficulty,
for Ashbery as for his readers, is how to construct something upon which to
rejoice when you are the heir of this tradition, yet reject both privileged
moments of vision and any privileged heightenings of rhetoric in the deliberately subdued and even tone of your work. Stevens is difficult enough in this

kind of poem, yet for him there are times of unusual excellence, and he momentarily will yield to his version of the high style in presenting them. For Ashbery, the privileged moments, like their images, are on the dump, and he wants to purify them by clearly placing them there. Say of what you see in the dark, Stevens urges, that it is this or that it is that, but do not use the rotted names. Use the rotted names, Ashbery urges, but cleanse them by seeing that you cannot be apart from them, and are partly redeemed by consciously suffering with them. Stevens worked to make the visible a little hard to see; Ashbery faces: "a blank chart of each day moving into the premise of difficult visibility." The sounds of nature on this suburban sunrise have a hard tone: "this deaf rasping of branch against branch." These too are the cries of branches that do not transcend themselves, yet they do concern us:

> They are empty beyond consternation because
> These are the droppings of all our lives
> And they recall no past de luxe quarters
> Only a last cube.
> The thieves were not breaking in, the castle was not being stormed.
> It was the holiness of the day that fed our notions
> And released them, sly breath of Eros,
> Anniversary on the woven city lament, that assures our arriving
> In hours, seconds, breath, watching our salary
> In the morning holocaust become one vast furnace, engaging all tears.

Where "The Course of a Particular" rejects Ruskin's Pathetic Fallacy or the imputation of life to the object world, Ashbery uncannily labors to make the fallacy more pathetic, the object world another failed version of the questing self. Yet each day, his poem nobly insists, is holy and releases an Orphic "sly breath of Eros," to be defeated, and yet "engaging all tears." If a poem like this remains difficult, its difficulty arises legitimately from the valuable complexity of its vision, and not from the partial discontinuity of its rhetoric.

The thematic diffidence of "Sunrise in Suburbia" is transformed in the superb short poem "Parergon", which gives us Ashbery's version of pure Shelleyan quest, *Alastor* rather than its parody in *The Comedian as the Letter C*. As in "Evening in the Country", Ashbery begins by affirming, without irony, a kind of domestic happiness in his artist's life of sitting about, reading, being restless. In a dream-vision, he utters the prophecy of the life he has become: "we need the tether/ of entering each other's lives, eyes wide apart, crying." Having done so, he becomes "the stranger", the perpetual uncompromising quester on the model of the Poet in Shelley's *Alastor*:

> As one who moves forward from a dream
> The stranger left that house on hastening feet
> Leaving behind the woman with the face shaped like an arrowhead,
> And all who gazed upon him wondered at
> The strange activity around him.

How fast the faces kindled as he passed!
It was a marvel that no one spoke
To stem the river of his passing
Now grown to flood proportions, as on the sunlit mall
Or in the enclosure of some court
He took his pleasure, savage
And mild with the contemplating.
Yet each knew he saw only aspects,
That the continuity was fierce beyond all dream of enduring,
And turned his head away, and so
The lesson eddied far into the night:
Joyful its beams, and in the blackness blacker still,
Though undying joyousness, caught in that trap.

Even as the remorseless Poet of *Alastor* imperishably caught up the element in Shelley that was to culminate in *Adonais* and *The Triumph of Life*, so "Parergon" portrays the doomed-poet aspect of Ashbery, of whom presumably we will hear more in his later life. One of the few ironies in Ashbery is the title, which I assume is being used in the sense it has in painting, something subsidiary to the main subject. Yet the poem is anything but bywork or ornamentation. As beautiful as nearly anything in Ashbery, it is central to his dilemma, his sorrow and his solace.

With reverence and some uneasiness, I pass to "Fragment", the crown of *The Double Dream of Spring* and, for me, Ashbery's finest work. Enigmatically autobiographical, even if it were entirely fantasy, the poem's fifty stately ten-line stanzas, orotundly Stevensian in their rhetoric, comment obliquely upon a story never told, a relationship never quite a courtship, and now a nostalgia. Studying this nostalgia, in his most formal and traditional poem, more so than anything even in *Some Trees*, Ashbery presents his readers, however faithful, with his most difficult rumination. But this is a wholly Stevensian difficulty, neither elliptical nor obscure, but a ravishing simplicity that seems largely lacking in any referential quality. I have discussed the poem with excellent and sympathetic students who continue to ask: "But what is the poem *about*?" The obvious answer, that to some extent it is "about" itself, they rightly reject, since whether we are discussing Shelley, Stevens, or Ashbery, this merely distances the same question to one remove. But though repeated readings open up the referential aspect of "Fragment", the poem will continue to inspire our uneasiness, for it is profoundly evasive.

What the all-but-perfect solipsist *means* cannot be right, not until he becomes perfect in his solipsism, and so stands forth as a phantasmagoric realist (one could cite Mark Strand, a superb poet, as a recent example). "Fragment", I take it, is the elegy for the self of the imperfect solipsist, who wavered before the reality of another self, and then withdrew back into an interior world. The poem being beautifully rounded, the title evidently refers not to an aesthetic incompleteness, but to this work's design, that tells us only part of a story, and to its resigned conclusion, for the protagonist remains alone, an "anomaly" as he calls himself in the penultimate line.

The motto to "Fragment" might be from Ashbery's early "Le Livre est sur la table" where much of the enigma of the poet's mature work is prophesied. Playing against the mode of *The Man with the Blue Guitar*, Ashbery made a Stevensian parable of his own sorrows, stating a tentative poetic and a dark version of romance. The overwhelming last stanza of "Fragment" comes full circle to this:

> The young man places a bird-house
> Against the blue sea. He walks away
> And it remains. Now other
>
> Men appear, but they live in boxes.
> The sea protects them like a wall.
> The gods worship a line-drawing
>
> Of a woman, in the shadow of the sea
> Which goes on writing. Are there
> Collisions, communications on the shore
>
> Or did all secrets vanish when
> The woman left? Is the bird mentioned
> In the waves' minutes, or did the land advance?

As the table supports the book, this poem tells us, so deprivation supports "all beauty, resonance, integrity," our poverty being our imaginative need. The young poet, deprived of a world he can only imagine, and which he is constrained to identify with "the woman," learns that the sea, Stevensian emblem for all merely given reality, must triumph. Yet, if he is to have any secrets worth learning in his womanless world, it must come from "collisions, communications on the shore," where his imagination and the given meet. "Collisions, communications" is a fearfully reductive way of describing whatever sustenance Eros grants him to live, and is part of an open question. The final question can be read more as a rhetorical one, since the poems got written, and the later work of Ashbery proves that the land did advance.

We need to read this against the splendid final stanza of "Fragment":

> But what could I make of this? Glaze
> Of many identical foreclosures wrested from
> The operative hand, like a judgment but still
> The atmosphere of seeing? That two people could
> Collide in this dusk means that the time of
> Shapelessly foraging had come undone: the space was
> Magnificent and dry. On flat evenings
> In the months ahead, she would remember that that
> Anomaly had spoken to her, words like disjointed beaches
> Brown under the advancing signs of the air.

He has learned that there are indeed "collisions, communications on the shore," but this apparently crucial or unique instance saw two people "collide in this dusk." Yet this was not failure; rather, the advent of a new time. The stanza's balance is precarious, and its answer to the crucial earlier question, "Did the land advance?" is double. The brown, disjointed beaches seem a negative reply, and "the advancing signs of the air" a positive one.

In the context of Ashbery's development, "Fragment" is his central poem, coming about a year after "The Skaters" and just preceding "Clepsydra", his last major poem written abroad. "Sunrise in Suburbia" and the powerful shorter poems in *The Double Dream of Spring* came later, after the poet's return to this country in the autumn of 1966. My own intoxication with the poem, when I first read it in *Poetry* magazine, led me on to the two recent volumes, and my sense of the enormous importance of this poet. Though I lack space here for any extended account of "Fragment" before I go on to *Three Poems*, I want to give an encapsulated sense of some of its meanings, and the start of the appreciation it deserves, as perhaps the first successful poem of its kind in English since Swinburne's "The Triumph of Time".

The poem opens, as it will close, with the unnamed woman of "a moment's commandment," whom Ashbery sometimes addresses, and sometimes describes in the third person. After a vision of April's decline, "of older / Permissiveness which dies in the / Falling back toward recondite ends, / The sympathy of yellow flowers," the poet commences upon one of these recondite ends, an elegy for "the suppressed lovers," whose ambiguous time together seems to have been only a matter of weeks.

Much of the difficulty, and the poignance, of "Fragment" is generated by Ashbery's quasi-metaphysical dilemma. Committed, like the later Stevens, to the belief that poetry and *materia poetica* are the same thing, and struggling always against the aesthetic of the epiphany or privileged moment, with its consequent devaluation of other experience, Ashbery nevertheless makes his poem to memorialize an intense experience, brief in deviation. This accounts probably for the vacillation and evasiveness of "Fragment", which tries to render an experience that belongs to the dialectic of gain and loss, yet insists the experience was neither. There are passages of regret, and of joy, scattered through the poem, but they do little to alter the calm, almost marmoreal beauty of the general tone of rapt meditation. Even the apparent reference to the death of a paternal figure, in the forty-seventh stanza, hardly changes Ashbery's almost Spenserian pace. The thirtieth stanza sums up Ashbery's inclination against the Stevensian tendency to move from a present intensity to a "That's it" of celebration, "to catch from that / Irrational moment its unreasoning." The strength of Ashbery's denial of "that Irrational moment" comes from its undersong of repressed desire:

> But why should the present seem so particularly urgent?
> A time of spotted lakes and the whippoorwill
> Sounding over everything? To release the importance

> Of what will always remain invisible?
> In spite of near and distant events, gladly
> Built? To speak the plaits of argument,
> Loosened? Vast shadows are pushed down toward
> The hour. It is ideation, incrimination
> Proceeding from necessity to find it at
> A time of day, beside the creek, uncounted stars and buttons.

Of story, "Fragment" gives almost nothing, yet it finds oblique means of showing us: "the way love in short periods / Puts everything out of focus, coming and going." Variations upon this theme constitute almost the whole of the poem's substance, and also its extraordinary strength, as Ashbery's insights in this area of perception seem endless. In its vision of love, "Fragment" hymns only the bleak truth of the triumph of absence:

> Thus your only world is an inside one
> Ironically fashioned out of external phenomena
> Having no rhyme or reason, and yet neither
> An existence independent of foreboding and sly grief.
> Nothing anybody says can make a difference; inversely
> You are a victim of their lack of consequence
> Buffeted by invisible winds, or yet a flame yourself
> Without meaning, yet drawing satisfaction
> From the crevices of that wind, living
> In that flame's idealized shape and duration.

This eloquent despair, Shelleyan in its paradoxical affirmation of love yet acknowledgement of love's delusiveness, ends precisely in Shelley's image of the coming and going of the Intellectual Beauty, "like darkness to a dying flame." Uniquely Ashberyian is the emphasis on *satisfaction*, despite the transitoriness of "living" in so purely "idealized" a shape and duration. "Fragment" alternately explores the saving crevices and the shape of love's flame. Progression in this almost static poem is so subtle as to be almost indiscernible until the reader looks back at the opening from the closing stanzas, realizing then that:

> . . . This time
> You get over the threshold of so much unmeaning, so much
> Being, prepared for its event, the active memorial.

The reader's gain is an intensified sense of "time lost and won," never more strongly felt than in the poem's erotic culmination, stanzas 13–20, where Ashbery seeks "to isolate the kernel of / Our imbalance." In stanza 16, Ashbery finds no satisfaction in satisfaction anyway, in the only stanza of the poem that breaks the baroque stateliness and artful rhetorical repetitiveness of its form:

> The volcanic entrance to an antechamber
> Was not what either of us meant.

> More outside than before, but what is worse, outside
> Within the periphery, we are confronted
> With one another, and our meeting escapes through the dark
> Like a well.
> Our habits ask us for instructions.
> The news is to return by stages
> Of uncertainty, too early or too late. It is the invisible
> Shapes, the bed's confusion and prattling. The late quiet,
>   This is how it feels.

"The volcanic entrance to an antechamber," as a dismissal of the inadequacy of phallic heterosexuality to the love meant, is a kind of elegant younger brother to Hart Crane's bitter characterization of this means of love as: "A burnt match skating in a urinal." Ashbery wisely does not pause to argue preferences, but accomplishes his poem's most surprising yet inevitable transition by directly following: "This is how it feels" with a return to childhood visions: "The pictures were really pictures / Of loving and small things." As the interchange of interior worlds continues, Ashbery attains a point of survey in stanza 36 where he can assert: "You see, it is / Not wrong to have nothing." Four years later, writing "Soonest Mended", this joined an echo of Lear's speech to Cordelia to become: "both of us were right, though nothing / Has somehow come to nothing." Expectation without desire is henceforth Ashbery's difficult, more-than-Keatsian attitude, not a disinterestedness nor any longer a renunciation, but a kind of visionary sublimation. This self-curtailing poetic *askesis* is performed as I think the dialectic of poetic influence compels it to be performed by a strong poet, as Ashbery has now become. That is, it is a revisionary movement in regard to the prime precursor, Stevens, who blends with what seems to be the dying figure of Ashbery's own father in the dense and exciting sequence of stanzas 38 through 49. These stanzas are Ashbery's version of Stevens' "Farewell to Florida" and recall its Spenserian image of the high ship of the poet's career being urged upon its more dangerous and mature course. Though Ashbery will back away from this ominous freedom in his final stanza (which I quoted earlier), the quest aspect of his career attains a wonderful culmination in stanza 49:

> One swallow does not make a summer, but are
> What's called an opposite: a whole of raveling discontent,
> The sum of all that will ever be deciphered
> On this side of that vast drop of water.
> They let you sleep without pain, having all that
> Not in the lesson, not in the special way of telling
> But back to one side of life, not especially
> Immune to it, in the secret of what goes on:
> The words sung in the next room are unavoidable
> But their passionate intelligence will be studied in you.

Here, as in so many passages having a similar quality, Ashbery reaches his own recognizable greatness, and gives us his variety of the American Sublime. The "parental concern" of Stevens' "midnight interpretation" (stanza 38) produced the grand myth of the Canon Aspirin in *Notes toward a Supreme Fiction*, where Stevens at last, detaching himself from the Canon, could affirm: "I have not but I am and as I am, I am." Ashbery, in his moment most akin to Stevens' sublime self-revelation, affirms not the Emersonian-Whitmanian Transcendental Self, as Stevens most certainly (and heroically) does, but rather "the secret of what goes on." This is not, like Stevens' massive declaration, something that dwells in the orator's "special way of telling," but inheres painfully in Ashbery's vulnerability. As a self-declared "anomaly," Ashbery abides in the most self-revelatory and noble lines he has yet written:

> The words sung in the next room are unavoidable
> But their passionate intelligence will be studied in you.

That the pathos of "Fragment", a poem of the unlived life, of life refusing revenge upon its evaders, could lead to so lucid a realization, is a vital part of Ashbery's triumph over his earlier opacities. In the recent *Three Poems*, written in a prose apparently without precursors, this triumph expands, though again large demands are made upon the reader. But this I think is part of Ashbery's true value; only he and Ammons among poets since Stevens compel me to re-read so often, and then reward such labor.

Though "The New Spirit", first of the *Three Poems*, was begun in November 1969, most of it was written January to April, 1970. In a kind of cyclic repetition, the second prose poem "The System" was composed from January to March 1971, with the much shorter "The Recital" added as a coda in April. This double movement from winter vision to spring's re-imagings is crucial in *Three Poems*, which is Ashbery's prose equivalent of *Notes toward a Supreme Fiction*, and which has the same relation as *Notes* to *Song of Myself*. Where Stevens reduces to the First Idea, which is "an imagined thing," and then equates the poet's act of the mind with the re-imaging of the First Idea, Ashbery reduces to a First Idea of himself, and then re-imagines himself. I am aware that these are difficult formulae, to be explored elsewhere, and turn to a commentary upon *Three Poems*, though necessarily a brief and tentative one.

I described "Evening in the Country" as a "convalescent's" displacement of American Orphism, the natural religion of our poetry. *Three Poems* might be called the masterpiece of an invalid of the Native Strain, even a kind of invalid's version of *Song of Myself*, as though Whitman had written that poem in 1865, rather than 1855. Ashbery's work could be called *Ruminations of Myself* or *Notes toward a Saving but Subordinate Fiction*. Whitman's poem frequently is address of I, Walt Whitman, to you or my soul. Ashbery's *Three Poems* are addressed by *I*, John Ashbery writing, to *You*, Ashbery as he is in process of becoming. *I*, as in Whitman, Pater, Yeats is personality or self or the *antithetical*; *You*, as in the same visionaries, is character or soul or the *primary*. Ashbery's swerve away from tradition here is that his *You* is the re-imagining, while his *I* is a reduction.

"The New Spirit", the first poem's title, refers to a rebirth that takes place after the middle-of-the-journey crisis, here in one's late thirties or early forties:

> . . . It is never too late to mend. When one
> is in one's late thirties, ordinary things—like a
> pebble or a glass of water—take on an expressive
> sheen. One wants to know more about them, and one
> is in turn lived by them . . .

This "new time of being born" Ashbery calls also "the new casualness," and he writes of it in a prose that goes back to his old rhetorical dialectic of alternating ellipsis and the restored cliché. Indeed, "The New Spirit" opens by overtly giving "examples of leaving out," but Ashbery then mostly chooses to stand himself in place of these examples. Why does he choose prose, after "The Skaters" had shown how well he could absorb prose into verse at length? It may be a mistake, as one advantage, in my experience, of "The New Spirit" over "The System" and "The Recital", is that it crosses over to verse half-a-dozen times, while they are wholly in prose. I suppose that the desire to tell a truth that "could still put everything in" made Ashbery wary of verse now, for fear that he should not be as comprehensive as possible. Speaking again as the poet of "Fragment" he defines his predicament: "In you I fall apart, and outwardly am a single fragment, a puzzle to itself." To redress his situation, the New Spirit has come upon him, to renovate a poet who confesses he has lost all initiative:

> . . . It has been replaced by a strange kind of happiness within the limitations. The way is narrow but it is not hard, it seems almost to propel or push one along. One gets the narrowness into one's seeing, which also seems an inducement to moving forward into what one has already caught a glimpse of and which quickly becomes vision, in the visionary sense, except that in place of the panorama that used to be our customary setting and which we never made much use of, a limited but infinitely free space has established itself, useful as everyday life but transfigured so that its signs of wear no longer appear as a reproach but as indications of how beautiful a thing must have been to have been so much prized, and its noble aspect which must have been irksome before has now become interesting, you are fascinated and keep on studying it. . . .

This, despite its diffidence, declares what Emerson called Newness or Influx, following Sampson Reed and other Swedenborgians. Sometimes the *Three Poems*, particularly "The System", sound like a heightened version of the senior Henry James. But mostly Ashbery, particularly in "The New Spirit", adds his own kind of newness to his American tradition. At first reading of "The New Spirit", I felt considerable bafflement, not at the subject-matter, immediately clear to any exegete aged forty-two, but at the procedure, for it was difficult to see how Ashbery got from point to point, or even to determine if there were points. But repeated reading uncovers a beautiful and simple design: first, self-acceptance of the minimal anomalies we have become, "the color of the filter of the opinions and ideas everyone has ever entertained about us. And in this form we must prepare, now, to try to live." Second, the wintry reduction of that conferred self is necessary: "And you lacerate yourself so as to say, These wounds are me." Next, a movement to the *you* and to re-imagining of the *I*, with a realization that the *you* has been transformed already, through the soul's experience as a builder of the art of love. With this realization, the consciousness of the New Spirit comes upon the *I*, and self and soul begin to draw closer in a fine lyric beginning: "Little by little / You are the mascot of that time" (pp. 33–34). An event of love, perhaps the one elegized in "Fragment", intervenes, illuminates, and then recedes, but in its afterglow the New Spirit gives a deeper significance to the object-world. After this seeing into the life of things, the growth of the mind quickens. But the transparency attained through the new sense of wholeness "was the same as emptiness," and the sense of individual culmination serves only to alienate the poet further from the whole of mankind, which "lay stupefied in dreams of toil and drudgery." It is at this point of realization that the long and beautiful final paragraph comes (pp. 50–51), ending "The New Spirit" with a deliberate reminiscence of the end of "The Skaters". Two visions come to Ashbery, to make him understand that there is still freedom, still the wildness of time that may allow the highest form of love to come. One is "the completed Tower of Babel," of all busyness, a terror that could be shut out just by turning away from it. The other is of the constellations that the tower threatened, but only seemed to threaten. They beckon now to "a new journey" certain to be benign, to answer "the major question that revolves around you, your being here." The journey is a choice of forms for answering, which means both Ashbery's quest for poetic form, and his continued accept-ance of an "impassive grammar of cosmic unravelings of all kinds, to be proposed but never formulated."

I think that is an accurate account of the design of "The New Spirit", but I am aware such an account gives little sense of how Ashbery has added strangeness to beauty in thus finding himself there more truly and more strange. The transcendental re-awakening of anyone, even of an excellent poet, hardly seems *materia poetica* anymore, and perhaps only Ashbery would attempt to make a poem of it at this time, since his aesthetic follows Stevens by discovering the poem already formed in the world. His true and large achievement in "The New Spirit" is to have taken the theme of "Le Monocle de Mon Oncle", already developed in "Fragment", and to have extended this theme to larger problems of the aging and widening consciousness. Men at forty, Stevens says, can go on painting lakes only if they can apprehend "the universal hue." They must cease to be dark rabbis, and yield up their lordly studies of the nature of man. "The New Spirit" is Ashbery's exorcism of the dark rabbi in his own nature. Its achievement is the rare one of having found a radiant way of describing a process that goes on in many of us, the crisis of vision in an imaginative person's middle age, without resorting to psychosexual or social reductiveness.

"The System" is Ashbery's venture into quest-romance, his pursuit as rose rabbi, of "the origin and course / Of love," the origin and course together making up the System, which is thus a purposive wandering. Since the poem opens with the statement that "The system was breaking down," the reader is prepared for the prose-poem's penultimate paragraph, that tells us "we are rescued by what we cannot imagine: it is what finally takes us up and shuts our story."

The account of the System begins in a charming vision too genial for irony, as though Aristophanes had mellowed wholly:

> From the outset it was apparent that someone had played a colossal trick on something. The switches had been tripped, as it were; the entire world or one's limited but accurate idea of it was bathed in glowing love, of a sort that need never have come into being but was now indispensable as air is to living creatures . . . if only, as Pascal says, we had the sense to stay in our room, but the individual will condemns this notion and sallies forth full of ardor and *hubris*, bent on self-discovery in the guise of an attractive partner who is *the* heaven-sent one, the convex one with whom he has had the urge to mate all these seasons without realizing it. . . .

This "glowing love" inevitably is soon enough seen as "muddle," and the first phase of quest fails: "Thus it was that a kind of blight fell on these early forms of going forth and being together, an anarchy of the affections sprung from too much universal cohesion." Rather than despair, or yield to apocalyptic yearnings, Ashbery consolidates upon his curious and effective passivity, his own kind of negative capability, becoming "a pillar of waiting," but Quixotic waiting upon a dream. As he waits, he meditates on "twin notions of growth" and on two kinds of happiness. One growth theory is of the great career: "a slow burst that narrows to a final release, pointed but not acute, a life of suffering redeemed and annihilated at the end, and for what?" This High Romanticism moves Ashbery, but he rejects it. Yet the alternative way, a Paterian "life-as-ritual" concept, the *locus classicus* of which we could find in the magnificent "Conclusion" to *The Renaissance*, he also turns from, or asserts he does, though I think he is more a part of this vision than he realizes. He fears the speed with which the soul moves away from others: "This very speed becomes a source of intoxication and of more gradually accruing speed; in the end the soul cannot recognize itself and is as one lost, though it imagines it has found eternal rest."

By evading both notions of growth, Ashbery rather desperately evades growth itself. Confronting two kinds of happiness, "the frontal and the latent," he is again more evasive than he may intend to be. The first is a sudden glory, related to the epiphany or Paterian "privileged moment," and Ashbery backs away from it, as by now we must expect, because of its elitism, he says, but rather, we can surmise, for defensive reasons, involving both the anxiety of influence and more primordial Oedipal anxieties. The latent and dormant kind he seeks to possess, but his long espousal of it (pp. 73–86) seems to me the weakest sequence in *Three Poems*, despite a poignant culmination in the great question: "When will you realize that your dreams have eternal life?" I suspect that these are, *for Ashbery*, the most important pages in his book, but except for the lovely pathos of a dreamer's defense, they are too much the work of a poet who wishes to be more of an anomaly than he is, rather than the "central" kind of a poet he is fated to become, in the line of Emerson, Whitman, Stevens.

This "central" quality returns wonderfully in the last twenty pages of "The System", as the quest for love begins again. A passage of exquisite personal comedy, Chaplinesque in its profundity, climaxes in the poet's defense of his mask: "your pitiable waif's stance, that inquiring look that darts uneasily from side to side as though to ward off a blow—." Ashbery assimilates himself to the crucial Late Romantic image of the failed quester, Browning's Childe Roland, for the author of *Three Poems* now approaches his own Dark Tower, to be confronted there by every anxiety, as human and as poet, that he has evaded:

> . . . It is only that you happened to be wearing this look as you arrived at the end of your perusal of the way left open to you, and it "froze" on you, just as your mother warned you it would when you were little. And now it is the face you show to the world, the face of expectancy, strange as it seems. Perhaps Childe Roland wore such a look as he drew nearer to the Dark Tower, every energy concentrated toward the encounter with the King of Elfland, reasonably certain of the victorious outcome, yet not so much as to erase the premature lines of care from his pale and tear-stained face. Maybe it is just that you don't want to outrage anyone, especially now that the moment of your own encounter seems to be getting closer.

This version of Childe Roland's ordeal is an Ashberyian transformation or wish-fulfillment, as we can be reasonably certain that Browning's quester neither wants nor expects a "victorious outcome." But Ashbery feels raised from a first death, unlike Childe Roland, who longs for any end, and lacks a "quiet acceptance of experience in its revitalizing tide." Very gently, Ashbery accomplishes a Transcendental and open ending to "The System", complete with an Emersonian "transparent axle" and even an equivalent to the closing chant of Emerson's Orphic Poet in *Nature*, though Ashbery's guardian bard speaks to him in a "dry but deep accent," promising mastery (p. 99). Insisting that he has healed the sadness of childhood, Ashbery declares his System-wanderings are completed, the right balance attained in "what we have carefully put in and kept out," though a lyric" crash" may impend in which all this will be lost again. But, for now:

> The allegory is ended, its coils absorbed into the past, and this afternoon is as wide as an ocean. It is the time we have now, and all our wasted time sinks into the sea and is swallowed up without a trace. The past is dust and ashes, and this incommensurably wide way leads to the pragmatic and kinetic future.

This Shelleyan conclusion, akin to Demogorgon's dialectical vision, offers hope in "the pragmatic" yet menaces a return of the serpent-allegory (whose name is Ananke, in Ashbery as in Stevens or Shelley) in the still "kinetic" future.

The Coda of "The Recital" is a wholly personal apologia, with many Whitmanian and Stevensian echoes, some of them involuntary. "We cannot interpret everything, we must be selective," Ashbery protests, "nor can we leave off singing" which would return the poet to the living death of an unhappy childhood. Against the enemy (p. 111), who is an amalgam of time and selfishness, Ashbery struggles to get beyond his own solipsism, and the limits of his art. On the final page, an Emersonian-Stevensian image of saving transparence serves to amalgamate the new changes Ashbery meets and welcomes. This transparence movingly is provided by a Whitmanian vision of an audience for Ashbery's art: "There were new people watching and waiting, conjugating in this way the distance and emptiness, transforming the scarcely noticeable bleakness into something both intimate and noble." So they have and will, judging by the response of my students and other friends, with whom I've discussed Ashbery's work. By more than fifteen years of high vision and persistence he has clarified the initial prophecy of his work, until peering into it we can say: "We see us as we truly behave" and, as we see, we can think: "These accents seem their own defense."

Frank O'Hara's Poetry
by Susan Holahan

"ONE NEED never leave the confines of New York to get all the greenery one wishes—I can't even enjoy a blade of grass unless I know there's a subway handy, or a record store or some other sign that people do not totally *regret* life." This speaker in "Meditations in an Emergency" is, of course, Frank O'Hara's creation and not O'Hara himself, but he speaks (with some irony) for a poet who moved in New York as Marvell did in his garden, who made from details of the landscape an oddly significant vision.

O'Hara does not write about the city; he lives in it. In friendly reciprocity, a New York has come to live in the poems that no longer exists in fact. More likely it never existed. Knowing that once there was a Golden Griffin bookstore or a Ziegfeld Theatre, knowing that there is indeed a Seagram building not to mention an Allen Ginsberg, a literary tourist would be deceived into imagining that the whole of O'Hara's New York once had a geographical reality. His ceremonious naming makes the reader forget that the persons, places, things thereby gain meaning in a poetic universe rather than mass in a physical one.

Illusion suggests, even in many of his best-known poems, that the poetic narrative retails experience "as it happened." Behind this, however, stands a structure of personal encounters—their potentialities, their actualities, their aftermaths—working on all the senses to characterize his special world. O'Hara's New York has its own light, for example, rivalling the Florentine. As in the "luminous humidity" he discerned around the Seagram building, the silver hats of fortunate construction workers shine like literary lights, like magic, like love:

> we don't want to be in the poets' walk in
> San Francisco even we just want to be rich
> and walk on girders in our silver hats
> I wonder if one person out of the 8,000,000 is
> thinking of me as I shake hands with LeRoi
> and buy a strap for my wristwatch and go
> back to work happy at the thought possibly so
>
> ("Personal Poem")

In autumn "a cool graced light / is pushed off the enormous glass piers by hard winds" ("Khrushchev is coming on the right day!")—and it moves through the city. New York has its sound, too, which promises poetry: "a faint stirring of that singing seems to come to me in heavy traffic" ("Ode to

Michael Goldberg ('s Birth and Other Births)"). It is a necessary quality of this poetry that it speaks above or through the noise of cars and buses—in New York it's not volume but style that earns a hearing in a big cocktail party. ("One of the most startling things about Frank . . . was his ability to write a poem when other people were talking, or even to get up in the middle of a conversation, get his typewriter, and write a poem, sometimes participating in the conversation while doing so," his close friend the poet Kenneth Koch remembered for *Audit* in 1964.)

If light and sound might form part of anyone's description of his surroundings, New York for O'Hara has temperature and texture that make it a medium in which life continues only on the city's terms. In midtown Manhattan at the height of summer, heat rises from the pavement to meet what descends from sky and buildings at about face level. What is *in* this air you use as you walk around?

> Is it dirty
> does it look dirty
> that's what you think of in the city
>
> does it just seem dirty
> that's what you think of in the city
> you don't refuse to breathe do you
>
>   ("Song")

You can't refuse. There's always a possibility that someone might be waiting. The very thickness of the air might contain an encounter.

> though a block away you feel distant the mere presence
> changes everything like a chemical dropped on a paper
> and all thoughts disappear on a strange quiet excitement
> I am sure of nothing but this, intensified by breathing
>   ("Light   clarity   avocado salad in the morning")

Breathing here amounts to a commitment. The whole city breathes together or not at all, so an event in one part sends out its vibrations into another.

In this city small events develop an aura; small precisions delineate apocalypse:

> It is 12:20 in New York a Friday
> three days after Bastille day, yes
> it is 1959 and I go get a shoeshine
> because I will get off the 4:19 in Easthampton
> at 7:15 and then go straight to dinner
> and I don't know the people who will feed me
>
> I walk up the muggy street beginning to sun
> and have a hamburger and a malted and buy
> an ugly NEW WORLD WRITING to see what the poets

in Ghana are doing these days
                              I go on to the bank
and Miss Stillwagon (first name Linda I once heard)
doesn't even look up my balance for once in her life
and in the GOLDEN GRIFFIN I get a little Verlaine
for Patsy with drawings by Bonnard although I do
think of Hesiod, trans. Richmond Lattimore or
Brendan Behan's new play or *Le Balcon* or *Les Nègres*
of Genet, but I don't, I stick with Verlaine
after practically going to sleep with quandariness

and for Mike I just stroll into the PARK LANE
Liquor Store and ask for a bottle of Strega and
then I go back where I came from to 6th Avenue
and the tobacconist in the Ziegfeld Theatre and
casually ask for a carton of Gauloises and a carton
of Picayunes, and a NEW YORK POST with her face on it

and I am sweating a lot by now and thinking of
leaning on the john door in the 5 SPOT
while she whispered a song along the keyboard
to Mal Waldron and everyone and I stopped breathing
                              ("The Day Lady Died")

Merely listing a few trees or flowers, classical elegy could announce that with the poet-singer's death nature itself died. O'Hara walks and works to line out another world which will feel that mourning. Time is stopped from the first words; a moment extends itself over more and more space until, in the last lines, the feelings of the present instant—the instant of seeing her face or the instant of writing the poem—catch up those of the past ("I am sweating a lot by now and thinking of / leaning") to produce nature's classical tribute to the dead singer: "everyone and I stopped breathing."

As it occurs, the narrative of "The Day Lady Died" does seem, in the plainest terms possible, merely to occupy a lunch hour. "I don't know the people who will feed me" has a bravura effect: you calculate these small social risks against the likely benefits of new encounters and good dinners. In retrospect the same words may sound desperate, alienated, hysterical. While the poet and the poem keep moving, this hot, oppressed wandering in a vaguely unfamiliar city filled with small uglinesses seems the fault of the "muggy street beginning to sun," the vagaries of banktellers, the difficulties of bread-and-butter gifts. "After practically going to sleep with quandariness," anyway, the mood picks up. The wanderer can "just stroll" into a liquor store and "casually ask" for cigarettes, demonstrating his command of sprezzatura. Look back on this from the end, however, and the wandering seems to take place in an underworld. Strangely like Prufrock, the speaker starts to search through what has suddenly become the city of the dead. His casual strolling and asking barely hold in the tension of impending recognition.

And why so many references to France? They must make a pattern—so many can't be accidental—but surely each arises of itself. If Frank O'Hara happened to learn of the death of the great black singer Billie Holiday on July 17, 1959, when he chose among French books and purchased French cigarettes—all this is mere coincidence. Neither the poets in Ghana nor *Les Nègres* of Genet assert a necessary connection with the difficulties black musicians experience in the United States, though a year before O'Hara had ended his "Ode: Salute to the French Negro Poets":

> the only truth is face to face, the poem whose words become your mouth
> and dying in black and white we fight for what we love, not are

The appearance of coincidence works for O'Hara in the city as does a suggestion of surrealism, a dramatic style of conversation, and a musical notion of prosody. The city worked for him in providing not just the events and encounters but a special pace, a sense of gathering—images, tones, ideas. O'Hara placed himself at a center by working, throughout his poetic career, at the Museum of Modern Art. He had started out as a music student; by 1950, apparently, he was dividing his time between his poetry and others' painting. In addition to work (as curator by the time of his death in 1966) at the Museum, he wrote criticism for *Art News* and *Art & Literature*, art chronicles for magazines like *Kulchur*, a short book on Jackson Pollock. His close friendships with artists working in and near New York contributed to the book on Pollock, produced poems like his "Ode to Willem de Kooning", "Ode to Michael Goldberg ('s Birth and Other Births)", and the lithographs made with Larry Rivers. Rivers's description, in "Life Among the Stones", of the process by which they jointly created the "Love" stone might stand for a description of the relationship of poetry to painting in New York in the '50's:

> You say it is like the relationship between people who live under the same roof. There are moments where every feeling or action grows out of a direct response to what is said, to what is being done or who's got a hand somewhere. And then there are hours and days of solo. Everything is happening in the same space under similar conditions but the movements are barely responding to anything except what has been with you from birth and is turned in without fanfare at death.

O'Hara on Pollock seems truly to be talking to himself: "Surrealism," he notes, "enjoined the duty, along with the liberation, of saying what you mean and meaning what you say, above and beyond any fondness for saying and meaning." Saying and meaning like this demand activity on an appropriate scale and, toward the end of the essay, O'Hara describes Pollock's discovery of what came to be called Action Painting, when "the scale of the painting became that of the painter's body." As O'Hara extends this notion of "scale, and no-scale," he touches a reader's sense of the poet walking the city in "The Day Lady Died": what impresses itself as the shape and substance of the poem is, again in O'Hara's words for Pollock, "the physical reality of the artist and his activity of expressing it, united to the spiritual reality of the artist in a oneness which has no need for the mediation of metaphor or symbol."

Appraising Pollock, O'Hara could naturally allow himself much higher flights than he would in discussing poetry, particularly his own. For painting he could make claims. In poems "I am mainly preoccupied with the world as I experience it. . . . What is happening to me, allowing for lies and exaggerations which I try to avoid, goes into my poems." Very straightforward; but 1959, the year of many of his finest poems, the year of the Pollock book, the year of this manly and modest statement on poetics, also encompassed a contribution from O'Hara to LeRoi Jones's magazine *Yugen*. "Personism: A Manifesto" obliquely but obligingly reveals a major impulse for O'Hara's work.

> . . . to give you a vague idea, one of its minimal aspects is to address itself to one person (other than the poet himself), thus evoking overtones of love without destroying love's life-giving vulgarity, and sustaining the poet's feelings toward the poem while preventing love from distracting him into feeling about the person. . . . I was in love with someone. . . . I went back to work and wrote a poem for this person. While I was writing it I was realizing that if I wanted to I could use the telephone instead of writing the poem, and so Personism was born. . . . It puts the poem squarely between the poet and the person, Lucky Pierre style, and the poem is correspondingly gratified. The poem is at last between two persons instead of two pages.

O'Hara allows himself momentarily to sound a little like Holden Caulfield anxious to telephone Eustacia Vye, but he also glances at a source of energy in his poetry. He separates himself from other "New York" poets in his willingness to face, and to use, sentiment, even sentimentality—for its strength. His irony and his "drastic self-knowledge" (his phrase for Pollock) save the day. Dramatically, the reader participates in the poem without embarrassment. There's flattery in the "you", as there always is, but the energy-combine serves another end. Consider the personal/emotional structure of "Lana Turner has collapsed!":

> Lana Turner has collapsed!
> I was trotting along and suddenly
> it started raining and snowing
> and you said it was hailing
> but hailing hits you on the head
> hard so it was really snowing and
> raining and I was in such a hurry
> to meet you but the traffic
> was acting exactly like the sky

> and suddenly I see a headline
> LANA TURNER HAS COLLAPSED!
> there is no snow in Hollywood
> there is no rain in California
> I have been to lots of parties
> and acted perfectly disgraceful
> but I never actually collapsed
> oh Lana Turner we love you get up

At least three of us are at work here, carrying on a running argument about meteorology, hoping to meet, optimistically misreading the universe. Perhaps the force field of "personism" serves its benevolent purpose when all readers of scandalous headlines unite to lift their illusions back on to their empty pedestals, as similar energy works toward health in "Fantasy". O'Hara can use it for his own support; he does in poems like "Variations on Pasternak's 'Mein liebchen, was willst du noch mehr'" and "Poem / to Donald M. Allen". Toward what end he suggests in "A Poem in Envy of Cavalcanti":

> To be, Guido,
> a simple and elegant province all by myself
>
> like you, would mean that a toss of my head,
> a wink, a lurch against the nearest brick
>
> had captured painful felicity and all its opaque
> nourishment in a near and cosmic stanza, ah!

The magic of "envy" flashes him in—of all things—the mathematical center of this five-couplet poem ("a toss of my head, / a wink, a lurch") to his goal. Momentarily. The final couplet collapses like Lana Turner:

> But I only wither to the earth, my personal
> mess, and am unable to utter a good word.

O'Hara directed formidable technical resources toward his poetic goals. In his brilliant memoir, "Frank O'Hara and His Poems", Bill Berkson says, "An early notebook shows studies of Ronsard, Heine, Petrarch, Anglo-Saxon charms, Rilke, Jammes. There were imitations of Coleridge, translations of Hölderlin," and, one could add, references to Eliot as well as Olson, Stevens as well as Stein. O'Hara experimented with rhyme and off-rhyme in early poems like "After Wyatt" and "The distinguished / and freshly dusted Apollodorus-type." He developed a prosody that permitted the unobtrusively electric effects of even his most prosy works, but his intense artistic concern with syntax reached farthest and deepest.

O'Hara's remarkable way of making a sentence, or not-making a sentence, shapes his poems from 1951 on. Syntax covers anything from minute dependencies in a three-word sequence to massive interrelationships in the longest poem; it gives the poet a handle on time. O'Hara's sentences held firm around any range, any reference he reached for. He tests them in the long poem "Second Avenue" (1953), which gets from its syntax alone its structure and its constant hints of meaning. Times somehow mingle, in "Second Avenue"'s second sentence, placing the poem outside time, inside only syntax:

> This thoroughness whose traditions have become so reflective,
> your distinction is merely a quill at the bottom of the sea
> tracing forever the fabulous alarms of the mute
> so that in the limpid tosses of your violet dinginess
> a pus appears and lingers like a groan from the collar
> of a reproachful tree whose needles are tired of howling.

About two years later, the first sentence (also the first stanza) of "Sleeping on the Wing" defines another kind of reach. Syntax pushes space and time into parallels, floating them off at the end into a set of lucid but mysterious images:

> Perhaps it is to avoid some great sadness,
> as in a Restoration tragedy the hero cries "Sleep!
> O for a long sound sleep and so forget it!"
> that one flies, soaring above the shoreless city,
> veering upward from the pavement as a pigeon
> does when a car honks or a door slams, the door
> of dreams, life perpetuated in parti-colored loves
> and beautiful lies all in different languages.

No doubt the airline's comfortable upholstery encouraged these swoops, with the present embracing an historical past as it moves into the future. Later, the poems that broke time into fragments (like "The Day Lady Died") needed to contain all movement within the present moment, as does this first sentence/paragraph of "Personal Poem" (1959):

> Now when I walk around at lunchtime
> I have only two charms in my pocket
> an old Roman coin Mike Kanemitsu gave me
> and a bolt-head that broke off a packing case
> when I was in Madrid the others never
> brought me too much luck though they did
> help keep me in New York against coercion
> but now I'm happy for a time and interested

This syntax that contains the past has a way of resolving its disappointments by appreciating the present—"but now I'm happy for a time and interested." It will not make promises for the future.

O'Hara's poems after 1960 or so insist instead on separate moments. Syntax becomes a means of separating one moment's perception from another's, and the infrequent pattern that works like sentences signals a special occasion, a moment worth extending over time and space.

I am sitting on top of Mauna Loa seeing thinking feeling
the breeze rustles through the mountain gently trusts me
I am guarding it from mess and measure
                        it is cool
                        I am high
                        and happy
                        as it turns
                        on the earth
                        tangles me
                        in the air
the celestial drapery salutes an ordinary occurrence
                                        ("Biotherm," 1961–62)

Only rarely can one moment trust another, or one insight lead another, to this stability. Saying, earlier, could bring "seeing thinking feeling" together in syntax; when they mesh here, in a very long poem which signals its major transitions with the quasi-syntactic banners "NEVERTHELESS," "BUT," "AND," they give good cause for celebration.

Inevitably syntax involves time, and time held prizes for O'Hara throughout his career. It *acts* in his poetry dramatically. Some private sense of menace may have endowed him with enormous respect for time's paradoxical uses. The title of his second collection is from the prose poem of 1954: *Meditations in an Emergency*. Only a poet takes this chance with time, that crises will offer him perfect occasions for contemplation, in fact, for poetry. He may pay for his temerity.

The eager note on my door said "Call me,
call when you get in!" so I quickly threw
a few tangerines into my overnight bag,
straightened my eyelids and shoulders, and

headed straight for the door. It was autumn
by the time I got around the corner, oh all
unwilling to be either pertinent or bemused, but
the leaves were brighter than grass on the sidewalk!

Funny, I thought, that the lights are on this late
and the hall door open; still up at this hour, a
champion jai-alai player like himself? Oh fie!
for shame! What a host, so zealous! And he was

there in the hall, flat on a sheet of blood that
ran down the stairs. I did appreciate it. There are few
hosts who so thoroughly prepare to greet a guest
only casually invited, and that several months ago.
                                        ("Poem," 1950)

Just what worked upon the daring in this use of time O'Hara's later style

refuses to specify. In "A Step Away from Them" (1956), he walks somewhat
morosely in his city. Cabs look "hum-colored." He checks "bargains in
wristwatches," then "Everything / suddenly honks: it is 12:40." Somehow,
when the moment suddenly invades, takes over, what seemed hot and irritating
fills with possibility, even pleasure.

> A lady in
> foxes on such a day puts her poodle
> in a cab.
>   There are several Puerto
> Ricans on the avenue today, which
> makes it beautiful and warm. First
> Bunny died, then John Latouche,
> then Jackson Pollock. But is the
> earth as full as life was full, of them?
> And one has eaten and one walks. . . .

In the city, a moment can sustain a poet, as well as a glass of papaya juice.
Then moments jostle one another. The city seems "merely a kissed country, a
hamster of choices" in "Variations on Pasternak's 'Mein liebchen, was willst
du noch mehr?'" (1959). And:

> Walls, except that they stretch through China
> like a Way, are melancholy fingers in the snow
> of years
>   time moves, but is not moving in its strange grimace
> .   .   .   .
> what do you think has happened
> that you have pushed the wall and
>   stopped thinking of Bunny
>   you have let death go, you have stopped
>   you are not serene, you desire something, you are not ending
>   ("Variations")

This "not ending" augurs well. A centenarian can enjoy himself; "doom has
held off." From particular days and nights, poems will emerge, softened by
rain. They may not last. Time works on persons and poems, so that, by 1961:

> it seems that breath could easily fill a balloon and drift away
>
> scaring the locusts in the straggling grey of living dumb
> exertions then the useful noise would come of doom of data
> turned to elegant decoration like a strangling prince once ordered
> no there is no precedent of history no history nobody came before
> nobody will ever come before and nobody ever was that man
>   ("For the Chinese New Year & for Bill Berkson")

Who was that man? If the question, put this way, recalls the Lone Ranger,
fine. A mask enters it for O'Hara, too, and he always indulged his own penchant for references to radio, TV, and movie lore (concluding, "never argue

with the movies"). The question faced him constantly. He asked it in the past while he kept trying to answer it in the present.

> I am standing in the bath tub
> crying. Mother, mother
> who am I ? If he
> will just come back once
> and kiss me on the face
> his coarse hair brush
> my temple, it's throbbing!
>
> .   .   .   .   .   .
>
> roll back your eyes, a pool,
> and I'll stare down
> at my wounded beauty
> which at best is only a talent
> for poetry.
>
> .   .   .   .
>
> Now I am quietly waiting for
> the catastrophe of my personality
> to seem beautiful again,
> and interesting, and modern.
>
> ("Mayakovsky")

Merely ask the question and someone rebukes you with narcissism. Rebuke yourself, and the only solution is to wait. Meanwhile, as O'Hara says elsewhere, go on your nerve. Going on his nerve, he probes this issue in poem after poem, surrounding it with a cluster of images. Horses, for example, in an ancient fashion, have something to do with mastery of deep, instinctive forces (for self-protection); but the horse the poet learns to control in "Poem / to James Schuyler" has somehow turned into a terrible burden in "Ode";

> It's as if I were carrying a horse on my shoulders
> and I couldn't see his face. His iron legs
> hang down to the earth on either side of me
> like the arch of triumph in Washington Square.
> I would like to beat someone with him
> but I can't get him off my shoulders, he's like evening.
>
> Evening! your breeze is an obstacle,
>   it changes me, I am being arrested,
>   and if I mock you into a face
> and, disgusted, throw down the horse—ah! there's his face!
> and I am, sobbing, walking on my heart.

"It's as if" poses this answer to a complex situation, not a simple, single question. Some sort of face reveals itself—"*a* face," never quite delineated.

"In Memory of My Feelings" explores the many selves of a poet at length, and brilliantly. Images from earlier poems reappear; with old talismans and new O'Hara builds an impressive structure, moving toward "the serpent's turn" at the end. In the fourth of five sections he gives fullest, freest play to his vision of many in one:

> One of me is standing in the waves, an ocean bather,
> or I am naked with a plate of devils at my hip.
>   Grace
> to be born and live as variously as possible. The conception
> of the masque barely suggests the sordid identifications.
> I am a Hittite in love with a horse. I don't know what blood's
> in me I feel like an African prince I am a girl walking downstairs
> in a red pleated dress with heels I am a champion taking a fall
> I am a jockey with a sprained ass-hole I am the light mist
>   in which a face appears
> and it is another face of blonde I am a baboon eating a banana
> I am a dictator looking at his wife I am a doctor eating a child
> and the child's mother smiling I am a Chinaman climbing a mountain
> I am a child smelling his father's underwear I am an Indian
> sleeping on a scalp
>   and my pony is stamping in the birches,
> I've just caught sight of the *Nina*, the *Pinta* and the *Santa Maria*.
>
>   What land is this, so free?
>   I watch
> the sea at the back of my eyes, near the spot where I think
> in solitude as pine trees groan and support the enormous winds,
> they are humming *L'Oiseau de feu*!
>   They look like gods, these whitemen,
> and they are bringing me the horse I fell in love with on the frieze.

"Grace" happens to be the first name of the friend to whom the poem is dedicated. "The conception / of the masque barely suggests the sordid identifications," and the myriad-minded Indian encompasses the child, the mother, the Hittite, the Chinaman (a character who makes inscrutable appearances from time to time in several other poems), the graced poet, who recognizes himself midway as "the light mist in which a face appears."

"In Memory of My Feelings", whose title calls up Wordsworth's "emotion recollected in tranquillity", comes to this place of memory or recollection to make possible new poetry, "where I think / in solitude as pine trees groan and support the enormous winds." (The city reduces these winds to breath.) Memory can work further on this image: "Ode to Michael Goldberg ('s Birth and Other Births)" evokes memories and feelings (this poetic investigations too will surface vipers, Indians, journeys of discovery to foreign countries) and catches the same wind at home.

> Up on the mountainous hill

behind the confusing house
where I lived. . . .
.   .   .   .

the wind sounded exactly like
Stravinsky
          I first recognized art
as wildness, and it seemed right,
          I mean rite, to me
climbing the water-tower I'd
look out for hours in wind
and the world seemed rounder
and fiercer and I was happier
because I wasn't scared of falling off

nor off the horses, the horses!
to hell with the horses, bay and black

After the mastery claimed in this ode, the amazing series of poems in 1959—but there were other countries to visit, other languages to learn: someone, in "Hotel Particulier" (1960), seeks "the hostel where the lazy and fun-loving / start up the mountain." A poet investigates "How to Get There" through travel poem after travel poem, moving around in Europe, in New York, in memory and time. Sometimes he moves, more often he is being moved. In time he names the threat that pushes:

Behind New York there's a face
and it's not Sibelius's with a cigar
it was red it was strange and hateful
and then I became a child again
.   .   .   .

what do you think this is my youth
and the aged future that is sweeping me away
carless and gasless under the Sutton
and Beekman Places towards a hellish rage
it is there that face I fear under ramps
                    ("For the Chinese New Year")

New York hides a terror now. It's not a face the poet can identify with—perhaps it resembles the threatening face dimly remembered in "Mayakovsky". Fear only drives the poet harder to reach his reader, who is and is not the person directly addressed—personism looking over shoulders. Frighteningly private references inject themselves into stanzas without warning. They embarrass everyone; "personality" has dragged them in its train.

Being a poet, you "can adorn [the past] with easy convictions." How do you touch another *person* if your epigraph from D. H. Lawrence warns that "we fall apart / Endlessly, in one motion depart / From each other"? "I have

something portentous to say to you but which / of the papier-mâché languages do you understand," the poet asks. These must be the same "different
languages" that, in "Sleeping on the Wing" had the grace to perpetuate life
"in parti-colored loves / and beautiful lies." The odds against him have
mounted impossibly.

The poet, reluctantly facing "the season of renunciation," keeps "looking
for a million-dollar heart in a carton / of frozen strawberries." He awards
himself no points for persistence. Distracted questions interrupt his search;
mad alternatives to effort threaten to overwhelm him with lassitude, but self-
discovery dominates all other impulses.

> oh oh god how I'd love to dream let alone sleep it's night
> the soft air wraps me like a swarm it's raining and I have
> a cold I am a real human being with real ascendancies
> and a certain amount of rapture what do you do with a kid
> like me if you don't eat me I'll have to eat myself

Unheroically, the poet has entangled himself in the "Restoration tragedy" he
invented while "Sleeping on the Wing". If "In Memory of My Feelings"
seemed to open limitless possibilities, "For the Chinese New Year" insists on
closing them off again. The Hittite, adolescent girl, Chinaman, and Indian
who all made up one evolving person have faded into "strange fantoms I /
read about in the newspapers." (The rhetorical device is now simile rather
than metaphor.) The poem works toward forcing its speaker to confront his
single self, demanding as that confrontation may be. He threatens more than
once to foist this meeting off onto the shoulders of the person he addresses,
but that person, he discovers, finally will not permit this escape. Resolution
struggles against old favorite indulgences:

> I think it's goodbye to a lot of things like Christmas
> and the Mediterranean and halos and meteorites and villages
> full of damned children well it's goodbye then as in Strauss
> or some other desperately theatrical venture it's goodbye
> to lunch to love to evil things and to the ultimate good as "well"
>
> the strange career of a personality begins at five and ends
> forty minutes later in a fog the rest is just a lot of stranded
> ships honking their horns full of joy-seeking cadets in bloomers
> and beards. . . .

From this, many questions could arise, since someone takes leave here of all
O'Hara's subjects, his occasions, his deepest concerns. Have they threatened,
in the hectic atmosphere of this "desperately theatrical venture" to become
"data / turned to elegant decoration"? From beginning to end of this poem,
the speaker has felt torn: something lingers, but much has been lost. He
trembles between strenuous efforts to scrutinize this experience and violent
desires to dismiss it completely. At the end, easy success fails to make itself

available. Still, it's the New Year, of a sort (and "Chinese" has always equalled "mysterious" for O'Hara). Despite the omens and the apparent lack of received tradition, something might emerge; so the poet turns prophet:

> no there is no precedent of history no history nobody came before
> nobody will ever come before and nobody ever was that man
>
> you will not die not knowing this is true this year

Adrienne Rich: The Poetics of Change
by Albert Gelpi

THE DEVELOPMENT of a poet's themes, techniques and imagery is an instructive and moving study—if the poet is as compelling as Adrienne Rich is. Her first book was published twenty years ago, and she came into her own in the four collections which constitute her poems since the 'sixties; in sequence, the volumes point the drift of American poetry since the Second World War.

The poems which went into *A Change of World*, selected by W. H. Auden for the Yale Younger Poets Series in 1951, were written in the years just after the War, a period dominated by awesome figures: Eliot, Frost, Stevens, and so on. Poets of the generations after theirs—Auden and Tate, for instance, and later Robert Lowell—seemed to be substantiating Eliot's prediction that poetry should take a turn to a stricter formalism than was needed in the 'teens and 'twenties. Dylan Thomas had been a fascinating exotic; Pound was notorious; Williams represented the only major opposing force, but his influence was small compared to the combined presences of Eliot-Tate-Auden. In fact, American poetry was about to take a turn which would make Williams and Pound the presiding eminences for the new poets; the topography of American poetry looked astonishingly different by the end of the fifties, and even more markedly so by the mid-sixties. But there was little evidence of the impending shift in 1951 when Adrienne Rich, a Radcliffe senior, made a debut as early as it was auspicious.

In his "Foreword" Auden complimented the "younger poet" somewhat condescendingly for not seeking novelty and instead cultivating the "detachment from the self and its emotions" which makes for craftsmanship, as Eliot had observed. Thus the echoes of Frost, Yeats, Stevens, Robinson, Emily Dickinson and Auden himself in these first poems indicated her intelligence and discretion. Auden sums up the virtues of the poems with the statement that they "are neatly and modestly dressed, speak quietly but do not mumble, respect their elders but are not cowed by them, and do not tell fibs." In other words, the stereotype—prim, fussy, and schoolmarmish—that has corseted and strait-laced women-poets into "poetesses" whom men could deprecate with admiration.

Modest and understated as these poems are, they are—the best of them—more interesting than Auden's comments suggest, and the main concerns of the later mature work are adumbrated from the start: the sense of imminent doom in "Storm Warnings", "Eastport to Block Island" and "The Ultimate Act"; the relations between man and woman in "An Unsaid Word" and

"Mathilde in Normandy"; the difficulty and necessity of communication in "Stepping Backward"; the metaphysical scepticism of "Air Without Incense" and "For the Conjunction of Two Planets"; the fact of mutability in "A Change of World" and "Walden 1950"; the consequent concentration on the passing moment which almost every one of these pieces exemplifies. Rich's reflex is consistent throughout: she seeks shelter as self-preservation. In "Storm Warnings", the first poem in the book, she prepares against the threats within and without by sealing off a comfortable, weather-proof sanctuary:

> I draw the curtains as the sky goes black
> And set a match to candles sheathed in glass
> Against the keyhole draught, the insistent whine
> Of weather through the unsealed aperture.
> This is our sole defense against the season;
> These are the things that we have learned to do
> Who live in troubled regions.

The only exposure is the keyhole that locks the door. So the finely poised paradoxes of "Afterward" note ruefully that a fond innocence must fall, as it will, to the recognition of limits:

> Now that your hopes are shamed, you stand
> At last believing and resigned,
> And none of us who touch your hand
> Know how to give you back in kind
> The words you flung when hopes were proud:
> *Being born to happiness*
> *Above the asking of the crowd,*
> *You would not take a finger less.*
> We who know limits now give room
> To one who grows to fit his doom.

Still, acknowledged limits can, *faute de mieux*, raise protective perimeters within which one can learn to operate: not just the walls that enclose the psyche but, by extension, the prosodic and technical conventions that shape the space and time of the poem. Aesthetic form rescues the moment from the flux, as "Designs in Living Colors" says, into a richer and repeated realization; besides, aesthetic form imposes the control that raw emotions demand: "A too-compassionate art is only half an art. / Only such proud restraining purity [as Bach has] / Restores the else-betrayed, too-human heart" ("At a Bach Concert").

The poems in *A Change of World* display a variety of meters, rhymes and stanzas, and each piece elaborates its convention symmetrically, as in the balance of unresolved dualities in "For the Conjunction of Two Planets". After a while the reader begins to wonder if the artifice, no matter how skillfully wrought, may serve as a partial evasion of the conflicts which are the subject of the poem. The verbal expression may camouflage a refusal to do what "The Ultimate Act" urges: commit that act "beneath a final sun." Limits which are hard to accept may become, in the end, too easy to accept. The precariousness of one's situation makes for the insistence on remaining unattached and unharmed; hence the decorous reserve of the woman toward the man in "An Unsaid Word", "Mathilde in Normandy" and "Stepping Backward". It's "you and I in our accepted frame," and poetry is itself a frame for viewing at a relatively safe distance a changing world divided from and against itself.

The Diamond Cutters (1955) is filled with travel poems, written on a Guggenheim in Europe and describing famous places and monuments with the acute eye of the tourist. Even such home scenes as Walden and the Charles River take on the detachment of tourist-views. What makes them more than genteel impressions is the developing metaphor which implies that we are all aliens in a fallen world. The first section of the book is called "Letter from the Land of Sinners": Europe littered with the ruins of time which still conjure up an era of greater beauty and order, perhaps even an arcadia when myths seemed true and we "listened to Primavera speaking flowers." But underneath the nostalgia there is the recognition that the fall into history was so original that Primavera is beyond recall, and we visit the ruins without inhabiting them. In "Ideal Landscape": "The human rose to haunt us everywhere, / Raw, flawed, and asking more than we could bear." In "The Celebration in the Plaza", after the balloon has popped and the fireworks fizzed out: "*But is that all?* some little children cry. / *All we have left*, their pedagogues reply." At the remains of the "Villa Adriana": "His perfect colonnades at last attain / The incompleteness of a natural thing."

What then remains? In "Lucifer in the Train" the poet repeats the journey from paradise and proposes, in the accents of Stevens, the old question about the fallen world: "What bird but feeds upon mortality, / Flies to its young with carrion in its claws?" The unconvincing answer comes in a prayer to Lucifer:

> O foundered angel, first and loneliest
> To turn this bitter sand beneath your hoe,
> Teach us, the newly-landed, what you know;
> After our weary transit, find us rest.

Were rest possible, we could make

> another kind of peace,
> And walk where boughs are green,
> Forgiven by the selves that we have been,
> And learning to forgive. Our apples taste
> Sweeter this year; our gates are falling down,
> And need not be replaced.
>
> ("Letter from the Land of Sinners")

"Landscape of the Star" draws this secular moral from the quest of the Magi for the Christ-child:

> Our gifts shall bring us home: not to beginnings
> Nor always to the destinations named
> Upon our setting-forth. Our gifts compel,
> Master our ways and lead us in the end
> Where we are most ourselves. . . .

The echoes of Yeats and Stevens and Eliot in all these lines only accentuate the effect of willed conclusion.

For the individual, the dilemma of a "change of world" comes down to the question of "Persons in Time", the title of the second section of *The Diamond Cutters*. Framing this set of narrative and dramatic poems, reminiscent of Frost and the Lowell of *The Mills of the Kavanaghs*, are two reflective pieces. "Concord River" cites Thoreau in an argument for so intense a commitment to the moment that it makes the elements of process into the "absolutes" of a "perfected hour." "The Insomniacs" poses the problem specifically for the artist. Is he merely an actor whose "voice commands the formal stage" to hold off "beyond the wings" "all formless and benighted things / That rhetoric cannot assuage"? The conclusion—and it is merely postulated— points beyond such escapism to postulate an art daring enough

> To live in time, to act in space
> Yet find a ritual to embrace
> Raw towns of man, the pockmarked sun.

However, the later revisions of these lines indicate something of the personal and political commitment which Rich's poetry would, in time, learn to make:

> To live in time, to act in space
> And yet outstare with truthfulness
> New slums of man, the pockmarked sun.

The last section of the volume recapitulates the major concerns: poems (such as "The Snow Queen", "A Walk by the Charles", and "The Tree") in which the individual is the epitome of his mortal and corrupt world; poems (such as "Love in a Museum", "Colophon" and "The Diamond Cutters") which commend the demands of art for forcing the moment to fulfilment in completed form. The poet's continuing attitude toward the submission of experience to the artistic process is revealed in phrases like "distance," "imagination's form so sternly wrought," "incisions in the ice," "tools refined": the hard, cold, clear surface of the engraved and faceted diamond.

Snapshots of a Daughter-in-Law (1963) is the transitional book in Adrienne Rich's development. Eight years had intervened between volumes, and they were years of great change, so that the book begins in one place and ends in another. What happens is the crucial event in the career of any artist: a penetration into experience which makes for a distinguishing style. Her themes—

the burden of history, the separateness of individuals, the need for relationship where there is no other transcendence—begin to find their clarifying
focus and center: what she is as woman and poet in late-twentieth-century
America. The first poems in the book are still quite regular; even so striking
a piece as "The Knight" is something of a tour de force in its proportioned
elaboration of a conceit. But by the time the reader encounters the title poem,
he knows he is dealing with a sensibility tough, restless, capable of unpre-
dictable leaps and turns:

> Your mind now, mouldering like wedding-cake, . . .
> crumbling to pieces under the knife-edge
> of mere fact. In the prime of your life.
>
> . . . .
>
> A thinking woman sleeps with monsters.
> The beak that grips her, she becomes.
>
> . . . .
>
> The argument *ad feminam*, all the old knives
> that have rusted in my back, I drive in yours,
> *ma semblable, ma soeur*!
>
> . . . .
>
> *Dulce ridens, dulce loquens*,
> she shaves her legs until they gleam
> like petrified mammoth-tusk.

This thinking woman paraphrases Baudelaire, parodies Horace to register
the pressures that make the mind moulder. The shock of the imagery is due
not merely to its violence (each of the passages refers to a cutting edge) but to
an accuracy so unsparing that the imagination reacts psychosomatically:
muscles tighten and nerves twinge. The ten sections of "Snapshots" com-
prise an album of woman as "daughter-in-law," bound into the set of roles
which men have established and which female acquiescence has re-enforced.
Women-artists—Emily Dickinson, Mary Shelley, Fanny Burney—stand out
as images of resistance and achievement, and they herald the image of fulfilment in the last lines:

> Well,
> she's long about her coming, who must be
> more merciless to herself than history.
> Her mind full to the wind, I see her plunge
> breasted and glancing through the currents,
> taking the light upon her
> at least as beautiful as any boy
> or helicopter,
> poised, still coming,
> her fine blades making the air wince
> but her cargo

no promise then:
delivered
palpable
ours.

The self-image projected here is archetypical, at once individual and collective: a signal of forces which would become a national movement within the decade.

Adrienne Rich's earlier poems were praised for their subtlety of rhythm and tone, and these unmetered lines lose none of their subtlety for being more strongly stressed and more freely paced. But in becoming more concrete, her poetry was becoming primarily visual rather than aural, and she has been increasingly successful at imprinting images so indelibly that they convey the meaning without comment or conclusion. The words "eye" and "see" recur insistently (some thirty times) throughout the *Snapshots* volume, and there can be no mistaking her purpose: to "outstare with truthfulness" each moment in the flux of time and thereby live as keenly as her powers of perception make possible. To be is to see; I am eye. Poetry functions as the vehicle for seeing and for fixing what one comes to see. It is the camera with lens and focus, and poems are snapshots.

Not that art provides a satisfactory alternative to time. Fixing an image dates it, and in the *Snapshots* volume Rich began her custom of dating each poem. The poet outlives the poem, can be dated only on his tombstone; yet each marker points the end. The first section in a sequence called "Readings of History" states her ambivalence about the snapshot-poem by calling the camera "The Evil Eye":

> Your camera stabs me unawares,
> right in my mortal part.
> A womb of celluloid already
> contains my dotage and my total absence.

At the same time the fact of mortality generates the urgency to see: "to know / simply as I know my name / at any given moment, where I stand" ("Double Monologue"); and, with others, to

> spongelike press my gaze
> patiently upon your eyes,
> hold like a photographic plate
> against you my enormous question.
>   ("Merely to Know")

To use time redeems it as best we can. Through the cultivation of consciousness we can live through time without merely being its victim. Adrienne Rich recognized the risks and responsibilities; "Prospective Immigrants Please Note" warns the reader of the categorical choice: safe security or a dangerous passage.

Either you will
go through this door
or you will not go through.

If you go through
there is always the risk
of remembering your name.

Things look at you doubly
and you must look back
and let them happen.

If you do not go through
it is possible
to live worthily

to maintain your attitudes
to hold your position
to die bravely

but much will blind you,
much will evade you,
at what cost who knows?

The door itself
makes no promises.
It is only a door.

It is indicative that this poem, written in 1962, comes just at that point in
Adrienne Rich's life when Jung says that a person in his thirties, having
accomplished his initial set of goals (career, marriage, family), may be called
by an inner necessity to the painful and exacting process of individuation.

"The Roofwalker", the last poem of *Snapshots*, is a redefinition of psychological and poetic perspective. No longer does it seem "worth while to lay— /
with infinite exertion— / a roof I can't live under," and the previous strate-
gems seem "blueprints, / closings of gaps, measurings, calculations"—all
useless now that

A life I didn't choose
chose me: even
my tools are the wrong ones
for what I have to do.

Already she has begun to try out a language more expressive of the uncer-
tainties of a bold conception of selfhood;

I'm naked, ignorant,
a naked man fleeing
across the roofs

> who could with a shade of difference
> be sitting in the lamplight
> against the cream wallpaper
> reading—not with indifference—
> about a naked man
> fleeing across the roofs.

The marvellous pun on "difference/indifference" effects the transition from the literate observer to the roofwalker, "exposed, larger than life, / and due to break my neck." The phrase "larger than life" suggests not just his heroism but the recognition that, ignorant as he is, he is exposing himself to the dangers and mysteries not just of personal destiny but of existence itself.

The "difference" in perspective calls into question society's assumptions about men and women both separately and in relation to each other. "A Marriage in the 'Sixties" refuses the clichés of conjugal devotion and brings love complicated by intelligence to a separate yet shared existence. "Antinöus: the Diaries" and "Rustication" express, even more viscerally than "Snapshots", a revulsion against the middle-class, suburban life which traps women, either willingly or helplessly, in gestures and postures. In "Antinöus" Rich speaks through the mask of a man, but as the favorite of the Emperor Hadrian, memorialized in busts for his sensual beauty, Antinöus becomes the perverted image of the object of man's lust, and so a mirror of a decadent society.

> If what I spew on the tiles at last,
> helpless, disgraced, alone,
> is in part what I've swallowed from glasses, eyes,
> motions of hands, opening and closing mouths,
> isn't it also dead gobbets of myself,
> abortive, murdered, or never willed?

In reaction against the definitions of "woman" allowed by the rules of the game Rich at first identifies the new possibilities of self-realization with "masculine" qualities within herself and so with images of men in several poems near the end of the book. In "Always the Same" Prometheus "bleeds to life" and his heroic song is described in a phrase from Lawrence. In "Likeness" the good man whom the song tells us is hard to find is "anarchic / as a mountain freshet / and unprotected / by the protectors." The "larger than life" roofwalker is a naked man. Their masculine strength derives not from mere physical courage but from the power of mind and will and judgment. "Ghost of a Chance" pits a man's discriminating intellect against the backward suck of the female sea, undifferentiated and undifferentiating:

> You see a man
> trying to think.
>
> You want to say
> to everything:

Keep off! Give him room!
But you only watch,
terrified
the old consolations
will get him at last
like a fish
half-dead from flopping
and almost crawling
across the shingle,
almost breathing
the raw, agonizing
air
till a wave
pulls it back blind into the triumphant
sea.

The rhythms of the middle lines imitate the strained effort to emerge into air, and the monosyllable of the last word-line, climaxing the long drag of the previous line, suggests the satisfaction which comes from the oblivion of the sea's triumph—a satisfaction which makes resistance all the more urgent. At the end of "Snapshots" the woman, cutting cleanly through the currents, is linked with "mind" and "light": "A woman sworn to lucidity," as Adrienne Rich would later describe herself.

In Jungian psychology the poet is at this point imagining herself in terms of her "animus," the archetypally "masculine" component in the woman's psyche which corresponds to the "anima" or archetypally "female" component in the man's psyche. Each person, man or woman, is a combination of—or, more accurately, an interaction between—male and female characteristics; the anima in the man and the animus in the women express the dynamism of that interaction, which, if creative, will open the passage to an accommodation of opposites in an identity. So for the man the anima is the key to the whole area of feeling and intuition and passion; "she" represents his relationship with matter, with sexuality, with the dark and formless unconscious. Correspondingly, for a woman the animus represents her affinity with light as mind and spirit and her capacity for intellection and ego-consciousness. In the process of individuation, then, activation of and engagement with the animus or anima is generally the first major, and potentially dangerous, phase; it marks the transition into a fuller realization of one's psychological being and stands as the mediating point—one way or the other—which makes hard-won selfhood possible. Whether initial differences between men and women in psychological character and orientation are inherent or acculturated is a matter for specialists to continue to investigate. Meanwhile Jung's terms provide at least a descriptive, if not prescriptive, frame of reference within which to sort out the different psychological dynamism through which men and women, even sophisticated and aware men and women, struggle towards androgynous wholeness.

One manifestation of this dynamic which neither Jungians nor critics have yet examined is the fact that, with a frequency too regular to be ignored, artists have identified themselves, especially in their capacity as artists, with their anima or animus, as the case may be. One would not want to insist on this connection rigidly, but the tendency is strong enough to suggest a pattern. And the reason would seem to be that the artistic process, a function of the process of self-realization, is thereby a function of the anima or animus in the psyche: the man breaking open the categories of consciousness to the ebb and flow of the unconscious, submitting the light to the darkness; the woman drawing the inchoate into shape, submitting emotion to the discriminating light. Poetry as a function of the anima or of the animus helps to illuminate the difference, for example, between Walt Whitman and Emily Dickinson or, to cite two contemporary poets who have been closely associated with each other, the difference between Robert Duncan and Denise Levertov. The fact that the Muses are women and anima-figures is just a sign that up till now art has been a dominantly masculine domain.

The psychological and artistic point which the *Snapshots* volume dramatises is Adrienne Rich's rejection of the terms on which society says we must expend our existence and her departure on an inner journey of exploration and discovery. As a woman-poet, she finds herself, perhaps unconsciously to a large extent, making the initial discoveries in the dimension and through the lead of her animus. So in "Face" she finds her reflection in the painting of a man whose "eye glows mockingly from the rainbow-colored flesh." Yet this mirror-image is himself "a fish, / drawn up dripping hugely / from the sea of paint." The metaphor, with the pun on "drawn," establishes the connection between the artistic process and the intereaction of consciousness and the unconscious. The unconscious is the reservoir whose elements need to emerge into conscious comprehension and definition, and the artist must draw them up into the "glow" and "flash" of the light "out of the blackness / that is your true element."

Such an attempt at reorientation has inevitably made tremendous differences in the kind of poem Adrienne Rich has been writing. She was herself very aware of the fact that a radical shift had occurred in her conception of the technique and construction of poems. In a previously unpublished introduction to a poetry reading given in 1964, between *Snapshots* and *Necessities of Life*, she summed up the transition. It deserves quotation in full as one of the remarkable statements about contemporary poetry; it describes not just the direction she would increasingly explore but also the controlling impulse of most of the poetry now being written.

> In the period in which my first two books were written I had a much more absolutist approach to the universe than I now have. I also felt—as many people still feel—that a poem was an arrangement of ideas and feelings, predetermined, and it said what I had already decided it should say. There were occasional surprises, occasions of happy discovery that an unexpected turn

could be taken, but control, technical mastery and intellectual clarity were the real goals, and for many reasons it was satisfying to be able to create this kind of formal order in poems.

Only gradually, within the last five or six years, did I begin to feel that these poems, even the ones I liked best and in which I felt I'd said most, were queerly limited; that in many cases I had suppressed, omitted, falsified even, certain disturbing elements, to gain that perfection of order. Perhaps this feeling began to show itself in a poem like "Rural Reflections", in which there is an awareness already that experience is always greater and more unclassifiable than we give it credit for being.

Today, I have to say that what I know I know through making poems. Like the novelist who finds that his characters begin to have a life of their own and to demand certain experiences, I find that I can no longer go to write a poem with a neat handful of materials and express those materials according to a prior plan: the poem itself engenders new sensations, new awareness in me as it progresses. Without for one moment turning my back on conscious choice and selection, I have been increasingly willing to let the unconscious offer its materials, to listen to more than the one voice of a single idea. Perhaps a simple way of putting it would be to say that instead of poems *about* experiences I am getting poems that *are* experiences, that contribute to my knowledge and my emotional life even while they reflect and assimilate it. In my earlier poems I told you, as precisely and eloquently as I knew how, about something; in the more recent poems something is happening, something has happened to me and, if I have been a good parent to the poem, something will happen to you who read it.

In other words, Rich has developed, as a poet, from a singleminded identification with the animus as a controlling consciousness which could secure itself in forms and suppress the threats to that security, to a reliance on the animus as the power within herself through which psychic experience with all its unknown turbulences and depths can emerge into articulation as the images and rhythms of the poem. Anne Bradstreet, our first poet, referred to herself, half playfully, as the mother of her poems; Adrienne Rich gives herself the more comprehensive role of parent. At the same time the animus is only the mediating point within the psyche; no matter how active it is, Adrienne Rich writes as a woman. "The Knight" describes the negative and destructive aspects of identification with the animus: an encasing of the flesh and nerves and even the eye in armor as cold as it is glittering. By contrast, perhaps the most dramatic image in *Snapshots* is the figure of the woman at the climax of the title poem. A 1964 poem published in *Necessities of Life* returns to Emily Dickinson and addresses her almost as the type of the woman-poet:

> you, woman, masculine
> in single-mindedness,
> for whom the word was more
> than a symptom—

> a condition of being.
> Till the air buzzing with spoiled language
> sang in your ears
> of Perjury
>
> and in your half-cracked way you chose
> silence for entertainment,
> chose to have it out at last
> on your own premises.

The pun on "premises" makes Dickinson's retreat to the family household a consequence of her resolution to live and write on her own terms in the face of public incomprehension like the critic Higginson's, and the irony is that her determination only made her seem "half-cracked" to Higginson, complacent in his masculine assumptions about what women and poets are.

Necessities of Life (1966), *Leaflets* (1969) and *The Will to Change* (1971) are better books than *Snapshots*; they move steadily and with growing success towards making a poetry which is not just an activity consonant with life but an act essential to it. "The Trees" is a good example of the development:

> The trees inside are moving out into the forest,
> the forest that was empty all these days
> where no bird could sit
> no insect hide
> no sun bury its feet in shadow
> the forest that was empty all these nights
> will be full of trees by morning.
>
> All night the roots work
> to disengage themselves from the cracks
> in the veranda floor.
> The leaves strain towards the glass
> small twigs stiff with exertion
> long-cramped boughs shuffling under the roof
> like newly discharged patients
> half-dazed, moving
> to the clinic doors.
>
> I sit inside, doors open to the veranda
> writing long letters
> in which I scarcely mention the departure
> of the forest from the house.
> The night is fresh, the whole moon shines
> in a sky still open
> the smell of leaves and lichen
> still reaches like a voice into the rooms.
> My head is full of whispers
> which tomorrow will be silent.

Listen. The glass is breaking.
The trees are stumbling forward
into the night. Winds rush to meet them.
The moon is broken like a mirror,
its pieces flash now in the crown
of the tallest oak.

Rich has commented on the importance of Williams' example in her learning not to be "self-protective" like Frost and thereby to "take the emotional risk as well as the stylistic risk." But the emotional and psychological quality of her verse is utterly her own, and the prosody shows none of the posturing of much "experimental" verse and none of the halting choppiness which too deliberate a preoccupation with "breath-unit" imposes on some of Williams' followers. In "The Trees", the rhythms trace out the psychic movement, doubling back on itself as it proceeds through a sequence of images. The images, vivid and preternaturally clear, are not descriptive in the usual sense. That is, they do not paint as actual scene or set up a narrative situation; they compose an internal landscape, eerie but strangely recognizable. Images of "eye" and "camera" persist through *Necessities of Life*, but increasingly in the later volumes dream and dream-imagery occur. And, as in a dream, the details are so present that they convey the poet's involvement with the particulars of experience from which the dream-poem derives.

What, then, does the poem trace out? A movement from within out, so that the empty forest "will be full of trees by morning." The psyche is a house, a structure suggesting now a plantation and now a hospital or sanatorium; but the house is filled with the natural and primitive shapes of trees rooted in the earth beneath the floor-boards and straining with a life of their own. While the conscious ego (the "I" of the poem) conducts its accustomed correspondence, the trees disentangle themselves and break out under the cover of darkness into the open air, "like newly discharged patients / half-dazed, moving / to the clinic doors." Not that the external world appears merely as the mirror of the individual psyche; the night and moon and forest are out there from the beginning, and "the smell of leaves and lichen" reaching "like a voice into the rooms" seems to have initiated the trees' movement and the internal "whispers / which tomorrow will be silent." The forest is empty to the individual until he realizes it, and the realization involves a distinctly personal and human awareness such as the forest cannot attain in and of itself. The poem ends, as it began, in mystery, and the trees are the exemplification of the mystery—the seemingly related mystery—of the internal and external worlds. One becomes aware of the complexities of one's becoming aware as well as of the complexities of the things perceived. Now the moon that had shone whole in the empty sky "is broken like a mirror, / its pieces flash now in the crown / of the tallest oak." The poem has not unriddled the mind or "reality" but rendered the encounter in a dreamscape for the reader to encounter for himself.

At the same time the entire thrust of the poem is a clarification of the un-comprehended or inadequately comprehended by recreating what *exists* beyond paraphrase or abstraction; in the imagery of several poems in *Necessities* light pierces darkness. Even here the moon, shattered by the branches of the trees, still illuminates the night, and the sun is the source of the rare moments of happiness and release in the book: "In the Woods", "The Corpse-Plant", and "Noon". In "Focus" Rich comes as close as she ever has to an explicitly religious dimension in one's perception of things. Caught in the "veridical light," falling on her desk-top through a skylight,

> an empty coffee-cup,
> a whetstone, a handkerchief, take on
>
> their sacramental clarity, fixed by the wand
> of light as the thinker thinks to fix them in the mind.
>
> O secret in the core of the whetstone, in the five
> pencils splayed out like fingers of a hand!
>
> The mind's passion is all for singling out.
> Obscurity has another tale to tell.

The intensity of Rich's poems since the late 'fifties stems precisely from the mind's passion and from the fact that in her mind and passion test and con-firm each other. The sacrament is the flash of the mind as it fixes, camera-like, the everyday things caught in this unusual light.

For Rich, however, a deepening subjectivity does not mean withdrawal, as it did for Dickinson, but, on the contrary, a more searching engagement with people and with social forces. "Necessities of Life", the first poem in that volume, notes her re-entry into the world after a time of guarded isolation. A world still marred by mutability ("Autumn Sequence", "Not Like That", "Side by Side", "Moth Hour"), still scarred by the violences of human relationship ("The Parting", "Any Husband to Any Wife", "Face to Face") and by the abuse of the environment ("Open Air Museum", "Breakfast at a Bowling Alley in Utica, N. Y."), increasingly menaced by politics and war ("Spring Thunder"): in short, stained, as "The Knot" tells us, by the blood-spot at the heart of things. *Necessities of Life* is filled with elegies ("After Dark", "Mourning Picture", "Not Like That"), and the title was meant, among other things, "to suggest the awareness of death under everything that we are trying to escape from or that is coloring our responses to things, the knowledge that after all time isn't ours." Existence is persistence, but these poems are affirmations, in the extremity of our situation, of the will to persist. "Like This Together", one of the best poems in the book, concludes:

> Dead winter doesn't die,
> it wears away, a piece of carrion
> picked clean at last,

> rained away or burnt dry.
> Our desiring does this,
> make no mistake, I'm speaking
> of fact: through mere indifference
> we could prevent it.
> Only our fierce attention
> gets hyacinths out of those
> hard cerebral lumps,
> unwraps the wet buds down
> the whole length of a stem.

Again against "indifference," "our fierce attention": only through that can the world last into the next season; we survive or perish together.

As an expression of this conviction, Rich's politics have taken clearer shape. The rejection of bourgeois mores voiced in *Snapshots* has led to a more radical view of the necessity, for life, of re-ordering social values and structures. But even the political poems in *Leaflets* and *The Will to Change* (for example, "For a Russian Poet", "Implosions", the "Ghazals", "The Burning of Paper Instead of Children") are not, in the end, propaganda leaflets. They remain poems because Rich has too powerful a sense of "original sin" to make the utopian mistake of externalizing evil by projecting it on others. The poems compel us precisely because they record how excruciating it is to live in this time and place; the politics is not abstracted and depersonalized but tested on the nerve-ends. The psychological and political revolutions are interdependent, because personal and public tragedy are linked, as "The Burning of Paper Instead of Children" and "The Photograph of the Unmade Bed", as well as the title poem, declare. Individually and collectively we need "the will to change."

As the ultimate challenge to her initial assumptions, Adrienne Rich raises the dreaded question for a poet: the very validity and efficacy of language. Is art the act of clarification and communication that we say it is? As early as "Like This Together" in 1963 she was worrying that "our words misunderstand us." Now in "The Burning of Paper":

> What happens between us
> has happened for centuries
> we know it from literature
>
> still it happens
>
> . . . .
>
> there are books that describe all this
> and they are useless

If language has no power to affect the given, then is the resort to language an evasion of action, as the revolutionaries charge? The epigraph to the poem quotes Fr. Daniel Berrigan: "I was in danger of verbalizing my moral impulses out of existence." Only unsparing honesty permits an artist to contemplate such a dangerous question, but Rich confronts it again and again through the last two books. "Shooting Script" speaks of "the subversion of choice by language." "The Burning of Paper" imagines "a time of silence / or few words," when touch might be more immediate, and quotes Antonin Artaud: "*burn the texts.*"

Yet this damning self-examination is conducted in the words of poems which are urgent, even desperate attempts at clarification and communication. Not that the questioning has been vain: there must be no blinking away the dangers of language as escape or the tenuousness of any attempt at articulation. But in the acknowledgment of all these limits, language remains a human *act* which makes other actions and choices possible: "Only where there is language is there world," "We are our words" ("The Demon Lover"); "Our words are jammed in an electric jungle; / sometimes, though, they rise and wheel croaking above the treetops" ("Ghazals"); "I am thinking how we can use what we have / to invent what we need" ("Leaflets"); "I wanted to choose words that even you / would have to be changed by" ("Implosions"). So, even in "The Burning of Paper", "this is the oppressor's language / yet I need it to talk to you." The conclusion is not to stop speaking and writing but to make words penetrate to the will as well as the mind and heart: "the fracture of order / the repair of speech / to overcome this suffering" ("The Burning of Paper").

In other words, persistence requires relocation. Much has intervened between *A Change of World* and *The Will to Change*. In "Storm Warnings" Rich had strategically enclosed herself within protective walls; now with the apocalypse perhaps about to break over our heads, she insists that we not merely submit but actively commit ourselves to change, as persons and as a people.

The poem as snapshot is no longer enough: stasis is death. "Pierrot Le Fou" begins:

> Suppose you stood facing
> a wall
>   of photographs
> from your unlived life
>
> as you stand looking at these
> stills from an unseen film?

It quickly beomes clear that the poem is concerned with, and is working as, film rather than photograph; "Pierrot le Fou" is itself a film by Jean-Luc Godard. Not that there is more narrative in these new poems; in fact, there is generally less, just as in most serious films there has been a reduction, almost an elimination, of plot for the imaging of a psychic dream-world. So in Rich's poetry there is a tendency toward longer poems or more sustained sequences of pieces; and they operate, even more exclusively than before, as a juxtaposition of images, spaced out on the page so that the sensibility can react and make connections. The poems of *The Will to Change* are a refinement of the imagistic technique worked out in the "Ghazals" of *Leaflets*, about which Rich has observed that "the continuity and unity flow from the associations and images playing back and forth. . . ." The title of the volume is from Charles Olson, and without being in any way an imitation of Olson these poems are Rich's exploration of "composition by field" so that the poem occupies the page on which it is placed as the ideogrammic expression of how her mind occupies the world in which and on which it operates. One of the purest instances of the technique is the first section of "Shooting Script":

> We were bound on the wheel of an endless conversation.
> Inside this shell, a tide waiting for someone to enter.
> A monologue waiting for you to interrupt it.
> A man wading into the surf. The dialogue of the rock with the breaker.
> The wave changed instantly by the rock; the rock changed by the wave
>   returning over and over.
> The dialogue that lasts all night or a whole lifetime.
> A conversation of sounds melting constantly into rhythms.
> A shell waiting for you to listen.
> A tide that ebbs and flows against a deserted continent.
> A cycle whose rhythm begins to change the meanings of words.
> A wheel of blinding waves of light, the spokes pulsing out from where we
>   hang together in the turning of an endless conversation.
> The meaning that searches for its word like a hermit crab.
> A monologue that waits for one listener.
> An ear filled with one sound only.
> A shell penetrated by meaning.

The effect is not a static list of images but a flow of interacting and mutually clarifying images: at once linear and encircling, defining temporally an area of dreamscape or poemscape.

"The Photograph of the Unmade Bed" explicitly distinguishes the poem from the snapshot: the poem says, or should say, "This could be"; the photograph says "This was," and is therefore a "photograph of failure." "Images for Godard", the succeeding poem in the book, is important for sketching out her developing intentions. Section 1 renders the search for meaning through language in the familiar cinematic metaphor of driving through a contemporary city. Section 2 compiles a montage of camera-shots. Section 3 links love with the ability to change and move toward the other person; love is, or ought to be, a kind of movie, but it is constantly being "stopped," so that connections are only achieved at moments. So Section 4 admits the limitations of what the artist, Godard in particular, has been able the achieve thus far; he ends his film *Alphaville* with the words "I love you" but cannot proceed from there because by his own declaration he cannot make a movie about love, only about the striving toward love. But the final section projects the possibility of the movie-poem that Godard had failed at:

the mind of the poet is the only poem
the poet is at the movies

dreaming the film-maker's dream but differently
free in the dark as if asleep

free in the dusty beam of the projector
the mind of the poet is changing

the moment of change is the only poem

But is the change only dream? Are dreams realities? "Shooting Script" is the scenario for the movie-poem. It consists of two parts of seven sections each. Part I intimates a "fresh beginning" but is dominated by a sense of past failures which trap the mind and immobilize "simple choice." Section 8, the opening of Part II, sees what has gone before as "a poetry of false problems, the shotgun wedding of the mind, the subversion of choice by language" and from this point on there is greater and greater insistence on the future as the dimension of choice. The past is associated with photographs (section 10) and even with film (section 9), or at least with a mere "Newsreel" of where one has been. In "Images for Godard", the movement of love had been "stopped, to shoot the same scene / over & over." "A Valediction Forbidding Mourning" referred to "the experience of repetition as death." Now the last section of "Shooting Script" rejects "whatever it was, the image that stopped you, the one on which you came to grief, projecting it over & over on empty walls," gives up "the temptations of the projector," and ends with the charge to move on: "To pull yourself up by your own roots; to eat the last meal in your old neighborhood." The shooting of the movie-poem has been so functional that it has had the effect of making the vital connection between art and life. As early as "The Diamond Cutters" Rich had warned the artist to concentrate on the work ahead rather than past achievements. But this is something more: here the poem is necessary as the moment of change, and it validates itself by propelling the poet, and us, past the poem into that open space where some act besides words may map out the future.

In approaching the point of individual decision the words act as outward thrusts of communication. This is a poetry of dialogue and of the furious effort to break through to dialogue: "I want your secrets—I *will* have them out" ("The Demon Lover"); "We're fighting for a slash of recognition / a piercing to the pierced heart. / Tell me what you are going through—" ("Leaflets");

I'd rather
taste blood, yours or mine, flowing
from a sudden slash, than cut all day
with blunt scissors on dotted lines
like the teacher told.
                    ("On Edges")

The poems probe at the lesions between "I" and "you," and the "you" addressed is a particular person, or the reader, or an aspect of the poet—or all three at once. The aggressiveness of the imagery is a measure of the poet's frustrated animus; but the violence measures as well the effort at contact and release, and the point of verbal contact, if achieved, is the moment of identification and change which is the aim and function and end of language.

The imagery associated with self shifts in the last two books: a sign from the deeps. The animus is the cross-over point, leading in the direction of a fuller comprehension and integration of the self; so crucial is the stimulus it provides that, as we have seen, the individual at first tends to see herself in terms of the animus. After a time, however, she begins to see that the animus represents only an element, or range of capacities, to be assimilated into her identity as a woman. The poems of *Leaflets* and *The Will to Change* render just that transition in the conception of the self. "Orion", the first piece in *Leaflets*, is an animus poem. In reaction against the entanglements of domestic routine ("Indoors I bruise and blunder") Rich projects her sense of identity on the masculine presence of the constellation Orion, as she had since girlhood: first as her "genius" ("My cast-iron Viking, my helmed / lion-heart king in prison"); then as her "fierce half-brother," weighed down by his phallic sword; now as her mirror-image and apotheosis. Moreover, she is specifically identifying herself as poet with Orion; while writing the poem, she had in mind an essay by the German poet Gottfried Benn on the plight of the modern artist.

"The Demon Lover", written two years later, presents a more complex analysis. Here "he" is the "other": both the animus and the man who in refusing to recognize her animus compounds her own sense of division; the whole question is whether an accommodation with "him" is possible internally or externally:

> If I give in it won't
> be like the girl the bull rode,
> all Rubens flesh and happy moans.
> But to be wrestled like a boy
> with tongue, hips, knees, nerves, brain . . .
> with language?

Her animus is the sticking-point: for her to insist upon and for the man to negate. Her contention is not to be a man but a whole woman and as a woman to be taken fully into account. But the circumstances show "him" as adversary; not only does the "man within" appear as "demon lover," but the masculine lover becomes a demon because he clings to the simple opposition between mind and body which makes for the simple distinction between man and woman. In denying her mind and spirit, he must deny his passions and debase his body to lust. The quandary within and without remains unresolved; "he," animus and lover, refuses her his secrets and consigns her to the female element: "Sea-sick, I drop into the sea."

Although to the demon lover she has seized on the terms which make connection most difficult, she has defined the only terms on which relation is possible. Neither man nor woman can be free until each has acknowledged the other. Adrienne Rich's new poems show an absorption of animus-powers into a growing sense of identity as woman and identification with women, and consciousness is the key. "Women" describes three images of self as "my three sisters," and comments: "For the first time, in this light, I can see who they are." "Planetarium" evokes the atronomer Caroline Herschel, her fame eclipsed by her brother William, as a heroine in the history of women's coming to consciousness, the light of her "virile" eye meeting the stellar light; of herself, Rich concludes:

> I am an instrument in the shape
> of a woman trying to translate pulsations
> into images for the relief of the body
>
> and the reconstruction of the mind.

In a hypnotic poem called "I Dream I'm the Death of Orpheus", she adapts imagery from Jean Cocteau's movie about Orpheus to depict herself as a woman whose animus is the archetypal poet:

> I am a woman in the prime of life, with certain powers
> and those severely limited
> by authorities whose faces I rarely see.
>   I am a woman in the prime of life
> driving her dead poet in a black Rolls-Royce
> through a landscape of twilight and thorns.
> A woman with a certain mission
> which if obeyed to the letter will leave her intact.
> A woman with the nerves of a panther
> a woman with contacts among Hell's Angels
> a woman feeling the fullness of her powers
> at the precise moment when she must not use them
> a woman sworn to lucidity
> who sees through the mayhem, the smoky fires
> of these underground streets
> her dead poet learning to walk backward against the wind
> on the wrong side of the mirror

The strong, incantatory rhythms—a significant new development in some of the recent poems—work their magic. What the dream-poem traces out is the resurrection of Orpheus through the woman's determination to resist all depersonalizing forces—psychological, political, sexual—arrayed against the exercise of her powers. The animus-poet comes alive again within the psyche, and his return is a sign of, and a measure of, her ability to "see through" and move forward on her "mission": not the course laid out by the "authorities" as the safe way to remain intact but the one intimated by "the fulness of her powers" as the only way to deliver herself whole. At this point in her life and in history such a purpose puts her against prevailing conditions and makes for lonely dislocation. Orpheus revives within her "on the wrong side of the mirror," "learning to walk backward against the wind."

But the contrary direction is not negative; bent on affirming life's possibilities, it makes the friction bearable and transfiguring. "We're living through a time / that needs to be lived through us," she writes in "The Will to Change", and that is the reverse of Matthew Arnold's perception of the modern paralysis as the feeling that everything is to be endured and nothing to be done.

The process is not, of course, completed, nor can it be: selfhood is the motive and end of the journey. But the fact that hers is not merely a private struggle but a summons to us all—at least to all of us who enter the door and cross the threshold into the psyche—informs the poetry with a mythic dimension in a singularly demythologized time. A myth not because her experience has been appended, by literary allusion, to gods and goddesses, but because her experience is rendered so deeply and truly that it reaches common impulses and springs, so that, without gods and goddesses, we can participate in the process of discovery and determination. It is existentialism raised to a mythic power, and the myth has personal and political implications. The result is a restoration to poetry of an ancient and primitive power, lost in the crack-up which the last centuries have documented. The power of the bard in his tribe has long since declined with the power of prophecy. Adrienne Rich's mission is to live out her dream of a society of individual men and women. By challenging us to a more honest realization, she has recovered something of the function of the poet among his people: not by transmitting their legends and tales but by offering herself—without pretensions, with honest hesitations—as the mirror of their consciousness and the medium of their transformation. In effect, her poetry has come to represent a secular and unillusioned version of the poet as prophet and the prophet as scapegoat living out individually the possibilities of the collective destiny. By long tradition in the patriarchal culture this tribal function has been the prerogative of male poets, but there is something peculiarly clarifying and liberating about confronting ourselves through the mind and imagination of a woman. Equally so for men as for women, because the work of a woman-artist is much more likely than the work of most men to present the counter-image essential to his wholeness and to activate and call into play that whole area of emotion and intuition within himself which is the special province of the "woman within."

All this accounts for the centrality of Adrienne Rich's work in the contemporary scene, for the electric immediacy of the reader's or hearer's response, and for the finally healing effect of poems wracked with the pain of awareness and the pain of articulation.

A Note on James Dickey
by Michael Mesic

JAMES DICKEY has been attempting to write, during the last decade, what none of his contemporaries seems capable of or interested in attempting—a poetry of the common man: about his obsessions, failures, uninspiring everyday life and attempts to escape it, and above all, his successes, which would not perhaps have been considered as such in another age or country. I think it is important to recognize in Dickey's work much of the American experience that other poets have been unfamiliar with, uninterested in, or ashamed of, and have therefore not preserved or perfected. We have Stevens' enlightened, philosophical inner world, Eliot's shadowy and often grotesquely beautiful religiosity, Pound's eclectic verbosity, Frost's chilly common sense, and others, but we lack in our poetry the fever of conquest, the sense of confrontation with nature and other men, and the overriding concern with and pride in success which are certainly parts of that experience. Dickey is proud to be an American and often proud of himself, but I do not think that he would be quite as proud to be a writer, had he not been a celebrated one.

America has never paid much attention or even lip service to its poetic products. The people who conquered a continent and its natural riches seldom had the time to notice how or whether their accomplishments were recorded. It is unfortunate that so many American readers believe that poetry is written for an elite, but in practice a very small proportion of them read or wish to read poems. Though our poets' isolation is much more the result than the cause of this lack of interest, even fewer people than ever today read serious poetry, because much of it has become, in isolation, unintelligible and boring. That Dickey has tried to bridge this "gap", not because of principles, but because he is much more a product and a part of middle America than his colleagues, is worth our consideration; but I cannot accept as valid a view of life based on a sad coupling of the assumptions of the entrepreneur, competitive athlete, dominant male, and glory seeker—the hero in contrived heroic situations. Dickey seems never to question the mythology on which most of the American male's life is based; and his unquestioning acceptance is at first annoying, and then suspect. Dickey was, the dust jacket of his *Poems 1957-1967* informs us, "a star college athlete (football, hurdles); a night fighter pilot with over one hundred missions in World War II and Korea; a hunter and woodsman; and a successful advertising executive in New York and Atlanta"—all this before becoming a professional poet, as he calls himself. It occurs to me that Wallace Stevens was probably just as successful an executive in the insurance business, but we are not forced by the dust jacket of his *Collected Poems* to recognize the fact. One would like to think that a man of Dickey's experience could not have lived his life without doubting at least once that his assumptions about that life were rigorously correct. Yet Dickey never audibly questions the values of the cult of masculinity: physical strength and health, unswerving determination, and above all success, be it sexual, financial, or otherwise. He does worry often and hard about his ability to *pass the test*, even when no test, at the moment, presents itself.

James Dickey was thirty-seven when his first book of poems appeared in 1960. What remains of *Into the Stone* in *Poems 1957–67* is little more than half of the original book. Though I prefer to abide by Dickey's editorial decisions and not discuss the earlier poems which he excluded from the collected volume, I would respect these decisions more if he had consistently pared down the later collections. Perhaps because he was more unsure of his abilities and intentions, many of Dickey's early poems are confidential, intense descriptions: of war-time experiences, memories of his family, and sorties into the woods, which provide the bulk of his subject matter; though the subject of the poem is sometimes no more than the occasion for a flood of reaction and impressions, as in "The Enclosure":

> I thought I could see
> Through the dark and the heart pulsing-wire,
>
> Their dungarees float to the floor,
> And their light-worthy hair shake down
> In curls and remarkable shapes
> That the heads of men cannot grow,
> And women stand deep in a ring
> Of light, and whisper in panic unto us
> To deliver them out
> Of the circle of impotence. . .

When he relies heavily on a situation or story, the poems are stark and disturbing, as in "The Performance", about a captured pilot during the Second World War, who had

> Come, judged, before his small captors,
>
> Doing all his lean tricks to amaze them—
> The back somersault, the kip-up—
> And at last, the stand on his hands,
> Perfect, with his feet together,
> His head down, evenly breathing,
> As the sun poured up from the sea
>
> And the headsman broke down
> In a blaze of tears, in that light

Of the thin, long human frame
Upside down in its own strange joy,
And, if some other one had not told him,
Would have cut off the feet

Instead of the head. . .

Though there is only one phrase of any imagination in this, the poem captures the scene and the absurd dignity of the captive precisely and cold-bloodedly. The total effect, as so often in this first book, is more than the sum of the parts, combining fairly incisive details with an adequate, though unfortunately not masterful, sense of the line.

Wallace Stevens wrote somewhere that a poet has only one or two ideas, and in every poem attempts their perfect expression. One of Dickey's recurrent themes is first articulated in "The String". One italicized line is repeated at the end of all but one of the seven line stanzas.

Except when he enters my son,
The same age as he at his death,
I cannot bring my brother to myself.
I do not have his memory in my life,
Yet he is in my mind and on my hands.
I weave the trivial string upon a light
Dead before I was born.

What seems most important in this poem is not what I expected—a sense of brotherhood which was not and never could be realized except in imagination —but rivalry, almost a challenge to the poet's position as his parents' son.

I believe in my father and mother
Finding no hope in these lines.
Out of grief, I was myself
Conceived, and brought to life
To replace the incredible child
Who built on this string in a fever
Dead before I was born.

A confession, of course, not of guilt, but of purpose, hovers among the string-laden fingers which perform the same tricks to prove, perhaps, their equal competence, if only to themselves. Again, I wonder about the personality behind the lines. One has very little choice when confronted with the confessional, or quasi-confessional poems of our era, but to react to the personality as well as the poetry. Dickey seems to feel that his existence is threatened on all sides, and therefore must aggressively compensate for what he may lack by "making it". The goal of his continual striving becomes clearer in the last and title poem of the first book:

Each time, the moon has burned backward.
Each time, my heart has gone from me

And shaken the sun from the moonlight.
Each time, a woman has called,
And my breath come to life in her singing.
Once more I come home from my ghost.
I give up my father and mother;
My own love has raised up my limbs:

I take my deep heart from the air.
The road like a woman is singing.
It sings with what makes my heart beat
In the air, and the moon turn around.
The dead have their chance in my body.
The stars are drawn into their myths.
I bear nothing but moonlight upon me.
I am known; I know my love.

Into the Stone he went, all alone with his memories of people not as large as himself, or even as large as life, so that when he came out, we were allowed to see of them only their reflection of or relationship to the poet. But in *Drowning with Others*, Dickey seemed a little to realize their concerns, not merely as his own, and they sometimes came to life.

The "Owl King", for example, is not only one of the longest, but one of the best poems in the book. Divided into three sections, the father, the owl king, and the blind child tell a story of mystical sight and communion within the forest's darkness.

Through the trees, with the moon underfoot,
More soft than I can, I call.
I hear the king of the owls sing
Where he moves with my son in the gloom.
My tongue floats off in the darkness.
I feel the deep dead turn
My blind child round towards my calling,
Through the trees, with the moon underfoot. . .

The owl king seems to have learned more about the boy than the father, because, as he says, "I swore to myself I would see / When all but my seeing had failed."

Each night, now, high on the oak,
With his father calling like music,
He sits with me here on the bough,
His eyes inch by inch going forward
Through stone dark, burning and picking
The creatures out one by one,
Each waiting alive in its own
Peculiar light to be found. . .

The most interesting section of the poem, "The Blind Child's Story", gains much because in it Dickey's almost invariable three beat line is allowed some freedom, is allowed to be something other than itself. I, for one, sigh with relief whenever that occurs, and not because the two beat lines are better, but because they break the nearly unbearable monotony of the rough unimaginative anapestic trimeter.

> I can hear it rising on wings.
> I hear that fluttering
> Cease, and become
> Pure soundless dancing
> Like leaves not leaves;
> Now down out of air
> It lumbers to meet me,
> Stepping oddly on earth,
> Awkwardly, royally.

The climax of the poem is dulled a bit by the addition of the boy's return to his father, which seems to me quite unnecessary after:

> Our double throne shall grow
> Forever, until I see
> The self of every substance
> As it crouches, hidden and free.
> The owl's face runs with tears
> As I take him in my arms
> In the glow of original light
> Of Heaven. I go down
> In my weight lightly down
> The tree, and now
> Through the soul of the wood
> I walk in consuming glory
> Past the snake, the fox, and the mouse:
> I see as the owl king sees,
> By going in deeper than darkness.
> The wood comes back in a light
> It did not know it withheld,
> And I can tell
> By its breathing glow
> Each tree on which I laid
> My hands when I was blind.

This technique of speaking in an assumed voice is one that Dickey takes up more fully later, and in many poems he imagines the thoughts of his characters, but explains them from a more objective point of view.

I could, I suppose, go on with a chronological discussion of the other volumes contained in *Poems 1957–67*, but that course seems to me unprofitable, because so many of the later poems—in *Drowning with Others*, *Helmets*, and even the volume which won the National Book Award, *Buckdancer's Choice*—

merely repeat, if not always the subject matter of *Into the Stone*, then the tone, often plodding, and the attitudes, much too self-concerned when there seems little in that quarter to be concerned with, of *Drowning with Others*. There are, of course, some fairly good poems scattered among those others which could have been allowed the anonymity of the notebook without much regret on my part. "On the Coosawattee", from *Helmets*, clearly prefigures Dickey's novel, *Deliverance*, and is worth considering at least for its differences from and similarities to the novel's prose. Prose, I think, has proved to be for Dickey a more profitable medium, artistically, and certainly, financially. "The Fire-bombing" and the convincingly sympathetic portrait of a peeping tom, called "The Fiend", from *Buckdancer's Choice*, are also curious, because unprecedented, examples of Dickey's abilities.

What seems to me most striking, however, reading over all of Dickey's poems, is the great change, not entirely in style, but obviously in format of the work in such a short period of time. When I mentioned earlier that Dickey attempted to write a poetry of the common man, it was because the attempt seems particularly to have engaged his subconscious. Though in his first book he did not entirely succeed in the attempt, in each successive volume, culminating in the latest—the title of which, *The Eye-Beaters, Blood, Victory, Madness, Buckhead and Mercy*, seems designed to attract the divergent desires of as many readers as possible—he has moved farther and farther towards the common man and away from poetry, as if admitting that the two are just not compatible, but trying, nonetheless, to stretch the definition of the latter because the former is not, unfortunately, as malleable. The result of this movement away from the focus of poetry has been to center Dickey's ellipse about the common man and his preferences, and the poet has given up even the pretense of indentation and line break and told again the story of one of his poems, dressed up and dressed out, in prose, with an almost too appropriate title, *Deliverance*, and deliverance it surely is, from any responsibility— no matter how little there was to begin with—for the placement of his words in a stricter order than their sense.

Examples from each of Dickey's collections will, I think, show clearly this movement and its unpleasant result. This selection is taken from "The Underground Stream" (lines 9–21), from *Into the Stone*.

> The motion by which my face
> Could descend through structureless grass,
> Dreaming of love, and pass
> Through solid earth, to rest
> On the unseen water's breast,
> Timelessly smiling, and free
> Of the world, of light, and of me.
> I made and imagined that smile
> To float there, mile on mile
> Of streaming, unknowable wonder,

> Overhearing a silence like thunder
> Possess every stone of the well
> Forever, where my face fell. . .

The meter of this passage is basically the same as that of the majority of the poems in the book—apparently, anapestic trimeter, though seldom do more than two of the three feet adhere strictly to the expected pattern. Though it is certainly permissable to omit one unstressed constituent of a foot here or there, Dickey's plodding diction does not indicate that any attempt was made to alter the rhythm of the lines, to make them more musically interesting, for instance, but that he was content when each of them had three stresses and enough non-stresses sprinkled in between to render the sense and avoid— what therefore becomes one of the most metrically interesting lapses in this selection, between lines 10 and 11 and lines 13 and 14—two consecutive stresses. The only explanation I can see for not adhering more strictly to what must be one of the meters closest to American speech, the anapestic, is that it was even easier for Dickey to express the sense of his thoughts without the confinement of any strict pattern. It is obvious, as well, that the sort of freedom Dickey takes to excess, when used sparingly, in the midst of pat-terned language, is a much more effective, because unexpected, device. One of the reasons I chose this selection is the simple couplet rhyme scheme em-ployed almost through the poem. Dickey has seldom used rhyme, and only in his first book, and never any system more complicated than this. It is no wonder, by thunder, that he hasn't, since the rhymes—this is true of so many feeble attempts at rhyme by modern poets—add nothing in their obviousness but a comical tone to poems that we are asked to believe are serious in intent.

The following passage—the first eleven lines of "The Heaven of Animals"— is not entirely representative of *Drowning with Others*, since many of the poems in the second book employ the same metrical, if that is the word, principles as in the first, but it does indicate Dickey's ever-decreasing use of even an appropriate meter. The contention of the poem as a whole is that in the heaven of animals some beasts hunt while the sole occupation of others is to be hun-ted, gladly and compliantly!

> Here they are. The soft eyes open.
> If they have lived in a wood
> It is a wood.
> If they have lived on plains
> It is grass rolling
> Under their feet forever.
>
> Having no souls, they come,
> Anyway, beyond their knowing.
> Their instincts wholly bloom
> And they rise.
> The soft eyes open.

It is sad how little sense of movement the short sentences allow. We are given little music with the sense of the words, less music even than we might expect from well-written prose.

  Helmets, likewise, presents many poems in the same approximate ana-pests, but this selection from "On the Coosawattee" (part three, lines 7–18), seems at first to present us with a new pattern, at least visually.

> And there is another stone, that boiled with white,
> Where Braselton and I clung and fought
> With our own canoe
> That flung us in the rapids we had ridden
> So that it might turn and take on
> A ton of mountain water
>
> And swing and bear down through the flying cloud
> Of foam upon our violent rock
> And pin us there.
> With our backs to the wall of that boulder,
> We yelled and kept it off us as we could,
> Broke both paddles, . . .

  There is, more's the pity, no new pattern here. There is, in fact, no pattern at all, except that the third and sixth lines of each stanza are shorter than the others. And what difference does it make where the lines end? This whole poem could be printed as prose and the story would be no less interesting or clear because of the different arrangement, and I doubt that anyone not familiar with the poem as it stands could indicate the line breaks of the original. This discussion of the line breaks in a poem may be old hat, but Dickey obviously saw some point to it, because his next book, *Buckdancer's Choice*, introduces a new format altogether, one, not surprisingly, which looks and reads like prose, so much so, in fact, that I am tempted to call it that. Here are the first seven lines, then, of "The Fiend".

> He has only to pass by a tree   moodily walking   head down
> A worried accountant   not with it   and he is swarming
> He is gliding up the underside light of leaves   upfloating
> In a seersucker suit   passing window after window of her building.
> He finds her at last, chewing gum   talking on the telephone.
> The wind sways him softly   comfortably sighing   she must bathe
> Or sleep.   She gets up, and he follows her along the branch. . .

Who calls this verse? or poetry? Not I.

  But the final indignity is the poems in *The Eye-Beaters* . . . etc., in which all the lines are centered after being divided without regard to sense. I can only guess that Dickey became weary of the previous trick, as who wouldn't, after using it quite regularly in *Buckdancer's Choice*, and in the poems, otherwise unpublished in book form, which appeared in *Poems 1957–*

67, and hit on the following type of form as anyone might hit the tab stop on a typewriter. The first poem in *The Eye-Beaters* . . ., "Diabetes", will suffice as an example (lines 10–20).

> The doctor was young
>
> And nice. He said, I must tell you,
> My friend, that it is needles moderation
> And exercise. You don't want to look forward
> To gangrene and kidney
>
> Failure   boils blindness infection skin trouble falling
> Teeth coma and death.
>   O.K.
>   In sleep my mouth went dry
>   With my answer and in it burned the sands
> Of time with new fury. . .

To note that Dickey has been reduced to such marvellous and sensitive descriptions as, "The doctor was young and nice," and such inventive phrases as, "the sands of time," is to contemplate the total collapse of what poetic ability he demonstrated earlier.

It is possible that James Dickey will concentrate, in future, on writing more outdoor adventure stories like *Deliverance*, and will write less and less of this sort of "poetry". When he started writing poems in the late 'fifties there was no one quite like him, and therefore his sort of poetry, better then than it is now, was interesting, as novel. Some of the earlier poems may last as examples of his style—some are good enough even as poems, compared to so much of what has been passed off in the past decade. But, as is true of almost any unusual, personal style, imitations abound as soon as it succeeds in attracting much attention, and those styles which are personal to begin with— if they are not also based on personal perception, and a thorough knowledge of poetic practice, which assures that few would-be mimics will be competent enough for the forgery—are taken over quickly by a crowd. Dickey's style has been imitated excessively already, so that if he does not again write the massive number of poems he once did, our loss will be compensated by the many poems of others written after his fashion. As fashions go (and this one will like so many others) this is not the most attractive that America produced in the 1960's.

James Dickey's poetry appeared like a tidal wave to flood the poetic land-scape of the 'sixties, washing inland as far as it could, but then settled into one of the lowest depressions in that landscape, producing one of our newest imaginative swamps, where the imitative bull-frogs have taken up residence and taken up the cry, exchanging their stories in indistinguishable croaks.

Staring from her Hood of Bone:
Adjusting to Sylvia Plath
by J. D. McClatchy

ALTHOUGH SYLVIA PLATH'S career ended in 1963, her notoriety has been a product of the decade since her death. No other poet's reputation in that time was so abruptly startled into fame. Her prophets and disciples, imitators and initiates, swarmed over the quarterlies. Among *Life*'s burning babies and beauty queens, between the fashions and gossip in those slick women's magazines she had scathingly satirized, there were hushed evocations of her genius and her torture, accompanied by ironically smiling snapshots. Her few poems were instantly established in anthologies; reverent essays were collected; the faithful accumulated. Robert Lowell approved and encouraged the mystique, and A. Alvarez has now awesomely mythologized her last days, huddled in a frozen flat, her head rested in the oven for a final warmth.

Such literary cults, their white goddesses, their high priests and totems are not uncommon—they can be as genteel as Virginia Woolf's or as hermetic as Hart Crane's. But Sylvia Plath's suicide and the posthumous publication of *Ariel* bred a cult of extraordinary passion and directness. One critic's phrase will serve as its theme: Plath was "sacrificed to her plot." The poet's own intensity became that of her admirers, as they insisted on reading her poems as personal rather than aesthetic risks. Critical evaluation gave way to existential celebration, authenticity replaced integrity, and each line of *Ariel* became a last breath. Stephen Spender could be chosen the spokesman to summarize the predominant view of the poems: "Their power, their decisiveness, the positiveness and starkness of their outline, are decided not by an identifiable poetic personality expressing herself, but by the poet, a woman finding herself in a situation, out of which she produces these disconcerting, terrifying poems. The guarantees of the authenticity of the situation are insanity (or near-insanity) and death. . . . She is writing out of a pure need of expression, certified, as I say, by death." Those words are, of course, as unfair as they are misleading, however strong the temptation to indulge them that the poet's end invites. Perhaps such a response is symptomatic of the same conditions that have made Sylvia Plath a cultural, as well as a literary, phenomonon. Alternately heroine or victim or martyr, she has been symbolized so hauntingly in the cultural consciousness that it is difficult not to read her life—with its gestures of defiance, courage, compulsion and despair—rather than her work in which those gestures are reflected or re-imagined. The reasons can be sifted. Certainly in the last fifteen years the taste has been created by which she is so appreciated— with critics madly urging the Extremist visions of madness, and the new energies released by the increasing acceptance by poets and readers of the confessional mode. The way we live now, as well, must be counted: the context of a decade stalked by public violence and private nightmare, the lip-service paid to women as a class, and our desperate national psychoses that are run like films out of sequence. There is this and more, and none of it enough.

Some of the more obvious damage caused by this aghast, retrospective piety has been done to Plath's first, and now overpraised, collection, *The Colossus*. There is about this volume the self-consciousness of beginnings. It is poetry of chosen words, of careful schemes and accumulated effects; its voice is unsteady, made-up. It leans heavily on its models and sources; there are broad hints of help from Roethke and Stevens, and even Eliot is echoed without parody: "In their jars the snail-nosed babies moon and glow." Ted Hughes seems also to have been a strong influence, but one need only compare her "Sow" to his "View of a Pig" (or to any of his other early animals) to sense the more natural ease with which he urges and controls his language and the power it draws from strangeness. The awkward refinement which separates her from Hughes is evident as well in the literary cast of many poems which borrow Oedipus or Gulliver, Byron or Medea, Gabriel or Lucina for their authority, and in the stiff, stale diction which rattles around in them: cuirass, wraith, descant, bole, ambrosial, bruit, casque, ichor, pellicle. Too often the poems show their seams, and carry with them the musty smell of the underlined Thesaurus which Hughes remembers always on her knee at this time. It is not merely the expected *Gemäldegedichte*—on Brueghel's *The Triumph of Death* or Rousseau's *Charmeuse de Serpents*—that lead one to call most of the poems in the collection *compositions*. The reductive eye dominates the book and its slow figures, blocked landscapes and primary colors. There are times, though, when another vision intrudes, when the "moony eye" is "needled dark" and transformed to the "Red cinder around which I myself,/ Horses, planets and spires revolve" ("The Eye-Mote"). It is then that she sees most clearly, and at the same time allows us access to her deepest concerns. For the book's value seems finally to lie not in the promise or accomplishment of its verse, but in its introduction of themes that would recur more forcefully in later work.

The second vision, which scans "a place, a time gone out of mind," is part of a larger series of double views of experience. "The Two Sisters of Persephone" and "The Spinster" detail the "heart's frosty discipline" against the patterns of the rich, real world, while "Night Shift" opposes the organic and the mechanical. But most often, Plath is careful to modulate one view into the other; the natural world is internalized, its contours and meanings shifting into new significance. This technique can be handled archly, as it is in the metamorphic "Faun", or it can merely play over memories and moods, as in "Departure", where green thoughts in green shades are dulled by "The leaden slag of the world." But in other, better poems, the technique becomes theme and opens out towards the ambiguous power of vision. Her "Snake-charmer" is the poet whose solipsism is unconscious and still crafted:

> As the gods began one world, and man another,
> So the snakecharmer begins a snaky sphere . . .
>
> He pipes a world of snakes,
> Of sways and coilings, from the snake-rooted bottom
> Of his mind. And now nothing but snakes
>
> Is visible. The snake-scales have become
> Leaf, become eyelid; snake-bodies, bough, breast
> Of tree and human. And he within this snakedom
>
> Rules the writhings which make manifest
> His snakehood and his might with pliant tunes
> From his thin pipe.

There is nothing alien for this poet since his vision has no consequences beyond his control of it. The menace of The Other presses elsewhere; the dead clutch, and mummies or mushrooms or the thin people can escape "the contracted country of the head." And these finally are seen to assume the natural world; landscapes collapse into sleepless dreams, and another world is imagined real:

> They sing
> Of a world more full and clear
>
> Than can be. Sisters, your song
> Bears a burden too weighty
> For the whorled ear's listening
>
> Here, in a well-steered country,
> Under a balanced ruler.
> Deranging by harmony
>
> Beyond the mundane order,
> Your voices lay seige.
>
> ("Lorelei")

And again, in "The Burnt-Out Spa", from a sag-backed bridge

> Leaning over, I encounter one
> Blue and improbable person
>
> Framed in a basketwork of cat-tails.
> O she is gracious and austere,

Seated beneath the toneless water!
It is not I, it is not I.

No animal spoils on her green doorstep.
And we shall never enter there
Where the durable ones keep house.
The steam that hustles us

Neither nourishes nor heals.

Her dead, watery self—The Other transformed into an identity—is located at last in a Byzantium of still perfection, beyond the process of vision. Poetry is not an escape but a confirmation, an approach to completion, "A brief respite from fear/ Of total neutrality" ("Black Rook in Rainy Weather"). The "rare, random descent" of that angel (which may possibly derive from Rilke's, but probably recalls Stevens's Angel in his luminous cloud) is strongly felt in "Sculptor", whose bald, bulky, chiseled bodies—no longer the sensuous evanescence of snakes—dwarf us:

Our bodies flicker

Toward extinction in those eyes
Which, without him, were beggared
Of place, time, and their bodies.
Emulous spirits make discord,

Try entry, enter nightmares
Until his chisel bequeaths
Them life livelier than ours,
A solider repose than death's.

The book's final sequence of poems, whose verse is more assured, stands as an anxious meditation on the dilemma of her conviction: "I am becoming another. . . . I must swallow it all. . . . Tell me my name." The world of the senses, breath and beauty, is reduced by impatient scorn:

This shed's fusty as a mummy's stomach:
Old tools, handles and rusty tusks.
I am at home here among the dead heads.

Let me sit in a flowerpot,
The spiders won't notice.
My heart is a stopped geranium.

If only the wind would leave my lungs alone.
Dogbody noses the petals. They bloom upside down.
They rattle like hydrangea bushes. . . .

This is a dull school.
I am a root, a stone, an owl pellet,
Without dreams of any sort.

Mother, you are the one mouth
I would be a tongue to. Mother of otherness
Eat me. Wastebasket gaper, shadow of doorways.

                                                     ("Who")

The consolations of artifice are inadequate: "I inhabit/ The wax image of myself, a doll's body" ("Witch Burning"). And the poet's last vision of her self dismisses most of the poems that precede it:

The mother of pestles diminished me.
I became a still pebble.
The stones of the belly were peaceable,

The head-stone quiet, jostled by nothing.
Only the mouth-hole piped out,
Importunate cricket

In a quarry of silences.
The people of the city heard it.
They hunted the stones, taciturn and separate,

The mouth-hole crying their locations. . . .

This is the after-hell: I see the light.
A wind unstoppers the chamber
Of the ear, old worrier. . . .

Love is the bone and sinew of my curse.
The vase, reconstructed, houses
The elusive rose.

Ten fingers shape a bowl for shadows.
My mendings itch. There is nothing to do.
I shall be good as new.

                                                     ("The Stones")

There is a sense of vicious, if still incomplete, achievement about these last poems that appears again in the tone of *Ariel*, just as the longing for "perfection" becomes more acute in the later volume. The other, potential self envisioned in *The Colossus* is more profound and traditional than the adjective "schizophrenic" describes, though that is what it may eventually become. Here, at least, it carries the thematic burden, and its images that yet fresh images beget turn on the bitter furies of complexity.

Crossing The Water and *Winter Trees* gather most of Plath's uncollected "transitional" poems, and while a few of them predict *Ariel*, most are more or less uncertain efforts to secure a new voice. At one extreme, Yeats lurks behind her "Magi", and at the other, there is a wholly unsuccessful attempt at swagger:

> It's violent. We're here on a visit,
> With a goddam baby screaming off somewhere.
> There's always a bloody baby in the air.
> I'd call it a sunset, but
> Whoever heard a sunset yowl like that?
> ("Stopped Dead")

But generally, the lines are fuller and less studied than those in *The Colossus*, and her cadences are less tense, more closely adjusted to the speaking voice. She herself admitted the change to an interviewer in 1962, while discussing some of these poems: "These ones that I have just read, the ones that are very recent, I've got to say them, I speak them to myself, and I think that this in my own writing development is quite a new thing with me, and whatever lucidity they may have comes from the fact that I say them to myself, I say them aloud." Perhaps this is due to the delayed influence of Robert Lowell—to whom she also admits a debt for his confessional "breakthrough." Lowell's own shift from his early densely wrought lines to a charged colloquialism may have been Plath's example here. Certainly one senses a close study of Lowell has filtered back into several of these poems: his Lady of Walsingham, who "Expressionless, expresses God," prefigures her Lady of the Shipwrecked:

> Our Lady of the Shipwrecked is striding toward the horizon,
> Her marble skirts blown back in two pink wings.
> A marble sailor kneels at her foot distractedly, and at his foot
> A peasant woman in black
> Is praying to the monument of the sailor praying.
> Our Lady of the Shipwrecked is three times life size,
> Her lips sweet with divinity.
> She does not hear what the sailor or the peasant is saying—
> She is in love with the beautiful formlessness of the sea.
> ("Finisterre")

Her own voice, the shrill, sharp sound that soars in *Ariel*, can be heard in such poems as "Whitsun", "Zoo Keeper's Wife", or in "Surgeon at 2 A.M." where the body is described as "a Roman thing":

> It is a statue the orderlies are wheeling off.
> I have perfected it.
> I am left with an arm or a leg,
> A set of teeth, or stones
> To rattle in a bottle and take home,
> And tissues in slices—a pathological salami.
> Tonight the parts are entombed in an icebox.

> Tomorrow they will swim
> In vinegar like saints' relics.
> Tomorrow the patient will have a clean, pink plastic limb.

The poems in *Winter Trees*—poems like "Purdah", "Childless Woman", "By Candlelight" and "Thalidomide"—are closer still to the hard exactness of tone in *Ariel*; they read like the negatives from which the later poems were printed. The images used to enclose personal relationships are more carefully worked, and poems like "The Babysitters", "Leaving Early" and "Candles" demonstrate her increasing ability to accommodate facts into poetry, to discover her experiences rather than merely to display her feelings about them. Like the surgeon, "now a tattooist," she is no longer content

> Tattooing over and over the same blue grievances,
> The snakes, the babies, the tits
> On mermaids and two-legged dreamgirls.
> The surgeon is quiet, he does not speak.
> He has seen too much death, his hands are full of it.
>
> ("The Courage of Shutting-Up")

The same longings that loom in *The Colossus* are again present, though without the consistency with which they appear in her two "finished" collections. In *Winter Trees*, her long experiment, "Three Women: A Poem for Three Voices", written for radio broadcast, deals with the new, alien life her characters swell with and discharge:

> Dark tunnel, through which hurtle the visitations,
> The visitations, the manifestations, the startled faces.
> I am the centre of an atrocity.
> What pains, what sorrows must I be mothering?

Other poems in the volume as well recircle her concern: the "Mystic" who has been "Used utterly, in the sun's conflagrations" and must still live with a heart that has not stopped, or the woman in "Purdah" whose veils are only "visibilities" that conceal a Clytemnestra, or the monstrous potential in "Thalidomide". *Crossing The Water* offers more explicit, if less striking, examples with "Face Lift", "In Plaster", "Crossing The Water", and "Small Hours":

> I imagine myself with a great public,
> Mother of a white Nike and several bald-eyed Apollos.
> Instead, the dead injure me with attentions, and nothing can happen.
> The moon lays a hand on my forehead,
> Blank-faced and mum as a nurse.

That moon—the dead, silent stone, chilled with false light and shadowed scars—comes to dominate the later poems, as the sea had her earlier work.

Perhaps the easiest way to approach *Ariel* is to trace some of the recurrences of a single concern—her father, The Father—through to its treatment in the book's most famous poem, "Daddy". The plain prose version is in her autobiographical novel, *The Bell Jar*, whose narrator, Esther Greenwood, "had a great yearning, lately, to pay my father back for all the years of neglect, and start tending his grave." It is only a simple sense of loss, of the horrible distance between the living and the dead, that is then revealed:

> At the foot of the stone I arranged the rainy armful of azaleas I had picked at a bush at the gateway of the graveyard. Then my legs folded under me, and I sat down in the sopping grass. I couldn't understand why I was crying so hard.
> Then I remembered that I had never cried for my father's death.
> My mother hadn't cried either. She had just smiled and said what a merciful thing it was for him he had died, because if he had lived he would have been crippled and an invalid for life, and he couldn't have stood that, he would rather have died than had that happen.
> I laid my face to the smooth face of the marble and howled my loss into the cold salt rain.

Given the point-of-view, the emotion here is left distanced and unaccountable, and is told with the restraint which Plath uses throughout the novel to draw out slowly its cumulative effects of disorientation and waste.

"The Colossus" resumes the pose, but further develops the metaphor: the girl clambers in helpless self-absorption over the mammoth ruins of her father: "Thirty years now I have labored/ To dredge the silt from your throat./ I am none the wiser." But the mystery of loss and betrayal, the secretive sexual fantasies, the distortions of knowledge and memory, are left unexplored, dependent solely on the poem's figurative force:

> Nights, I squat in the cornucopia
> Of your left ear, out of the wind,
>
> Counting the red stars and those of plum-colour.
> The sun rises under the pillar of your tongue.
> My hours are married to shadow.
> No longer do I listen for the scrape of a keel
> On the blank stones of the landing.

"The Beekeeper's Daughter", also addressed to "Father, bridegroom," moves towards the final statement, the whole relationship, in its line, "My heart under your foot, sister of a stone," but not until *Ariel* is Plath able to open up the experience and manage its depths and intricacies. The language and movement of "Daddy" are most strikingly different: instead of slow, careful gestures, the poem races its thickly layered and rhymed language into some strange, private charm to evoke and exorcise a demon-lover. The short lines—which Plath reads with tremulous contempt in her recording of the poem—have a formulaic quality appropriate to the murderous ritual which the poem enacts: "Daddy, I have had to kill you./ You died before I had time." But what is most extraordinary about this poem is the amount and complexity of experience which it can convincingly include. In Freudian terms, if "The Colossus" dealt with remorse, "Daddy" deals in guilt. The poem veers between love and hate, Eros and Thanatos. Imagining herself as a Jew and her father as a Nazi, or her husband as a vampire and herself as a maiden, the poet languishes in the need for punishment to counter the loss of love. The ambivalence of identification and fear is used to reveal more than "The Colossus" even hints at:

> Every woman adores a Fascist,
> The boot in the face, the brute
> Brute heart of a brute like you. . . .
>
> At twenty I tried to die
> And get back, back, back to you.
> I thought even the bones would do.
>
> But they pulled me out of the sack,
> And they stuck me together with glue.
> And then I knew what to do.
> I made a model of you,
> A man in black with a Meinkampf look
>
> And a love of the rack and the screw.
> And I said I do, I do.

The macabre *Liebestod*, the "model" marriage confirming tortures finally felt in a real marriage, the degradation of her father (which doubles as the origin of guilt in the murder of the primal father) as a form of self-loathing, the loss of father and husband like two sad suicides that leave the poet furiously fingering her scars—"Daddy" astonishes a reader by the subtle fury of its hurts, and it shows to best advantage what Plath had learned in her troubled interval. The strong personality through which the experience of "Daddy" emerges is, above all, the accomplishment of *Ariel*.

That personality is a stylistic one, first of all. Ted Hughes has described the style of *Ariel* as one of "crackling verbal energy." But the exuberance is of a special sort. One hesitates to term it "American," except that Plath herself does, in her 1962 interview: "I think that as far as language goes I'm an American, I'm afraid, my accent is American, my way of talk is an American way of talk." The dynamics, the sharp, quick tonal contrasts, the hard exactness of word and image, the jaunty slang, the cinematic cutting—these are what she is pointing to. Even in poems—like "Tulips"—with quieter long lines, she sustains a new tension of menace and energy:

> My body is a pebble to them, they tend it as water
> Tends to the pebbles it must run over, smoothing them gently.
> They bring me numbness in their bright needles, they bring me sleep.

> Now I have lost myself I am sick of baggage—
> My patent leather overnight case like a black pillbox,
> My husband and child smiling out of the family photo;
> Their smiles catch onto my skin, little smiling hooks.

But in the book's best poems, the lines are pared down, at times to a stark, private code, but always with purity and precision. Paradoxically, this taut, new control often creates effects of singular primitivism. She may have sought these; Hughes recalls her reading African folktales "with great excitement." They may also owe something to her marked identification of the imagination with the unconscious. Poems like "Getting There", "Medusa", and "Little Fugue" splay psychic scraps across dream landscapes with the mastery of Ingmar Bergman. The Gothic, or merely grotesque, aspects in the late poems which critics have commented on seem to be the weaker signs of this tendency, and the several mystical plunges she takes—for example, in "The Night Dances", "The Moon and the Yew Tree", and "Poppies in July"— are also attempts to approach, through the unconscious, higher states of being and art. Plath confesses the influence of Blake on these later poems, and like Blake she often seems to compel her vision through the poem.

That vision, again, is one of "perfection"—a term as central to Plath as "circumference" is to Emily Dickinson. Though "Ariel" and "Years" offer terrified, exultant arguments against "great Stasis," and "The Munich Mannequins" presents an ambiguous image of those bloodless idols to the self, the relentless hunt for a still completion, a condition beyond "the aguey tendon" of mortality, beyond the Shelleyan veils of life, continues:

> If you only knew how the veils were killing my days.
> To you they are only transparencies, clear air.
>
> But my god, the clouds are like cotton.
> Armies of them. They are carbon monoxide. . . .
>
> Only let down the veil, the veil, the veil.
> If it were death
>
> I would admire the deep gravity of it, its timeless eyes.
> I would know you were serious.
>   ("A Birthday Present")

That timelessness is the peace of the "Paralytic":

> I smile, a buddha, all
> Wants, desire
> Falling from me like rings
> Hugging their lights.

It is, as well, the peace of the dead and of the moon:

> The woman is perfected.
> Her dead
>
> Body wears the smile of accomplishment,
> The illusion of a Greek necessity
>
> Flows in the scrolls of her toga,
> Her bare
>
> Feet seem to be saying:
> We have come so far, it is over. . . .
>
> The moon has nothing to be sad about,
> Staring from her hood of bone.
>
> She is used to this sort of thing.
> Her blacks crackle and drag.
>
> ("Edge")

Strong assertions of this yearning structure other poems too—"Sheep in Fog", "Tulips", "Medusa", "The Moon and the Yew Tree"— and in the Bee poems, the impenetrable detachment of the poet from her experience creates another dualistic series that probes the middle state between "these people at the bridge" and "The mausoleum, the wax house."

The familiar dilemma and longing in *Ariel*, however, take on an urgency and poignance that the earlier volumes lack. Part of it lies in a despair with the very language the poet now finally controls:

> Years later I
> Encounter them on the road—
>
> Words dry and riderless,
> The indefatigable hoof-taps.
> While
> From the bottom of the pool, fixed stars
> Govern a life.
>
> ("Words")

Perhaps this is her frequent distrust of voice, but the poem, which closes *Ariel* except for the last blank page, implies that the vision forever escapes the language that alone can restore it. The silence that "perfection" demands, like the trusting, completed silence of her infants, becomes then a source of confusion for the poet, as though to contemplate an action were already to have accomplished its consequences. What she substitutes for the contradictory silence is "purity," the process towards perfection: "Pure? What does it mean?" Again, her technique is shaped into her theme, and purity, the spoken silence of great suffering and of the mystics, becomes a central concern among some of the book's strongest poems:

I am too pure for you or anyone.
Your body
Hurts me as the world hurts God. I am a lantern—

My head a moon
Of Japanese paper, my gold beaten skin
Infinitely delicate and infinitely expensive. . . .

I think I am going up,
I think I may rise—
The beads of hot metal fly, and I, love, I

Am a pure acetylene
Virgin
Attended by roses,

By kisses, by cherubim,
By whatever these pink things mean.
Not you, nor him

Not him, nor him
(My selves dissolving, old whore petticoats)—
To Paradise.

("Fever 103°")

"Lady Lazarus", which seeks out its purification in an achieved death, seems though to be an earlier poem and an uncertain one, admittedly "theatrical." Its sense of performance lets it lapse into mere rhetoric at times; her pain and its necessity are checked by their publicity. But it serves to measure the absolute purity that her last poems approach.

Sylvia Plath's suicide, which some critics read as her last, inevitable poem, has led most critics to assume a greater degree of fulfilment and completion in her work than it can justly claim. Her consistency, instead, lies in her experimentations with voice, and in her reworkings of the dilemma of the divided mind. That she was able, in *Ariel*, to include so much more of her experience and of her most persistent theme, in a voice equal to their demands and significance, does not mean that she might not have continued to seek a style that would have allowed her to write from beyond the limits of her longing. Her last poems are just arriving.

Another Side of this Life:
Women as Poets
by Peggy Rizza

A POET'S SEX likely deserves no more attention than any other autobiographical fact. But critics of every sort, since time immemorial, have arduously pointed out the woman who managed to tear herself away from vacuuming the rug or breast-feeding to do something else, something unexpected. And this amazed attention extends to women poets, who, although they have walked off with their share of Pulitzer Prizes and National Book Awards, are not infrequently considered peculiar, a class of their own.[1] It shall be no easier to find themes or characteristics common to women poets than it would be for any especially random selection of poets. As unique individuals, the women poets mentioned herein have little in common outside of gender. Yet as women, all share the experience of having a certain role fulfilment expected of them, and of being regarded in the light of certain sexual stereotypes.

In the following pages I shall discuss four poets who have written distinguished work in the 1960's: Elizabeth Bishop, who lives in Brazil and in the United States, and whose *Complete Poems* won the National Book Award in 1970; Anne Sexton, a Boston poet who won the Pulitzer Prize in 1967 for *Live or Die*, her third volume; Maxine Kumin, also a Boston poet and friend of Anne Sexton, author of three books of verse, two novels, and many children's books; and Mona Van Duyn, winner of numerous significant awards (most recently, a National Book Award), who lives in St. Louis. References to Sylvia Plath, whose remarkable work sometimes provides the most appropriate examples for my discussions, will occur here and there. There are other outstanding poets who are omitted due only to lack of space and scope—Denise Levertov, Diane Wakoski, Adrienne Rich, Jean Valentine, Marianne Moore, Jane Shore, Sandra Hochman, Louise Glück. The treatment will not be complete, but, I hope, representative. Ideally, I would like to discard the question whether these poets differ from male poets. I would like to prove beyond doubt that distinction—laudatory or derisive—automatically granted women writers on account of their sex is, more frequently than not, fatuous. Without being fashionably psychoanalytic about each poet's particular sex-role adjustment, I must say that the women poets of the 'sixties are affected more by the taste and manners of their decade (autobiography, confessionalism, and formal elegance), and by their own isolated senses of art, than by their sexual self-concepts. But quite possibly, these poets are influenced, however unconsciously (here we allow for speculation), by sexual stereotypes, sex role models, or sexist attitudes, and this should be kept in mind.

In *Thinking About Women*, Mary Ellmann has set forth what she interprets as the most common sexual stereotypes for women, some of which can be applied instructively to the particular concerns of the four poets at hand. The first and most ironical stereotype (Formlessness) is the one which claims that whereas men are ingenious, synthesising, and reasoning, women, like nature, are indiscriminate and formless. This concept may find proof in disorderly kitchen cabinets or pocketbooks, but never in the work of any woman poet mentioned on these pages. Each of them has demonstrated fierce technical discipline in writing, capably and with grace, in restricted forms (quatrains, alexandrains, sonnets, villanelles, the improbable sestina); and, although many male poets do not currently write formally disciplined verse, for some reason all of these women have used—and some continue to use—rigorous verse forms long after achieving first fame.

A second stereotype, Feminine Hysteria, derives from that common notion that all of woman's experience is seen through the hazed filter of her own self-concept or her own emotion, and that the emotion is without objective correlative, self-generated, hysterical (from the Greek *hystera*, or womb). It is impossible to determine the ratio of self-generated (and thus excessive, unnecessary) emotion in the poetry of women to that in the poetry of men. It is probable that the ex-soldier war poet describes a more externally caused grief than does the suicidal housewife poet (or does he?). But since poets who venture beyond supportive structural categories (such as war) are involved in the most self-reliant, egocentric, even narcissistic of the arts, one for which they themselves are the only essential material, a certain amount of self-enchantment is inevitable. Furthermore, the 1960's was a decade of autobiography and confession in poetry. With Robert Lowell's *Life Studies* as the precedent and Sylvia Plath's *Ariel* as one probable culmination, poetry had become a medium for intense, often agonising self-discovery, self-appraisal, and revelation. In the context of the age one may no more indict women for egocentricity or its selection of moods than men.

Our final sexual stereotype, that of Female Confinement, conceives of woman as so absorbed in domestic life, in the details of food and feeding, cleaning and childcare, that she is aware of little outside of the four walls of her own household. As Mrs Ellmann illustrates it,

> Even falling off a cliff, the mother thinks, 'Mother of Three Falls Off Cliff.' And drowning, she cannot review her life as she should, her concern being entirely confined to the now forever unshaken towel on the beach. (pp. 89–90)

Women, inevitably, have reacted to these stereotypes in various ways, by accommodating and internalising them, or by rebelling against them. Writing formally disciplined verse, for example, might be interpreted as rebellion against the accusation of Formlessness (or as a self-induced sort of Confinement). As poets, women have shown themselves capable of originality, iconoclasm, and utter candor (though Plath in doing so earned for herself and her sex this dubious praise from Robert Lowell: "This character is feminine rather than female, now fanciful, girlish, charming, now sinking to the strident rasp of a vampire" [p. ii, Introduction to *Ariel*.]). And enough poems by women have been violent, relentless, exacting descriptions of horrible events, Nazi war crimes, pain and suicide, so that so connotatively prissy a title as "poetess" seems hardly to apply to the writers. Great emotional honesty in women's writing has occasionally been resented as hysteria. Arch-baiter of witch-hunters, Anne Sexton has wickedly flaunted the internal generative mysteries of womanhood, and in a concentration of self-study, has written such poems as "In Celebration of My Uterus" and "Menstruation at Forty". She risks excess in these poems, an excess of personal femininity that her readers may be unable or unwilling to assimilate. There is some question whether Anne Sexton has crossed the obscure line separating honesty from excessively personal, and therein uninformative, disclosure.

Elizabeth Bishop seems never to approach the questionable, whether in matters of good taste or topic or intention. She corresponds to none of the feminine stereotypes: she is "confined" in neither her subject matter nor in her ways of seeing; hysterical emotion is hardly a consideration, since her poems seldom reveal her own emotions; her verse forms are at least as rigorous and consistent as those of Robert Lowell or Richard Wilbur. There is little autobiography in her poems that indicates that the writer is a woman. Yet, there is a delicacy of description, a certain mildness or innocence that might first be considered "girlish," though a deeper reading reveals a maturity and worldliness that has somehow failed to corrupt the writer's immaculate freshness. The pages of *The Complete Poems* offer constant alternations of type and form, on one page a song, and on the next, blank verse. And so it is with subject matter, a selection of garden flowers in a vase, none of them offensive or horrifying, all of them presented with considerate formality.

Great balance and integrity distinguish Miss Bishop's poetry. Neither subjective nor sterile, it possesses the qualities that we look for in writing: sensitivity, intelligence, artistry and compassion. We read poetry with the expectation that the poet will do a certain amount of fishing for us, so that, casting in unseen places, she will eventually serve us some undreamed of catch. We enjoy being surprised, but we also want to understand the poetry, we want to be touched exactly by the mention of something we might ourselves have experienced. Miss Bishop satisfies this wish by never writing about experiences limited to herself. She lets one feel that, in the special circumstance, one might have perceived the same thing.

Discipline is the key to Miss Bishop's achievement. And for her, discipline means not only writing in a specific form: it means avoiding the flamboyant statements of "apocalyptic" poets for whom reality warps to fit the metaphor or the imagination. Her discipline includes an almost objectivist restriction to the data perceived by the senses, described without recourse to abstraction. Always looking outward, she treats the visual world compassionately, but not sentimentally. The style is conversational, never flat or argumentative; it sometimes has the language but never the verbosity of prose, recalling the long, declarative, more colloquial lines of her friend, Marianne Moore:

> I have a friend who would give a price for those
>   long fingers all of one length—
> Those hideous bird's claws, for that exotic asp
>   and the mongoose—
>   (Moore, *Complete Poems*, p. 58)

Miss Bishop's descriptions demand careful deliberation, as though they were beautifully formed, internal dialogues. In an early but representative poem, the poet is studying a map, and discussing (in alternately rhymed stanzas) what is perceived:

> Land lies in water; it is shadowed green.
> Shadows, or are they shallows, at its edges
> showing the line of long sea-weeded ledges
> where weeds hang to the simple blue from green.
> Or does the land lean down to lift the sea from under,
> drawing it unperturbed around itself?
> Along the fine tan sandy shelf
> is the land tugging at the sea from under?

The poetry of our century, taking its cue from the Romantic Age, usually insists upon the duality of the subjective (i.e., the ego) and the objective (i.e., everything outside the self). But most moderns see all things as existing at the mercy of their own thought, as mere objects of their minds, objects whose reality is simply a reflection of the subjective ego. The mystical or apocalyptic imagination can conceive of a union of the two or of a reality which does not include the self. Without qualifying as "apocalyptic," Miss Bishop treats objects, natural things, people, as though she loves them for themselves, and not for how she can use them to reflect herself or her metaphors. She possesses what might be called an "objective imagination." Her animal poems are a clear demonstration of this respect for "other" things; they are absent of pathetic fallacy, and not quite anthropomorphic enough to be fables.[2] Yet the animals earn our sympathy. The Giant Toad of an early prose poem requests, "I am big, too big by far. Pity me." And in language just slightly slant of colloquial, he tells how some "naughty children" once picked him up and placed a lit cigarette in his mouth. ". . . when my slack mouth was burning, and all my tripes were hot and dry, they let us go. But I was sick for days."

In her meticulously brilliant poem "The Fish", Miss Bishop describes in minute detail "a tremendous fish" that she has just caught and is examining, as it hangs over the side of the boat, "a grunting weight,/battered and venerable/and homely." She is at first objective:

> I thought of the coarse white flesh
> packed in like feathers,
> the big bones and the little bones,
> the dramatic reds and blacks
> of his shiny entrails,
> and the pink swim bladder
> like a big peony.

But eventually she empathises with the fish in a near-negative capability, when she notices five old hooks and fish lines hung from his lower lip, decorations from five great escapes, and sees them as "a five haired beard of wisdom/ trailing from his aching jaw." Finally, she lets the fish go.

A single poem, "Going to the Bakery", assumes the vision of the depressed. Even here, however, emotion is conveyed not through personal lament, but through image and tone: "The bakery lights are dim . . . the round cakes look about to faint . . . The gooey tarts are red and sore . . . The loaves of bread/lie like yellow fever victims/laid out in a crowded ward."

Poets are explorers of the language: they become familiar with its terrain, and the brave ones attempt to alter it by inventing new uses for it. The poets discussed here are all highly skilled technicians, and creative in their application of technique. They often employ techniques of popular songs in poetry to obtain their desired effects. For example, in Miss Bishop's poem about walking by the ocean on a cold autumn evening ("At the Fishhouses"), the repetition of the line "cold dark deep and absolutely clear" evokes an almost physical sensation. For Maxine Kumin, the explorations of conventional as well as original formal techniques becomes an aspect of discipline. Her command of tricks and forms of the language, like Miss Bishop's, is vast and varied. To her son, she writes a poem whose two alternately repeated refrains sound like something he might sing with his guitar:

> Dreaming you travel light
> guitar pick and guitar
> bedroll sausage-tight
> they take you as you are.
>
> They take you as you are
> there's nothing left behind
> guitar pick and guitar
> on the highways of your mind.
>
> (*Nightmare Factory*)

She even uses the familiar form of the nursery rhyme, individualized by a simulated German accent. In her poem "Fraülein Reads Instructive Rhymes", she recalls a terrifying book probably read to her during her childhood in Germantown, Pennsylvania:

> Now look at Conrad, the little thumb-sucker.
> *Ach*, but his poor mama cries when she warns him
> The tailor will come for his thumbs if he sucks them.
> Quick he can cut them off, easy as paper.
>
> (*Halfway*)

Mona Van Duyn, in the final poem of *To See, To Take*, quotes lines from Great Literature in a way which is almost parody or paraphrase, an ironical device of the wilfully self-conscious literature: "A murderous rage is the force that through green fuses/drives the daisies of love . . . they dangle tatters of their worn out winter coats/and neither marry nor burn . . . he waits alone in bare/ruins of the choir where last she sang . . . Nemerov sparrows/make free with kings . . . I think of Jeffers'/obsessed will to arrive at the inhuman/view, of Dickey, who began to act out his own animal when he caught the eye of a panther."

Anne Sexton uses repetition as an emphatic device, an insistant repetition of the poem's most vivid line. In "Ballad of the Lonely Masturbator", each stanza returns to "At night, alone, I marry the bed." The rhymed lines contain short, emphatic sentences, leading relentlessly to the final refrain:

> I horrify
> Those who stand by. I am fed.
> At night, alone, I marry the bed.
>
> (*Love Poems*)

At times repetition becomes neither evocative device nor refrain, but the whole form of her poem. In "In Celebration of My Uterus", each line of one stanza begins with "one is," each line of the next with "let me"—

> Many women are singing together of this:
> one is in a shoe factory cursing the machine,
> one is at the aquarium tending a seal,
> one is dull at the wheel of her Ford,
> one is at the toll gate collecting,
> one is tying the cord of a calf in Arizona,
> one is shifting pots on the stove in Egypt, . . .
>
> let me carry a ten-foot scarf
> let me drum for the nineteen-year-olds,
> let me carry bowls for the offering . . .

The use of repetition here fails to provide emphasis, excitement, or a comforting lull; it simply allows the poet to write an extended list, and not an especially remarkable one. The fault, I maintain, lies not with the poet's talent, which is sizeable, but with the poet's immediate willingness to accept and to to propagate sexual stereotypes, both in her choice of subject matter and in what even a superficially formal technique cannot conceal as a disorderly and "formless" presentation. And the poet's profuse emotionalism (lack of artistic detachment) accomodates the stereotype of Hysteria.

Even without the threat of catcalls of hysteria, autobiographical poetry whose concerns are so intensely personal as to be only narrow and inward is ultimately unfathomable or tedious, alienating to the reader. Writing about one's uterus has only slightly more potential than writing about one's pancreas, and that only in the presently controversial stereotypes of sexuality. Granted, if there is anything that modern poetic theory has taught us, it is that there exists nothing that cannot be mentioned in a poem. The problem is less one of inappropriateness than of insignificance: in these poems, the self, its body, its depressions, become an obsession, and to us, there's little new or enlightening about it.

Suicide is an example of one of those topics which are palatable for just so long, and in just such discreet amounts. For Maxine Kumin, the attempted suicide of a friend, though eliciting her sympathy, seems outrageous, incomprehensible, an ungratefulness to life:

> There was a bed made for you
> there was a durable kitchen
> where almonds and apricots
> knocked in the cupboards
> there were waxed newel posts
> footsteps that listened and loved you
> ("Atlantic", August 1971)

For Sylvia Plath, suicide, like self-appraisal, was a subject which she treated with objectivity, control and originality:

> Dying
> Is an art, like everything else.
> I do it exceptionally well.

But for Anne Sexton, suicide, or madness, or the neurotic's sufferings, have been a fixation since her first book, *To Bedlam and Part-Way Back*. In her third book, *Live or Die*, she writes "Sylvia's Death":

> Thief!—
> How did you crawl into,
>
> crawl down alone
> into the death I wanted so badly and for so long?

The comparison must not be interpreted as invidious. Both poets write with energy and skill, and neither claims to be particularly devoted to coolness or logical development. But Anne Sexton follows and perhaps encourages the feminine stereotype of Hysteria by dwelling on emotions which seem to have no objective cause. Certainly, to write honestly one should call forth and use all of one's emotions. But not every emotion needs to be documented, and one must struggle to dispense with those which are groundless, fabricated or over-exploited. Out of touch with objective reality, poetry begins to depend completely on its words, which, without inner life, exceed their cause. In "The Break" (*Love Poems*), Anne Sexton's words seem excessive:

> My one dozen roses are dead.
>
> They have ceased to menstruate. They hang
> there like little dried up blood clots.

We feel like voyeurs, as though we have read something we hadn't quite intended to read, something which is revealing or even embarrassing but in no way instructive. The impact is not that of seeing a beautiful fish pulled out of deep water, but of finding the same fish dead on the beach.

In the realm of autobiography, though, the separation between confession and honest description is tenuous. Autobiography is not in itself destructive. One of the finest volumes in recent American poetry, Robert Lowell's *Life Studies*, marked a breakthrough for autobiographical writing, and may well have been the most revolutionary influence on Sylvia Plath (who veers radically toward the confessional between her first and second books). If anything, post-*Life Studies* poets were avoiding the fuzzy questions of Truth and Destiny that the Symbolists had made so chic, and were writing about immediate concerns. Autobiography still can seem refreshingly relevant, as long as it does not forsake such traditional values as artistic detachment, balance, audience, empathy and relationship to larger contexts.

Many autobiographical poems deal with the experience of mental or physical illness. Being in a hospital can be an alternately miserable and inspirational experience. To the unscientific of mind, it can be frightening: it threatens to remove one's individuality along with one's clothes and valuables. To the sensitive mind, the experience can be not only a threat to the ego, but a source of new sensations, emotions, and perceptions. In the hospital for what seems to be surgery, Sylvia Plath is hyper-sensitive:

> I didn't want any flowers, I only wanted
> To lie with my hands turned up and be utterly empty.
> . . .
> The tulips are too red in the first place, they hurt me.
> Even through their gift paper I could hear them breathe
> Lightly, through their white swaddling, like an awful baby.

In "Post-Op: Lying Flat", Maxine Kumin muses,

> I get a lot of thinking in, lying flat,
> mostly about myself, not necessarily
> about death waiting by the bear trap.

Mona Van Duyn has enough detachment for humor:

> In twenty-four hours, the hefty nurse, all smiles,
> carries out my urine on her hip like a jug of cider,
> a happy harvest scene . . .

And in illness, Anne Sexton seems detached, inspired:

> My sleeping pill is white.
> It is a splendid pearl;
> it floats me out of myself,
> my stung skin as alien
> as a loose bolt of cloth.

The rest of the autobiography in Anne Sexton's first book, from which these lines are quoted, is remarkable, quite as though the writer *had* been floated out of herself to observe her own life. At times her subjects have historical tenor, as when she describes her picturesque grandfather,

> who begat eight
> genius children and bought twelve almost new
> grand pianos . . .

And at times it is intensely personal, confessional, as in the touching poem to her baby, "Double Image":

> I needed you. I didn't want a boy.
> Only a girl, a small milky mouse
> of a girl, already loved, already loud in the house
> of herself. We named you Joy.
> I, who was never quite sure
> about being a girl, needed another
> life, another image to remind me . . .

But in her second book, *All My Pretty Ones*, the autobiographical style is occasionally obscure, inexact, even trite:

> A thousand doors ago
> when I was a lonely kid
>   . . . and it was summer
> as long as I could remember

In her third book, *Live or Die*, she admits in her preface that the poems "read like a fever chart for a bad case of melancholy." Although the book is worthy, it is obsessive, including such poems as "Wanting to Die", "Suicide Note", and a final hokey happy ending poem, "Live". She has moved so far inward that by her fourth book, *Love Poems*, her concerns are absolutely personal:

> And now I spent all day taking care
> of my body, that baby. Its cargo is scarred.
> I annoint the bedpan. I brush my hair,
> waiting in the pain machine for my bones to get hard,
>   . . . And the other corpse, the fractured heart,
> I feed it piecemeal, little chalice. I'm good to it.

For men and women both, autobiography in poetry seems to have been the predominant genre of the 'sixties. Some of the poems discussed here, like those of *Life Studies*, recall the poet's childhoods, usually in the semi-analytic memories of painful or formative events. Mona Van Duyn remembers her hypochondriac mother, confined and confining:

> Keeping me numb on the couch for so many weeks,
> if somehow a wiley cough or flu or pox
>
> got through her guard, my legs would shake and tingle,
> trying to find the blessed way back to school.

And sometimes the poems are love poems, for example, Mona Van Duyn's "Marriage, With Beasts":

> And treat me, my pet,
> forever after as what I seem; for it seems,
> and it is, impossible for me to receive,
> under the cagey wedlock of your eyes,
> what I make it impossible for you to give.

Or Maxine Kumin's "After Love":

> Afterwards, the compromise.
> Bodies resume their boundaries.
>
> These legs, for instance, mine.
> Your arms take you back in.
>
> . . .
>
> Nothing is changed, except
> There was a moment when
>
> the wolf, the mongering wolf
> who stands outside the self
>
> lay lightly down, and slept.

But usually, as is the way with the genre, the topics orbit around the poets' surroundings, their homes, marriages, children or egos; and may at times seem to support the convention of feminine Confinement, meaning by this a confinement of the mind and senses. Yet Lowell might suffer the same accusation. At home in the suburbs, the opportunities for introspection proliferate. A poet might find ample inspiration in such a situation, maintaining as she must an immaculate sensitivity, a fearless and naive habit of looking at things. One poet[3] writes to Sylvia Plath, "Your eyes would stare/at a normal broom in your hands/for hours." And to Emily Dickinson, a total recluse who cultivated loneliness ("That polar privacy:/A soul admitted to itself") and its pain ("A Wounded Deer—leaps highest"), he writes,

> When a circus passed your
> House, each color left you
> Speechlessly opened. The wind turnings each hour,
> So ordinary, you
>
> Found brilliant . . .

But when the confined poet's subjective ego predominates, the poems reveal only an over-described unhappiness, and its myopic, essentially incommunicable details.

And yet, female confinement is socially acceptable. For two generations now, Freud-worshippers have accused the woman who would not or could not accept a subservient or sublimated position of suffering penis-envy, castration-drive, or masculinity complex. Freud himself generously protected his wife from the world by insisting that she stay home where she belonged. A. Alvarez describes Sylvia Plath during the first year of her marriage as "effaced; the poet taking a back seat to the young mother and housewife"; and in his review of her first book, *The Colossus*, as "serious, gifted, withheld, and still partly under the massive shadow of her husband" (*New American Review* #12). Sylvia Plath's busy life of bee-keeping, house-keeping, potato-farming and babies should have stabilized her. But she lasted little more than a year, using her final time to make the first dive to the center of her self: her past, her mind and its visions, her coveted death.

Mona Van Duyn's poems often approach domestic details, and then with skill and grace, such that even a poem about shopping for food (for example) becomes a readable life study. In "Post-cards from Cape Split", a series of beautiful descriptions of aspects of her summer house, she is frequently "feminine," chatty, concerned with the garden, the food, the washing of the dog and of the dishes. But the poem does not bore or alienate us for a single line; we are constantly taken by the perfection of description, the fitness of metaphor:

> . . . I am dazzled by the man in boots.
> It is as if a heron stood in my dining room.

And something more: the sense that the poet is using her mind not as a room in which to dwell, but as a unique device for looking outward, at a world or earth which is vaster and ultimately more engaging than her own case history. In the cover notes for *To See, To Take*, James Dickey is quoted: "Mona Van Duyn is one of the best women poets around." We grind our teeth.

> . . . Reading these poems, we see that domesticity is filled not only with frustrations but with a very considerable amount of humor, and, even at its most maddening, with that human warmth that guarantees, if it is worked at during the day, a satisfying and renewing night together under the universal dark.

We cannot be sure that James Dickey intends this praise in quite the sense that I take it. But in his ever-so-slightly condescending way, he has uncovered an instructive truth: that one can be domestic without being confined, if one maintains a largeness of outlook, a certain "humor" or temperament. One can be "a sweating Proust of the pantry shelves" (Mona Van Duyn). If that is how one wishes to see oneself, without being neurotic about it.

Sandra MacPherson writes a surprising series about fruits and vegetables called "Three from the Market", in which she manages to view her objects with both detachment and an imaginative sense of their relationship to herself:

> Come radishes, rosy against your greens,
> crisp when I am soft with weakness.
>
> I, what there is of me, may be argued:
> but you may not. Your whole self struts,
> your leafiness flutters about your head
> like a crown of doves.
>
> No radish was ever terrified.
>
> (*Field*, #3, Fall 1970).

Maxine Kumin devotes a section of her last book, *The Nightmare Factory* to "Tribal Poems" which describe, address or devote themselves to her children. The writer is a fairly selfless figure, allowing the mother into the poems as though she were someone else. In praise of her daughters:

> the whole sweet smell of the house that holds them,
> the tropic disorder that they bring,
> the bright sherbet of their underwear drip-drying
> and the cargo of their redemptive creams
> that stain the bathroom porcelain
> with the ooze of crushed flowers.

Even involved, she keeps sight of a tragic grandeur in the mother's relationship with the first daughter:

> Too soon the huntsman will come.
> He will bring me the heart of a wild boar
> and I in error will have it salted and cooked
> and I in malice will eat it bit by bit
> thinking it yours.
> And as we both know, at the appropriate moment,
> I will be consumed by an inexorable fire
> as you look on.

The women poets of the 'sixties are more faithful to their individual art than to the sexual stereotypes (hysteria or confinement, or others) that seem occasionally to show up in their work. Strictly speaking, the connotations of "womanhood" provide a slim source of inspiration. In a stylistic or generic sense, any autobiographical poet inflicts on himself a certain confinement, and makes a tacit pact that he or she will be limited to writing about the joys and restrictions of the individual's experiences. It should thus be clear that those who have chosen the autobiographical approach are confined, due not to their sex roles, but to the inevitable demands of the genre. Above all, no matter what they write about, women poets must no longer be regarded as confined or hysterical women who write poetry in their spare time, but simply, as poets.

NOTES

¹ In *Thinking About Women*, Mary Ellmann has uncovered two useful quotes, one from Robert Lowell who commented when Marianne Moore won the Poetry Society's Gold Medal, "She is the best woman poet in English" (p. 33), and the other from a 1965 *Commentary* which says "A man would give his right arm to have written Flannery O'Connor's 'Good Country People,'" (Ibid, p. 31). Both are extensions of Dr. Johnson's over-quoted claim that a woman preaching is like a dog walking on its hind legs . . .

² Miss Bishop seems always to have taken the advice of Gary Snyder's poem, "What You Should Know To Be A Poet", the first line of which is, "All you can about animals as persons." (*New American Review* #8)

³ James Martin, a young American poet.

James Tate and Sidney Goldfarb and the Inexhaustible Nature of the Murmur
by R. D. Rosen

I.

FOUR YEARS AGO, I devised a culinary metaphor to describe the two varieties of poetry I thought were being written in America. There was "all-meat" poetry and "all-beef" poetry; that is to say, fatty, hybrid and on the whole unhealthy verse on one hand and a higher quality lyric on the other. The former, which flooded my desk then (as poetry editor of the *Harvard Advocate*) was the work of indiscriminate eaters and was by far in the majority. The latter, so much harder to uncover among the submissions, were the products of a few gourmets who had inherited a literary scrupulosity and palate from a previous generation of writers.

Eager to find myself in the second group, I was content to arrange such a simple distinction. To me it was either genuine beef or an indigestible "all-meat" hot dog that I was reading. I refused to acknowledge shades of excellence, those intermediate dishes that were tasty, even satisfying, though by no means memorable.

What I then took to be fatty all-meat verse has since become even more prevalent and the few poems that betrayed their authors' formal training and wish to imitate the mastery of Eliot or Jarrell or Lowell (before the *Notebooks*) or even the shrewdness of Wilbur or Snodgrass became fewer and fewer. Informality, careless images, and new forms of reticence had all worked their way into most poetry being published. Despite the terrible accumulation of words, a queer silence had fallen on poets, as though they were suddenly all afraid to interrogate their dead masters. Everyone failed to pay homage to the canon of literary heroes foisted on them in highschool and freshman year at college. Students just beginning to write contracted a certain superciliousness. No one bothered to inquire about technical skills; they just wrote, like a nervous habit. For some, poetry was as good a high as anything else, and an occasional publication was a real trip.

Reviewers and magazine editors who once may have winced at this new poetry, so effortlessly avant-garde, now had no choice but to accept it. Thanks to them, all poets became famous for half an hour. Richard Brautigan, skilful as a prose writer, decided to become a poet. When he came to Harvard to read in the fall of 1969 with his coterie of Gallo-drinking sycophants, a gasping sea of poetasters egged him on gleefully until he ended the evening by reading the same poem thirty times with different inflections. It was a more advanced stage of the same malady that was already in evidence in the 'fifties when Wallace Stevens came to Harvard and read to less than a dozen people.

Now everyone is impatient to transcribe his Xanadu. Poems sound like TV ads; and TV ads are unmistakably poems. L. E. Sissman, prominent advertising executive, began publishing in *The New Yorker* a while ago, glutting his poems with brand names, and he hasn't stopped. Erik Satie is played behind ads for Dutch Cleanser. All the falsified voices of technological America have crept into the last refuge of the word.

Out of the pack of all-meat poets (this distinction increasingly loses its charm and validity), James Tate and Sidney Goldfarb have emerged as writers of special note. If only because their voices seem more honest, they have managed to distinguish themselves from the general drone. Reading Tate's second book, *The Oblivion Ha-Ha*, one fears for his future. His past, however, is brighter. His first book, *The Lost Pilot*, which won the Yale Series of Younger Poets Award in 1967, is a precocious and often ingenious work. Although Tate's as well as Goldfarb's poetry appears to have roots in both the surrealism of the 'twenties and the Confessionalism of the 'fifties and 'sixties, it grows out of a more immediate contemporary condition. In *The Lost Pilot* Tate shares with Goldfarb that feeling of disengagement that now characterizes a morally homeless generation. We used to be simply against American politics; but after so much unsuccessful counter-movement, we are paralyzed and forced to live outside of those politics. We used to write directly against the war. Now we can only get at the war by writing about everything else. Many poets have outgrown Bly's penchant for war images, no matter how clever. A couple of years ago, poetry was still being exercised as a polemic against America; but now we content ourselves with the fact that poetry proves that at least the poet is still alive. We don't have to be reminded of Song My so much as we have to be reminded of ourselves. We are already too familiar with the transgressions of the world and only want to extricate ourselves, flee to some spacious, peaceful moment. Consider Tate's "Manna":

> . . . it was two
> o'clock in the morning in
> Pittsburg, Kansas, I finally
> coming home from the loveliest
> drunk of them all, a train chugged,
> Goddamn, struggled across a
> prairie intersection and
> a man from the caboose real-
> ly waved, honestly, and said,
> and said something like my name.

Then James Wright's "Outside Fargo, North Dakota":

> Suddenly the freight car lurches.
> The door slams back, a man with a flashlight
> calls me good evening.

Despite the obvious difference between Wright's tight, lean lines and Tate's poem, they are both moving in on the same moment. It's the slightest sign of coherence on one's universe that is lived for, that moment of anonymous recognition in the freight yard; all others are derealized, impeded by expectation, formality, personal and public holocaust. Maybe so many fine poets come out of the Midwest because there, on all that flat land at night, it is easiest to make those simple connections, to wave from your car to the only person in a ten-mile area, to be surprised and comforted by a sudden headlight, or to stop in a train in a small town at two in the morning.

The feeling of being a moral outlaw is as strong in Tate as it is in Wright or Bly. Tate longs to remove himself from the curious reality of wars to another world of more reasonable alternatives:

> Today I am falling, falling,
> falling in love, and desire
> to leave this place forever.

Wright longs

> . . . to be lifted up
> By some great white bird unknown to the police.

This explicit fear of authority is much deeper in Wright than it is in Tate or Goldfarb who, as members of a younger, investigated generation, are already inured to hassles, busts, and the small discomforts of living on the periphery of the American middle-class. Wright, though, is at times almost self-indulgent about his fear of authority. "The bulldozers will scrape me up after dark behind/the officers' club" ("Before a Cashier's Window in a Department Store"). The same thing is found in a poem by Robert Mezey called "A Confession" (in his volume *The Door Standing Open*):

> What would I say to a squad car
> if it came on its noiseless tires
> and picked me out with its lights, like
> a cat or rabbit? That I
> only wanted to see how people
> live, not knowing how? That I
> hadn't had a woman in months?

The embarrassment before bureaucrats, the apology for not knowing how to act, is less pronounced in Tate and in Goldfarb, who has "nothing to declare but energy!" But Tate's estrangement is deep, despite his refusal to dwell on it in the same terms as Wright. Tate's father was reported missing over Germany when the poet was five months old. His feeling of loss and fatherlessness is like an invitation to another world:

> I feel dead. I feel as if I were
> the residue of a stranger's life,
> that I should pursue you.
>
> ("The Lost Pilot")

The grief is less cultural here than personal. Tate's mother, forced to be his father as well, also became a stranger:

> I could never find the proper
> approach. I would have
> lent you sugar, mother.

In his second book, the desire to apprehend his heritage has become an exasperated wish to abandon it. In the poem, "Leaving Mother Waiting for Father":

> . . . I propped her against a hotel
> and left without any noise.

It is as though the family battle has become a model for the abandonment of America. In a poem in *The Oblivion Ha-Ha* entitled "Consumed", Tate reels off a succession of near clichés. Life is constant transformation. Home is nowhere. "The longing to be pure/ is over" because the world undermines our quest for absolutes. Every act is a capitulation to one system or another. Tate is

> . . . the stranger
> who gets stranger by the hour.

Goldfarb is also the stranger. But while Tate is wry, Goldfarb is warm. His humorous self-effacement is a pose that succeeds. His poems are like the monologues of winos in the bleachers or failed college graduates who corner you on the street with their shabby wisdoms. Goldfarb is the old man who wants to talk with you on the El platform. But despite the sense of age in some poems, Goldfarb, like Tate, is only in his late twenties. If Tate wants to leave this place forever, Goldfarb only wants to rejoin it. In *Speech, For Instance*, his first book, he has learned to live with vulnerability:

> I need a witness!
>
> I need a witness!
>
> I need a witness because I take up space!
>
> Recognition
>
> is only the beginning . . .
>
> My house will be your house there will be no houses
> We will be hungry for one another
> We will know where the food is
> I need a witness! . . .

and:

I
am a man
of deep
affection
and I want
to enter
the world.

The need for certifying of experience motivates writing itself. For
Goldfarb, it is mostly the experience of himself that he cannot totally account
for unless it is recognized. He cannot experience himself completely in the
world except through his writing; only his work invests "reality" with actual-
ity. The unverbalized, unclothed event is bare and outside of himself.

But that very need for certification in turn pulls the poet away from the
world of immediate experience. Much of Anais Nin's diaries deals with the
artist's familiar condition of "being outside the world." The artist is unable to
participate fully in life because life has endowed him with an art that has
created for him a more preferable realm of possibilities. The self of the poet,
with its schizoid tendencies, "as long as it is uncommitted to the objective
element, is free to dream and imagine anything."[1] Everything is possible
because nothing has been proven impossible in the universe of his own writing. Yet he struggles between his allegiance to his work and his loyalty to a
world outside that he finds odious and peopled. Lawrence knew his "societal
instinct" suffered at the hands of his writing. He wanted to give, but he could
not quite work himself back into the world. The world is too unlyrical, the
collision with it a shock that disrupts the fictive train of thought.

Goldfarb is hardly resigned to his condition. He wants in. But doesn't he
realize that, once back in the world, he would no longer be able to write his
poems? Perhaps he writes only *in order* to get back into the world. As it is, he
remains outside of it, continuing to write about getting back even though that
act of writing is primarily what is keeping him out. (Although perhaps it is
true that the self-conscious writer, living for so long outside of the world, will
eventually achieve enlightenment and suddenly find himself at its center.)

Beyond Goldfarb's sense of abused affection, of his dissociation from the
living of life (a familiar enough motif), he has witnessed to some extent the
fragmentation of his ego and the formation of personae useful to him in both
his life and his art. One doesn't feel that either he or Tate is playing out
archetypes in poetry, as Wright seems closer to doing with his "great white
bird," but rather that their voices are on the conscious level of personae, which
can be assumed and dropped at will. Largely, Tate's and Goldfarb's voices
are conscious manipulations, an exaggerated negative capability in which the
poet chooses to be someone else. The poet, on the other hand, through whom
an *unconscious*, archetypal form expresses itself, is not engaged in a deliberate
act. And it is that poet who knows of "no halfway stage between radical
isolation in self-absorption or complete absorption in all there is."[2] It is that

poet of whom Erich Neumann, the Jungian psychologist, said: "When unconscious forces break through in the artist, when the archetypes striving to
be born into the light of the world take form in him, he is as far from the
men around him as he is close to their destiny."[3] But Tate and Goldfarb
do not attain this state, they operate somewhere in between self-absorption
and complete absorption in all there is. Of the three examples from Goldfarb's work which follow, the first two are clearly conscious personae whereas
the third smells faintly of a primary, archetypal situation:

> I'm the man you just passed,
> There were words in my mouth.
>
> No I am not the skies of Paris.

and:

> On the midnight subway
> I fell on my knees
> Before a dead woman
> And proposed to her.

But Goldfarb's book, after all the compassion and experimentation with
different masks, ends with a sinking back into the self. It is as though he
finally realizes that not only are all his personae inadequate, but so is the poet,
the most terrifying persona of all. At the end, he cannot even help a dog
free itself from a chain-link fence:

> I have no stomach for any animal but myself.

Yet there is a moment in each of their books when Tate and Goldfarb do
appear to be experiencing something that approximates the moment "of
absorption in all there is." In *The Oblivion Ha-Ha*, Tate writes:

> . . . Almost
> everything is having some effect
> on me.

Then listen to Goldfarb's title poem, "Speech, for Instance":

> Everything
> has its effect:
> speech, for
> instance, or
> a girl
> coming out
> of the sea.

Both these excerpts were written at instants of sensitivity to the events of the
world, as though the synaptic thresholds were suddenly lowered to let in all
these rediscoveries. Tate:

> I have faith the air will

soon cohere or speak
tomorrow morning as you are

pulling on your boots,
my love, by the fire . . .

on either side of myself
the water is seldom

so navigable . . .

Goldfarb:

Everything
has its effect:
Sleep.
Breakfast.
Conversation.
. . . I
recognize the wind and
food and shelter most after
a plunge into the icy ocean. The sun
warm, the dune
warm . . .

Although the tone of Tate's poem is graver than Goldfarb's, both employ a manner of description rather than metaphor which suggests a sudden awakening to their environment. Eventually, the description itself becomes a metaphor for a condition of the psychosoma. But implicit is a horror at being a writer. The poems are trying to express an equivalency of all things, the complete unity that is endemic to psychedelic experience. The poem is no longer exalted as the indispensable camera. *Everything* has its effect; speech and the poem are just another experience, subordinate perhaps to the more original experience of the girl coming out of the sea or the juniper berries. All acts are equalized, and the "water is seldom so navigable." "Speech, for Instance" is a renunciation of words, of the poem, of the poet who is impelled to transcribe reality even after an intense immediate experience. The poem undermines itself; it is a recognition of the insufficiency of the secondary, certifying experience that it, being a poem, inevitably is. What Tate and Goldfarb would rather encompass is the immediate moment. But they can't. Their creative relationship is with themselves in the act of writing and not with the objects of their writing, animate or inanimate. Goldfarb writes in the middle of the poem, "All this/is written/in one form/or another." But Goldfarb insists on the word, which is his shield. Elsewhere, he writes, "Actually I'm under/a certain kind of cover." He is isolated by his own commentary. Perhaps that is the explanation of his line, "Description is loneliness."

II.

> If the surrealists made dreams, sickness, and madness the central content of
> art and tried to make their writing and painting flow directly from the un-
> conscious, this was merely a late caricature of what was suffered by the great
> creative personalities, for they all stand under the sign of Orpheus, who was
> rent to pieces by the maenads. And in consequence, the art which expresses
> our time seems to consist only of fragments, not of complete works.
>
> > Erich Neumann,
> > *Art and the Creative Unconscious*[4]

> Most of what the surrealists write is artificially produced by the mind, not by
> the unconscious. To place an umbrella on an operating table is incongruous
> but it is not an image from the unconscious.
>
> > *The Diary of Anais Nin*[5]

Tate has a weakness for the dream-image which is not convincing, but
"sounds right."

> . . . None of the little
> anthracite rabbits with carrot
> pink eyes are real . . .
> > ("The Descent")

> Kings and queens
> donkeying through the fractured
> gallery of my seasons.
> > ("In The Face of the Waters")

At times, he is silly, like Brautigan, unable to resist colloquialisms from
commercial modes of speech, from soap operas, ads, or radio talk shows:

> Then I thought of all the women
> I had ever had. I appreciate
> the patronage; thanks for dropping in.

or:

> I
> know what he will say:
> he's the fire hydrant
> of the underdog . . .

Fortunately, unlike Brautigan, Tate's little jokes are not usually the point
of the poem. They are only the posture of a single image. Contextually, of
course, lines like the above have their drama, and I should say that their use
attests not to Tate's silliness as much as his willingness to incorporate as
many speech idioms as he can into his voice, admirable enough when so
many poets, perhaps in deference to the confessionalists, are addicted to the
same emotional pitch in all their poems. Tate always seems to be shifting gears,
often without knowing it, driving through a wide range of tones.

Under control, he is innovative as in the following images which suggest that for Tate metaphor is the search for the ambiguous equality of two seemingly diverse experiences:

> She arranges the furniture
> so that it might resemble the beauty
> of the saliva on the lip of the slave
> when he thinks of her . . .
>> ("Mrs America")

> . . . Our gladness
> flares like a pheasant in an empty field.
>> ("Little Yellow Leaf")

This is operating with the notion that a quality can be transferred from one experience to another, no matter how preposterous the transfer may appear. And, when done well, this is where his surrealism succeeds. He seems to be tracing the logic of associations and using the condensation and displacement of dreams.

> The silent cameras of hemophilia . . .
>> ("Mrs America")

There are metaphors which totter on the edge of inanity, about to fall over; but they are usually saved by a sincerity reflected in the poem as a whole. Still, many of Tate's poems are marred by lines which don't belong, by an obscurity that is comic. To be sure, Tate is often aware of this predicament.

> The insular firebird
> (meaning the sun) . . .

He is embarrassed by his own abstruseness. It seems like an adolescent game. The poems that are farthest from confusion are conversational narratives like "Intimidations of an Autobiography" and "Uncle", both in *The Lost Pilot*. Tate is quiet and direct in these autobiographical poems as if real conscious remembrance moderates his surrealism, distils the profusion of metaphor. The simple nostalgia of the poems strengthens and justifies all the images.

Goldfarb's poetry is cleaner, more compassionate, the voice of someone wanting to be heard. Where Tate is the quiet promoter of his own moods, where his poems are often fragile because their sentiments are so delicate and uncertain, Goldfarb is the garrulous advertiser of his condition:

> I pretend I have to piss just to see
> if the bathroom still recognizes me.
>> ("Aubade: Thinking about You")

Tate isn't so sure of himself. Here is his poem "The Book of Lies":

> I'd like to have a word
> with you. Could we be alone

for a minute ? I have been lying
Until now. Do you believe

I believe myself ? Do you believe
yourself when you believe me ? Lying
is natural. Forgive me. Could we be alone
forever ? Forgive us all. The word

is my enemy. I have never been alone;
bribes, betrayals. I am lying
even now. Can you believe
that ? I give you my word.

Both Goldfarb and Tate complain about duplicity; both refuse to exempt themselves from the sins of America:

Then you're in a certain place
with people all around you,
interested, friendly people
in the way that a tribe of natives
might be interested and friendly
but you're completely alone;
out the window
isn't the building
he works in, she
doesn't do her
laundry down the street . . .
(Goldfarb, "To Make Them Monumental")

Goldfarb is always intelligible and what little surrealism or suspended imagery he uses is there to support or address a proposition already made. In his more difficult poems, though, Tate appears to begin with a prefabricated image and then allows his poem to develop its own proposition or statement. The immediate image precedes its intention. If one is going to be calculating, one should be calculating throughout. By putting down what image comes to mind, Tate is hoping that the inherent logic of his unconscious will necessarily be uncovered. But, in the absence of a poet continually willing to interview his own unconscious contents, the surrealist poem will just be a convoluted succession of inscrutable visions; not inscrutable in themselves, but inscrutable as a *pattern* of meanings which says something about the poet and his exposure to archetypes in himself. Tate only seems to be following André Breton's advice to put his "trust in the inexhaustible nature of the murmur."[6] Often, Tate just seems to be talking to himself.

It is one thing, in McLuhan's useful words, to "live consciously in the unconscious." It is another thing to translate haphazardly an unconscious tremor into the easiest, most available conscious language. I am afraid that too many poets are doing precisely the latter. The disappearance of a cultural canon with which to identify has encouraged a lot of would-be artists to identify with that absence of precedence and form. Neumann made the distinction:

> The great artists make *conscious* use of the situation, dissolving configured outward reality into a stream of feeling and action that, although coming from within, is nevertheless directed; this is equally true of Klee or Chagall, of Joyce, or Thomas Mann. [italics mine] The lesser artists make a program of this principle; they amuse themselves and the world with the literary and artistic expression of their incontinence, with an exhibition of their private complexes.[7]

Roman Jakobson recounts the story of an illiterate Serbian peasant who was able at will to recite native epics in accurate homeric meter. We have lost touch with those levels of our race unconscious, those reservoirs of rhythms, habits, and archetypes, that would enable us to summon rich histories. The primitive's decentralized ego, his profound collective experiences, are largely lost to us. What remains is the addiction to our own contemporaneousness and the slick craving for individuality. On one level, the poetry of Tate and Goldfarb is charming, skilful. On another, though, it is just one more sloppy example of the desire to be singled out.

NOTES

[1] R. D. Laing, *The Divided Self*, Pelican Books, London, 1965, p. 89.

[2] *Ibid.*, p. 91.

[3] Erich Neumann, *Art and the Creative Unconscious*, Bollingen Series LXI, Princeton University Press, 1959, p. 94.

[4] *Ibid.*, p. 116.

[5] *The Diary of Anaïs Nin*, Vol. 2, ed. Gunther Stuhlmann, Harcourt Brace and World, Inc., New York City, 1967, p. 178.

[6] André Breton, *The First Surrealist Manifesto*, in *Surrealists On Art*, ed. Lucy R. Lippard, Prentice-Hall, New Jersey, 1970.

[7] Neumann, p. 117.

A Conversation with Mark Strand

EDITOR'S NOTE.—The following interview with Mark Strand recapitulates, from an individual poet's perspective, many of the themes which the critics in this volume have discerned in poetry of the 'sixties. Strand's is one of the most impressive talents to have emerged during that decade. His three books of poems are *Sleeping With One Eye Open* (1964), *Reasons for Moving* (1968) and *Darker* (1970). (The last two of these are published by Atheneum.) By birth a Canadian (he was born in 1934 on Prince Edward Island), Strand has entered fully into the restlessness typical of the poet's life today in the United States. He turned to poetry after studying painting under Albers at Yale. Besides teaching for brief periods at many colleges in the United States he has taught in Brazil and has translated Latin American poetry. To define the flavor of Strand's work critics have invoked various influences: the writing of Borges and other illusionist masters, the techniques of modern film and of surrealist painting. But these poems, which explore with a deliberate, haunting simplicity the shifting boundaries of reality, provide their own best commentary. Here is one from *Darker* which seems to me representative:

The Prediction

That night the moon drifted over the pond,
turning the water to milk, and under
the boughs of the trees, the blue trees,
a young woman walked, and for an instant

the future came to her:
rain falling on her husband's grave, rain falling
on the lawns of her children, her own mouth
filling with cold air, strangers moving into her house,

a man in her room writing a poem, the moon drifting into it,
a woman strolling under its trees, thinking of death,
thinking of him thinking of her, and the wind rising
and taking the moon and leaving the paper dark.

This interview was taped in Athens, Ohio in 1971 and subsequently appeared in *The Ohio Review* (Vol. XIII, No. 2, 1972) as one of a notable series of talks with contemporary poets which that magazine has been publishing. The interviewers were the poets Wayne Dodd and Stanley Plumly. For this reprinting Mark Strand and I have made expansions and deletions in the text. For permission to use this material in an altered form I am grateful to the editors of *The Ohio Review*.

Interviewer: I think what we're going to do is to address your poems themselves. I wonder if you would comment on where you've come from. Where do you think you've come from, and where do you think you're going?

Strand: Well, I don't know where I'm going. If I knew where I was going I probably wouldn't go there. The idea is to—I wouldn't say surprise oneself . . . But I think you go, and then you discover where it is that you are, and writing is so . . .

Interviewer: It sounds like a line from one of your poems.

Strand: Maybe so. Where I started was—I started as a painter. I was a student of Joseph Albers at Yale, and somewhere early in my career there I discovered I wasn't destined to be a very good painter, so I became a poet. Now it didn't happen suddenly. I did read a lot, and I had been a reader of poetry before. In fact, I was much more given to reading poems than I was to fiction and the book that I read a lot, and frequently, was *The Collected Poems of Wallace Stevens*. And I think that a lot of American poets come from Stevens. The other book that had an influence on me was the *New Poets of England and America*, the Hall, Pack, Simpson anthology. I look back now and I read it, and I'm bored by a lot of the stuff, and some of it seems so forced and decorative. But I can still see why I was excited. There was an awful lot of "technical authority" in many of those poems, and it's something that I, as a beginning poet, lacked. And I went directly to measured lines and rhyme as a way of, you know, nailing down poems. I felt secure with rhyme and meter —secure is the wrong word—but if I worked within definable bounds I was, I thought, destined to come up with something decent.

Interviewer: In that sense then, what is it you want to do in a poem?

Strand: Well, I could answer that in a round-about way, saying what I want to do in a poem is discover what it is that I have to say.

Interviewer: It is an act of discovery?

Strand: Yes.

Interviewer: Having done it, what do you see that you have done?

Strand: Well, after the brief, and I think normal, period of exhilaration, there is a let-down. What I've done is written a poem. And what I have to do is write another one. Now I realize that . . . you see, what happens is, when I look back on my work I see my faults fairly clearly, and when I'm working on new poems, or the next poem, I try not to repeat myself, although I do, unconsciously. I don't have many things to say. I don't believe that many people do. I am limited because I'm one person, and I have, you know, one mind and one nervous system . . .

Interviewer: I think what I'm getting at is . . . Other people, in the reviews and the criticism, define what they perceive you as doing: I wanted to ask you what *you* perceived yourself as doing. I don't want to pose the question too naively, but I want to ask you what kind of poem it is you're making; the kind of poetry you are making is rather unique, I think, today.

Strand: That may be, although I have a very unclear sense of the kind of poem it is that I make. I have a clearer sense of the kind of poem other people make. If I tried to describe what it was that I did in a poem, I think I'd get in an awful mess, and I'd have a sick feeling that what I'd described wasn't in fact what I really am doing.

Interviewer: I think that's very good, and I think it's typical of the poem you're doing, as a matter of fact, the sense of withholding, the sense of silence, the sense of a great transparency in the language—that you're not even dealing in language.

Strand: Well, that's important. That's a good point. I think that one of the things I do try to do is call less attention to the verbal surface of the poem than I might have, had I been a poet of the 'fifties. There is a life in the poem that somehow comes through the language, or that the language points to, and it doesn't mean that it's not part of the language. It's just not part of the endless elaboration of language. It's a sort of direct language, suggestive and yet concrete. I deal with identifiable states of mind which are at the same time elusive. Does that make sense? I rely on dreams and on chance associations, as well.

Interviewer: A number of people of course have commented on the obvious fact of a severely plain vocabulary to your poetry, and . . .

Strand: It wasn't always that way.

Interviewer: Wasn't it? Well, actually I wanted to ask a kind of longwinded question, though I hope it's not just fatuous. Michael Hamburger, in his *The Truth of Poetry*, talks a good bit about what he calls the anti-poetry movement of the decades after World War I. I mean the movement in poetry which was a reflection surely of a kind of distrust that a lot of people felt, a distrust of the surface of poetry and everything, and I wondered to what extent you see that continuing in contemporary poetry and even in your own, in this talk about the lack of concern for the verbal surface.

Strand: Well, anti-poetry is really modern poetry. Contemporary poetry isn't modern poetry, and it isn't anti-poetry. I feel very much a part of a new international style that has a lot to do with plainness of diction, a certain reliance on surrealist techniques, a certain reliance on journalistic techniques, a strong narrative element, etc. Now I realize this doesn't cover all of contemporary poetry, but there does seem to be a connection between, say, Parra and Zbigniew Herbert and Jaime Sabines and Vasko Popa and Charlie Simic, to pick a few scattered poets. Auden would say there can be no international style because there is no international language, but maybe that's my point— that poets are connected by a similarity of interests. With the amount of translation going on there is an enormous sharing of points of view. And I think we read other poets in translation, oddly enough, for content. You might even say that poetry is what is retained in translation, not what is lost (though I say this almost jokingly—because reading poets in translation is, at the same time, not quite like reading poetry written in English. It's more relaxing. A certain pressure is missing). But I'm talking—and perhaps mistakenly—about a certain sort of poetry being written—vaguely surreal, vaguely narrative—as I said.

Interviewer: You write very narrative poems, for example.

Strand: Yes, well there are other people who do too, and I think that a poem is less a moment that's endlessly elaborated on, or one sensation that's endlessly talked about (and I don't mean that in a bad sense). A poem really moves very quickly from point A to B to C to D; and you have a sense that you're moving through time, as well as that you're moving over the expanse of space that connects them.

Interviewer: One of the things that question was wanting to get at, was to what extent you think there is very firmly embedded in contemporary poetry now, the poetry of today, a distrust of what once on a time would have been called "poetic conventions," and now which we would probably put in quotation marks.

Strand: Are you speaking about rhyme and meter?

Interviewer: I don't mean only that.

Strand: Well, I don't know. I can say that we distrust rhyme because it sounds a little tinny, a little false, a little decorative, and a little unnatural. The point of writing a version of plain-style verse, it seems, is to affect as much as possible the naturalness of conversation, or plain discourse, not overly-excited discourse. Rhymes would get in the way . . . I'm not talking about my own poetry when I say this, I'm sure Galway Kinnell and Robert Mezey, whom we mentioned at lunch, would not ever write in meters or rhyme.

Interviewer: Even though they have . . .

Strand: Even though they have, right. I still rhyme. I mean, I've rhymed fairly recently, and I find it useful. For instance, these lines from "The Way It Is":

> My neighbor's wife calls to me, her mouth is pressed
> against the wall behind my bed.
> She says, 'My husband's dead.'
> I turn over on my side,
> hoping she has not lied.

And I don't mind meters either. It sometimes seems quite natural to me.

Interviewer: Sure. I was wondering if you thought there might be a distrust of a kind of conventionalized stance that poetry so often brought to a situation which we would, today, consider a kind of falsification of it. I mean that's the kind of thing that Mezey objects to in his past poetry, in a lot of his poetry of the years rejected.

Strand: But that's something he, of course, is in a much better position to talk about than anyone else. I mean, I don't feel the same way about my early rhymed poems. If I dislike them, it's not because they were in rhyme, it's because they just weren't as, as . . .

Interviewer: As authentic . . .?

Strand: Well I'm not sure I would use the word "authentic". They just weren't in touch with the things that I now consider important. I mean I believe I was honest when I was writing those poems; it's just that I had an odd idea of what made me go. I don't have that idea now, and I think I perhaps was mistaken in those days. I had a very sentimental view of myself, which crops up now and again in my poems.

Interviewer: There is this ongoing, if I may coin a phrase, ontological conversation with yourself. It seems to be underneath almost everything you're doing. And so many poets, who are 10 years, 15 years older than you, seem to have come to a point of near madness in their work. They seem to be almost fragmenting, falling apart right in front of their poems, so to speak.

Strand: Yes, it's true.

Interviewer: But your work still has this sense of great—great control, great form, as if you were containing it. You're still very much in control, and yet your poems are just as mad, it seems to me, in their own way.

Strand: Well, I am really aware, too, that when I am writing a poem, I am writing a poem. I think that that makes certain demands. There are certain concessions made to that inner debate, artistic concessions, and they're important. You know, one of the horrifying things about many poets is that they lost, somewhere along the line, in the fervor of this inner debate, the idea of poetry.

Interviewer: That's a good point.

Strand: They become, in fact, "chroniclers" or "notators". They write notebooks or leaflets or what have you. As if to say, "I am connected to my times in this way, and I am connected to this debate in this way." But there's no sense of getting absorbed in the idea of the poem.

Interviewer: As if the poem is somehow in the way now; "I've got more truth to get at than that," they seem to be saying.

Strand: Poetry has always seemed to me the most truthful medium of all. To say that the poem gets in the way is to say that you don't trust what the poem can do. I mean I've always believed poems. Sir Thomas Wyatt's "They Flee From Me, That Sometime Did Me Seek" strikes me as terribly honest, yet it's a poem and a very formal one, and I certainly don't say, "Gee, I wish he'd written that as a confession and not as a poem, because as a poem it lacks reality," or "I don't believe it because it rhymes." And the same goes for Shakespeare's sonnets—they're very sad, and some of them are heart-breaking, and just because they're sonnets, that doesn't mean you can't believe them. And so on and so forth, right up to the present.

Interviewer: Well, that makes me aware of a question I want to ask you. I was recently reading a thing by Alain Bosquet about poetry in which he says, basically, that he thinks the act of perfecting the poem (after the poem has been roughly indited, finally making it accessible as a thing that is meant to be enjoyed and experienced by other people, and which will recreate in them what he calls the sense of "magnificent disarray" which the poet felt) is an act which necessarily impoverishes somewhat the experience or the emotion that the poem was trying to embody. To what extent do you think that is true?

Strand: Well, I was going to say that it is not necessarily true. It depends on your habits, it would seem to me. You take that initial emotion, or whatever it is that you want to create in the poem when you first sit down to write the poem, and to say that that is the one thing that must be preserved, and what comes out first is going to be closest to that is one way of solving the problem of writing a poem, it seems to me. I myself feel that I'm never sure about what it is that I'm talking about at the beginning. I have a rough idea and maybe a few images or a word, or just a mad desire to sit down and write; and in the process of writing, over an extended period of time—not only one sitting, but perhaps a couple of days or a few weeks—I develop a clear sense of what it is that I'm headed toward . . . and maybe not such a clear sense, maybe just enough sense so that I can direct my, my procedure, you know. I have on occasion written very quickly, and found it impossible to improve on what I've done, and I consider myself, in those cases, very lucky. It certainly saves a lot of work.

Interviewer: Yes, but it's unusual.

Strand: I think anyone who rewrites a poem or goes back and rearranges it, even if they do it a little, is saying the poem can be improved. So what's the difference, whether you spend 10 more hours, or 20 more hours improving it?

Interviewer: Or, as in Yeats' case, years.

Strand: Years, yes. Then you're saying that if you can improve it at all the original thing wasn't that holy and maybe it wasn't as perfect an indication of the emotional life that went into it as you might have wished. It's very lucky that you get that one-to-one relationship between what's done and what was intended.

Interviewer: I like your answer, and that's what I wanted you to talk about. I probably misrepresented, in my way of asking the question, Bosquet's position.

Strand: I probably misunderstood.

Interviewer: No, no! I think not. But certainly he wasn't suggesting that it shouldn't be rewritten. Indeed, he said that that rewriting has to be done over and over and over again, but that what you are doing then is making a poem that people can read, and that somehow or other the thing you wanted so desperately to do, (what that was you didn't know), doesn't make it fully into that poem. So then you have to write another one.

Strand: But maybe that thing you wanted to do so desperately was to sit down and write a poem. If it had been a fully thought-out poem that you wanted to write and you had it completed in your mind, you might not have written it. There wouldn't be that need perhaps. Look, if one sits down in a very mixed-up state of mind and very desirous of writing a poem . . . I mean the act of sitting there in a room in the quiet is going to take over at some point, you know. We don't stop when we have an emotion and it doesn't freeze us for the time it takes to write. There's a certain point at which we are *writing*, dealing with that emotion that compelled us to sit down in the first place.

Interviewer: In the context of the process and situation itself it's a type of transition.

Strand: Yes.

Interviewer: To particularize, then, from the earlier comments you were making (this is putting is awkwardly), what is the difference between *Reasons for Moving* and the more recent *Darker*?

Strand: Well, I would say that *Darker* is much more direct. There is less— the poems are less fables, something less allegorical about them.

Interviewer: Do you think it's more daring?

Strand: Well, I thought so when I wrote it.

Interviewer: I think so too.

Strand: I still believe it's a more daring book.

Interviewer: I get the sense, to interrupt your thinking here for a moment, that there's more Mark Strand in *Darker* than there is in *Reasons for Moving*, that you were moving to the kind of poem that Mark Strand would write and is writing there. I'm speaking as an outsider to the poems, of course, but I have a greater sense of speaking voice, say, direct to Mark Strand in *Darker*.

Strand: Well, I agree, but then I'm biased. There are other voices in *Reasons for Moving*. There are other voices in *Darker*, too, but I think that I don't rely on them; I think I use them with—I don't want to say greater control—but I use them because I've chosen to.

Interviewer: Yes, for example, a poem like "Courtship" as opposed to "Black Maps" or "The Sleep". I think that's a different voice, but yet a voice with which they are entirely compatible.

Strand: They are . . . They are different. When you put a book together, you have enormous misgivings about your voice. Suddenly it seems very scattered and things seem very different.

Interviewer: Yes, you're too many people all at once, and "How can that be?"

Strand: And then after a while you realize it's really quite unified, and the difference between "Black Maps" and "Courtship" isn't so great. I mean "Courtship" goes under the heading of poems I might call ugly poems. There is something . . .

Interviewer: Grotesque?

Strand: And it's funny.

Interviewer: Oh, I think it's hilarious. And also disturbing.

Strand: It's funny, and there's something unserious about it; it's a social poem. Not that social poems are necessarily less serious, but this one is. It's a poem that probably presents a false view of male-female relations, that a man to gain the confidence of a woman has to deny his manhood.

Courtship

There is a girl you like so you tell her
your penis is big, but that you cannot get yourself
to use it. Its demands are ridiculous, you say,
even self-defeating, but to be honored somehow,
briefly, inconspicuously in the dark.

When she closes her eyes in horror,
you take it all back. You tell her you're almost
a girl yourself and can understand why she is shocked.
When she is about to walk away, you tell her
you have no penis, that you don't

know what got into you. You get on your knees.
She suddenly bends down to kiss your shoulder and you know
you're on the right track. You tell her you want
to bear children and that is why you seem confused.
You wrinkle your brow and curse the day you were born.

She tries to calm you, but you lose control.
You reach for her panties and beg forgiveness as you do.
She squirms and you howl like a wolf. Your craving
seems monumental. You know you will have her.
Taken by storm, she is the girl you will marry.

Interviewer: I confess I don't believe that poem as much as I do a poem like, for example, "The Dreadful Has Already Happened", though they are strategically similar.

Strand: You shouldn't. "The Dreadful Has Already Happened" is a poem that is structured a little like it—but you could say that it's much more cinematic. There are many cuts (what I call cuts)—to landscape imagery, and then to this horrible scene being played out between the parents and the relatives. And it comes out of reading R. D. Laing's *The Politics of Experience*. It's about how we quickly learn how to participate in our own demise; how we pick up cues from our parents, and the world in general, that ultimately stifle us and destroy our imaginations and our individuality. And this was a poem that gave such standard goings-on character.

The Dreadful Has Already Happened

The relatives are leaning over, staring expectantly.
They moisten their lips with their tongues. I can feel
them urging me one. I hold the baby in the air.
Heaps of broken bottles glitter in the sun.

A small band is playing old fashioned marches.
My mother is keeping time by stamping her foot.
My father is kissing a woman who keeps waving
to somebody else. There are palm trees.

The hills are spotted with orange flamboyants and tall
billowy clouds move behind them. "Go on, Boy,"
I hear somebody say, "Go on."
I keep wondering if it will rain.

The sky darkens. There is thunder.
"Break his legs," says one of my aunts,
"Now give him a kiss." I do what I'm told.
The trees bend in the bleak tropical wind.

The baby did not scream, but I remember that sigh
when I reached inside for his tiny lungs and shook them
out in the air for the flies. The relatives cheered.
It was about that time I gave up.

Now, when I answer the phone, his lips
are in the receiver; when I sleep, his hair is gathered
around a familiar face on the pillow; wherever I search
I find his feet. He is what is left of my life.

I've always been attracted to the grotesque. When I was an artist, although a terrible one, I was in love with it, maybe because . . .

Interviewer: You don't paint anymore?

Strand: No I don't.

Interviewer: Well, you are a very visually oriented poet, certainly.

Strand: I learned a lot from painting.

Interviewer: I keep thinking of that line from "The Sleep": "Even the wooden sleep with the moon is possible . . ." "Wooden sleep" . . . that's a painter's way of saying it.

Strand: It is. You're right. Probably way back in my mind was Elizabeth Bishop's poem "The Monument", where everything is made out of wood. She's a very painterly poet.

Interviewer: Yes. A beautiful maker of images just by themselves. Let me ask you about, since we're doing this, about your habits as a writer. Do you go at it everyday?

Strand: No. Oh, I used to. I used to be a compulsive worker. I couldn't sleep at night unless I put in two or three hours of writing poetry. It's something I learned from my first teacher at Antioch College, Nolan Miller. He said you have to write two or three hours a day if you're going to be a writer. And I did, my first year at Antioch, when I though I would be a writer. And then when I was told I would never be a writer (by others at Antioch), I gave up. And later on when I went to Yale, I started putting in those hours again.

Interviewer : Do you now?

Strand : No. It's, it's—when I was writing when I lived in Iowa City and was teaching at the Workshop, I would write every day—maybe three hours, maybe one, but everyday, because I had a little study and it was quiet. I could get away and do that. But in the last few years, I only sit down and write when I feel like it. I write more quickly than I ever have, spend fewer hours on any poem, but I end up writing about as much. Or, it seems that way. Also, I publish more poems in magazines than eventually are included in my books. I throw them out because I think I've made mistakes in them, and I believe a book is important . . .

Interviewer: As a total entity ?

Strand : Yes. It's something that's going to be around for a while, and it's something that other people have to live with, and it should represent the best that I can give them. If I just thought, "Well, whatever I do is good and they just have to take it or leave it . . ." There are a lot of young poets that publish, I think, far too much. But I don't know what the reasons are. I don't believe it's because they want to be "the most published poet in America." For me, in recent years, magazine publication has become much less important. I mean, I've never written enough so that I would ever flood all the magazines in America at any one time, so I don't know what that feels like. But I do know that having a book come out is a distinctly different feeling. There's something about 2 years or 3 years or 4 years of work gathered together. And a book is also a way of putting a whole bunch of poems out of mind so that you have a sense you're beginning again. It's a bigger sense of beginning again than when you finish one poem and begin another. I, for one, work on several poems simultaneously—and I never have the sense that I'm finished, except when I have a book.

Interviewer : You indeed do write books of poems ?

Strand : I think it's coming to that. For instance, I've decided to do a pamphlet. I've written an elegy (which will be a pamphlet, just to have it be in the world by itself, you know; and then later be a section of my next book). And—I don't know what the shape of my next book will be or what it will look like. When I wrote *Darker,* I did know that there would be a lot of 3-stanzas, 12-line poems in it, and I knew that it would be made up mostly of very short poems (I had that sense because I wanted to continue writing those poems) and that it would conclude with "The Way It Is", the first poem I completed after *Reasons for Moving.* Now, I know that after *Darker,* the impulse was to write longer poems. I don't know why.

Interviewer : When you were talking about the elegy—I was thinking that you have other poems called "Elegy", or "Litany" or something . . .

Strand : Yes, "Litany."

Interviewer : . . . that refers to a sense of formal occasion in that poem, and I was thinking about, in my own weird way, about the style of line you do. It's not—I have the sense sometimes that you aren't even writing a line, but a sentence; you do really write sentences, and I can't think of another poet who is so conscious of the sentence.

Strand: Well, I think that it's just the way my ear works. I mean I don't want to destroy the . . .

Interviewer: Well, they're beautiful sentences.

Strand: . . . I don't want to destroy the unit of a sentence by making my lines overly important, nor do I want to destroy the line by playing too much with sentences. I try to get them working together instead of at odds. And without being boring. But there are times when, I admit, I do fiddle with the idea of a sentence, and even make fun of it. In the poem called "Letter" I wrote a sentence that wasn't a sentence because I felt I had to. Sometimes I feel I ought to break loose . . . but then I think, "Is not writing in whole sentences really breaking loose?" It's a difficult question. The "Litanies", for example, got a bit boring. That is, I didn't want to keep writing them. They're rhetorical and formulaic.

> Let the bodies of debutantes gleam like frigidaires.
> For they shall have sex with food.
> Let flies sink into their mother's thighs and go blind in the
>   trenches of meat.
> Let the patient unmask the doctor and swim in the gray milk of
>   his mind.
> For nothing will keep.
>   ("From a Litany")

And I love *Jubilate Agno*.

Interviewer: I was just going to ask you where you got the form for "The New Poetry Handbook".

Strand: That—I don't know. It probably comes out of reading. I read a lot of Whitman and Smart and Blake, and . . . I don't know. Oh yes, some friends at Irvine, Max and Carol Yeh, once showed me something they'd gotten from a publication of the American Philosophical Society. It was a dream book . . . I don't know which Near Eastern civilization it was . . . but anyhow, the line about "urine in your shoes" is something that came out of that. I kept it a long time.

Interviewer: I think that's "If a man publicly denounces poetry, his shoes will fill with urine." The beautiful thing about that poem is you seem the most unlikely candidate for such a description. But not only is it really fine in its own right as a poem, it has its didactic point to make. Of course, you're playing an ironical game with death but it does have great didactic sense, if you want to follow the absurdity of it.

> If a man lets his poems go naked,
>   he shall fear death.
>
> If a man fears death,
>   he shall be saved by his poems.

> If a man does not fear death,
>> he may or may not be saved by his poems.

> If a man finishes a poem,
>> he shall bathe in the blank wake of his passion
>> and be kissed by white paper.

Strand: It seems to me that in this poem—though perhaps not in the sections you've just quoted—I manage to equate poetry with some of the serious things that we experience in life.

> If a man conceives of a poem,
>> he shall have one less child.

> If a man conceives of two poems,
>> he shall have two children less.

If you can create ratios in which poetry can exist, in which a poem can exist, side by side with a child or with two children—it's convincing. I mean—it's not convincing because it's *true*, it's convincing because poetry is that *important.*

Interviewer: We talked a while ago about the sort of severity and simplicity of your poems, which everybody recognizes, but one of the things that strikes me and that I'd like to ask you something about is: whereas the present time does seem to be very clearly a time of marvellous riches in poetry, in the use of the simile and metaphor—I mean, this is just a great age of simile and metaphors—yet your own poetry, which is so much a part of our time, is a poetry that is somewhat reluctant, but I just wondered what would you say about that—if anything?

Strand: Well, I really don't know, since I believe—and I have a fuzzy picture of my own work—but I believe I use similes frequently. Perhaps not. But I do think the poem becomes an image, or sometimes the whole poem is a metaphor, or . . .

Interviewer: You don't have the sense that they are couched or posed as metaphors as such? They are very much what a poem is?

Strand: Right. It's very much the way Kafka's parables or paradoxes become metaphors. Kafka was—reading *Parables* and *Paradoxes* was a very big influence; reading Michaux was too. But there's something essentially uncontrolled about Michaux, and he really does go on quite long in those prose poems; but it was very liberating to read him.

Interviewer: Speaking of influences, I think probably Borges is the poet most influential to you.

Strand: Oh yes, but not his poetry, his fiction. Borges is such a marvellous writer, certain things in particular, *Funes, The Memorious* is a wonderful story and *Tlön, Uqbar, Orbis Tertius* is another one I particularly like. Also I mentioned Landolfi's stories at lunch. I used to enjoy reading psychoanalytic case histories, too.

Interviewer: How much does your reading come into your work?

Strand: Well, I get ideas from reading.

Interviewer: Well, obviously you read what you want to read and therefore . . .

Strand: I read . . . but I don't read a lot. I mean, people like Bill Merwin or Richard Howard are terribly well-read. They've read everything, it seems to me. And I read much less. But I do read, and I depend on what I read . . . There are certain key books. It's not how much, really, it's just what it happens to be. And I've been lucky in that I've stumbled across the right books or have a sort of instinctive ability to select. It was very important to read Bachelard or even Max Picard. Also to come across an anthology like *Post-War Polish Poetry*, you know, which is a fine anthology; or to suddenly find myself in a book store 12 years ago, and stumble across Alberti, and start reading Alberti, and decide that I wanted to translate him. That was an enormous stroke of good luck. Because I learned a lot from Alberti. I've translated a lot of his poems. I'm now reading a book on the movies by Stanley Cavell, and I think I'm lucky to be reading it at this very moment.

Interviewer: I'm tempted to ask you about surrealism, but I don't want to burden you with the responsibility.

Strand: I don't know much about surrealism.

Interviewer: I'm glad to hear you say that.

Strand: My attraction to surrealism, really, is not through surrealist poetry, which I've read a bit of and have translated some of, and don't really approve of. And even that great surrealist novel *Nadja* I found really quite boring. I'm much more interested in surrealist art—some of the collages of Max Ernst, or some of the paintings of DeChirico or Delvaux even, that sort of thing. Magritte is a painter I'm fascinated with. But I like painters who sort of skirt the edge, who aren't surrealists . . . Balthus, say, or Hopper.

Interviewer: That's what I meant. I didn't mean the surrealist movement, *per se*, but the technique itself. There is that aura about your poems. They have this echo, to me (without sounding precious about it), they do leave something, as being what I would call surreal.

Strand: I would sometimes refuse to make a distinction between the realistically observed and the imagined, and I . . .

Interviewer: Well, maybe that's the surreality I'm talking about.

Strand: Yes, well they both have equal power in my life. They both coexist and at almost any time I find myself wandering and doing other things while I'm in a room, sitting in a chair. I mean, I can be here and in France at the same moment. That's a banal way of saying it, but . . .

Interviewer: That double-self, that other self, of course, was everything in your work too, and everybody talks about that. (I get a little tired of it myself, reading this sense of self and anti-self, or whatever it is that the critics talk about.) But is what you are taling about something like that early scene in Updike's *The Centaur*, where the man goes in to teach the science class, and suddenly it becomes this kind of mixture of reality of nonreality, with the imagined activities of all these kids in there?

Strand: But it's not, it's not only that, you know. It's that I myself am an imagined character.

Interviewer: Okay, I like that better than what people have been saying it was. Imagined by yourself?

Strand: Well sure, and there's evidence of that, I mean in a concrete way, in dreams; but I also have an idea of myself which is not myself, you know.

Interviewer: In which that voice on the tape won't be true to either.

Strand: Yes, well there's always something . . . it's hard to talk about . . . one has a sense of parts of a life—we were talking about metaphor and simile before—and I have the feeling that I am a metaphor for my own being . . . The sense of self I have is coordinated and related in ways that depend on a high degree of selection. It is a chosen self. The way memory is chosen. But the raw self is me, too, just as I am also much more than I choose to remember at any given time. I'm in touch with only a small portion of my experience at any one time and this gives my life as it is verbalized an artificiality that experientially it doesn't have. Also, it could be said, I suppose, that the artificiality is real because it is all we know for sure. The rest is supposition—and may be metaphorical: that is, the true self may reside in the unremembered, unorganized, unthought-of. This would be a self defined by absence, and negatively reinforced. All I suppose I'm saying is that we know so little that what we do know in talking about the self seems hopelessly reductive and one-sided. One-sided in favor of perpetuating a self that will survive because it maintains the illusion of self-control.

Interviewer: That is the voice of the poems, is that what you're saying? Or are there several of these in several poems?

Strand: I would say . . . yes. But it doesn't have to be, you know. In a sense, Wordsworth's use of himself in the "Prelude" is kind of a metaphorical —I mean, you know, it's a self which is created out of, out of a vague feeling about self. It's not Wordsworth himself. If you're going to write about yourself and you sit down and begin a poem, you would be some kind of funky journalist if you said "I am Mark Strand, and I'm five foot two and eyes are blue".

Interviewer: But poets have done that, several recent ones have, you know, tried to speak to themselves directly in the poem, with the name and address, as it were, and so forth.

Strand: Well, that . . . you know, that's boring.

Interviewer: Yes, it is. I think it is.

Strand: I don't think writing about oneself need be a confession. I don't consider myself confessional, only because the "self" is an imagined "self". I mean it's not a notation on the actual self. You know, there's a difference between talking about the moccasins you sew or the pills you take and—you become a journalist after the fact of your life, in that respect. I mean most confessional poetry is very specific; there is no attempt to mythify the self. And I think that, perhaps, that's what I'm doing: creating a mythology of self.

Interviewer: Howard speaks of—not visionary, but he used the word vision, it's a construction from the word vision—and he goes back to it again and again in that piece he's done on you. And there is that great sense, I think in all your work, of a construct or a total metaphor, or of a total metaphysic, if you will, being addressed.

Strand: Well, largely through reading Wordsworth, I have a belief in the absorbing emblem of the self (that's a monstrous phrase) as a poetical possibility.

Interviewer: That's a great phrase. I'm not sure. I may have to think about it, of course, but it's kind of a beautiful phrase.

Strand: I mean the self in a sense is all we have left.

Interviewer: That's what your poems are, reductions, not retreats, but reductions—as if we had come down to this and it's all there is left.

Strand: Yes.

A Reading List

GENERAL NOTE:

The following lists include the titles of books which have been quoted from or referred to in each of the essays. Occasionally some extra references have been added. Criticism of the poetry of the 'sixties is perforce in an early stage. Of the poets studied here only Lowell so far has given birth to a critical industry, producing several full-length books—none, so far, very exciting. We may expect the same treatment to be given Plath and Berryman. Of more general studies the most useful (simply because it is so comprehensive) is Richard Howard's *Alone With America: Essays on the Art of Poetry in the United States since 1950* (New York: Atheneum, 1969). The prose style is regrettable, but the range is as one would wish. Among Howard's forty-one essays are pieces on many of the poets examined in the present volume: Ashbery, Bly, Dickey, Kinnel, Levertov, Merwin, O'Hara, Plath, Rich, Sexton, Snyder, Strand and Wright. The book also contains a useful bibliography. References are to American editions. British editions are indicated where they exist.

APPOINTMENTS WITH TIME: ROBERT LOWELL'S POETRY THROUGH THE "NOTEBOOKS"

Books by Robert Lowell: those marked * are published by **Faber & Faber**, London.
Land of Unlikeness. Cummington, Mass.: The Cummington Press. 1944.
Lord Weary's Castle. New York: Harcourt Brace. 1946.
The Mills of the Kavanaughs. New York: Harcourt Brace. 1951.
**Life Studies*. New York: Farrar, Straus & Cudahy. 1959.
**Imitations*. New York: Farrar, Straus & Cudahy. 1961.
**For the Union Dead*. New York: Farrar, Straus & Giroux. 1964.
**Near the Ocean*. New York: Farrar, Straus & Giroux. 1967.
**The Old Glory* (verse plays). New York: Farrar, Straus & Giroux. 1968.
Notebook 1967–1968. New York: Farrar, Straus & Giroux. 1969.
**Notebook*. (3rd edition revised and expanded) New York: Farrar, Straus & Giroux. 1970.

HOW TO READ BERRYMAN'S DREAM SONGS

Books by John Berryman: those marked * are published by **Faber & Faber**, London.
Short Poems. New York: Farrar, Straus & Giroux. 1967. (Includes the

previously published volumes *The Dispossessed* and *His Thought Made Pockets & the Plane Buckt*, together with the poem *Formal Elegy*.)
*Homage to Mistress Bradstreet. New York: Farrar, Straus & Giroux. 1956.
*77 Dream Songs. New York: Farrar, Straus & Giroux. 1964.
*Berryman's Sonnets. New York: Farrar, Straus & Giroux. 1967.
*His Toy, His Dream, His Rest. New York: Farrar, Straus & Giroux. 1968.
The Dream Songs. New York: Farrar, Straus & Giroux. 1969.
*Love & Fame. New York: Farrar, Straus & Giroux. 1970.
*Delusions, Etc. New York: Farrar, Straus & Giroux. 1972.

THE POETRY OF PROTEST

The poems quoted from in this essay appear in the following books:
Robert Frost, *In the Clearing*. New York: Holt, Rinehart & Winston. 1962.
Walter Lowenfels, ed. *Where Is Vietnam? American Poets Respond*. New York: Anchor Books. 1967.
Denise Levertov, *Relearning the Alphabet*. New York: New Directions. 1970. **Cape**, 1970.
Robert Lowell, *Near the Ocean*. New York: Farrar, Straus & Giroux. 1967. **Faber & Faber**.
Allen Ginsberg, *Howl and Other Poems*. San Francisco: City Light Books. 1956.
Robert Duncan, *Bending the Bow*. New York: New Directions. 1968. **Cape**, 1971.
Robert Bly, *The Teeth-Mother Naked at Last*. San Francisco: City Lights Books. 1970.
Adrienne Rich, *Leaflets*. New York: W. W. Norton. 1969. **Chatto & Windus**, 1972.

Addenda:

Two other typical anthologies of protest poetry are *The Writing on the Wall*, ed. Walter Lowenfels (Garden City, N.Y.: Doubleday, 1969) and *Campfires of the Resistance*, ed. Todd Gitlin (Indianapolis: Bobbs-Merrill, 1971).
Since this essay was written, poetry written by veterans returning from Vietnam has begun to be published. Two notable books are *Obscenities*, by Michael Casey (New Haven: Yale University Press, 1972) and the anthology *Winning Hearts and Minds: War Poems by Vietnam Veterans*, ed. Larry Rothman, Jan Barry and Basil T. Paquet (New York: McGraw-Hill, 1971).

LANGUAGE AGAINST ITSELF: THE MIDDLE GENERATION OF CONTEMPORARY POETS

Robert Bly.
Silence in the Snowy Fields. Middletown, Conn.: Wesleyan University Press. 1962. **Cape**, 1967.

The Light Around the Body. New York: Harper & Row. 1967. **Rapp & Whiting,** 1968.
"Looking for Dragon Smoke," in Berg and Mezey, *Naked Poetry*, Bobbs-Merrill, 1969.

Galway Kinnell.
What a Kingdom It Was. Boston: Houghton Mifflin. 1960.
Flower Herding on Mount Monadnock. Boston: Houghton Mifflin. 1964.
Body Rags. Boston: Houghton Mifflin. 1968. **Rapp & Whiting,** 1969.
The Book of Nightmares. Boston: Houghton Mifflin. 1971.

W. S. Merwin. (I omit Mr. Merwin's early books, which in no way enter my argument.)
The Moving Target. New York: Atheneum. 1963. **Rupert Hart Davis,** 1963.
The Lice. New York: Atheneum. 1967. **Rupert Hart Davis,** 1967.
The Carrier of Ladders. New York: Atheneum. 1970.

Gary Snyder.
Myths & Texts. Totem-Corinth Books, 1960.
Six Sections from Mountains and Rivers without End, Four Seasons Foundation, 1965. **Fulcrum,** 1967.
The Back Country. New York: New Directions. 1968. **Fulcrum,** 1967.
Earth House Hold: Technical Notes & Queries to Fellow Dharma Revolutionaries. New York: New Directions. 1969. **Cape,** 1970. (All prose quotations come from the included essay, "Poetry and the Primitive".)
Regarding Wave. New York: New Directions. 1970. **Fulcrum,** 1971.

James Wright.
The Green Wall. New Haven: Yale University Press. 1957.
Saint Judas. Middleton, Conn.: Wesleyan University Press. 1959.
The Branch Will Not Break. Middleton, Conn.: Wesleyan University Press. 1963.
Shall We Gather at the River. Middleton, Conn.: Wesleyan University Press. 1968. **Rapp & Whiting,** 1969.
Collected Poems. Middleton, Conn.: Wesleyan University Press. 1971.

DIMINISHING RETURNS: THE WRITINGS OF W. S. MERWIN

Books by W. S. Merwin
A Mask for Janus. New Haven: Yale University Press. 1952.
The Dancing Bears. New Haven: Yale University Press. 1954.
Green With Beasts. London: Rupert Hart-Davis. 1956.
The Drunk in the Furnace. New York: The Macmillan Company. 1960. **Rupert Hart Davis,** 1960.
The Moving Target. New York: Atheneum. 1963. **Rupert Hart Davis,** 1967.

The Lice. New York: Atheneum. 1967. **Rupert Hart Davis**, 1969.
The Carrier of Ladders. New York: Atheneum. 1970.
The Miner's Pale Children. New York: Atheneum. 1970.

JOHN ASHBERY: THE CHARITY OF THE HARD MOMENTS

Books by John Ashbery:
Some Trees. New Haven: Yale University Press. 1956.
The Tennis Court Oath. Middletown, Conn.: Wesleyan University Press. 1962.
Rivers and Mountains. New York: Holt, Rinehart and Winston. 1966.
The Double Dream of Spring. New York: Dutton. 1970.
Three Poems. New York: Viking Press. 1972.
Selected Poems. London: **Cape**. 1967.

FRANK O'HARA'S POETRY

Since this essay was written *The Collected Poems of Frank O'Hara*, edited by Donald Allen (New York, 1971) has been published by Alfred A. Knopf. O'Hara's poems, previously scattered through several small and hard-to-find selections are now most easily come by in this edition.

ADRIENNE RICH: THE POETICS OF CHANGE

Books by Adrienne Rich: those marked * are published by **Chatto & Windus,** London
A Change of World. New Haven: Yale University Press. 1951.
The Diamond Cutters & Other Poems. New York: Harper & Row. 1955.
*Snapshots of a Daughter-in-Law. New York: Harper & Row. 1963. Reprinted New York: W. W. Norton. 1967.
Necessities of Life. New York: W. W. Norton. 1966.
*Selected Poems. London: Chatto & Windus. 1967.
*Leaflets. New York: W. W. Norton. 1969.
The Will to Change. New York: W. W. Norton. 1971.
Diving into the Wreck. New York: W. W. Norton. 1973.

A NOTE ON JAMES DICKEY

Books by James Dickey:
Poems 1957–1967. Middletown, Conn.: Wesleyan University Press. 1967. **Rapp & Whiting,** 1968. (Includes most of the contents of the previously published books *Into the Stone, Drowning With Others, Helmets* and *Buckdancer's Choice*, together with additional poems.)
The Eye-Beaters, Blood, Victory, Madness, Buckhead and Mercy. Garden City, N.Y.: Doubleday. 1970.

From Babel to Byzantium: Poets and Poetry Now. New York: Farrar, Straus & Giroux. 1968. (Reviews and essays.)
Self-Interviews. Recorded and Edited by Barbara and James Reiss. Garden City, N.Y.: Doubleday. 1970.
Sorties. Garden City, N.Y.: Doubleday. 1971. (Journals and essays.)
Deliverance. Boston: Houghton Mifflin. 1970. **Hamish Hamilton**, 1970. (Novel.)

STARING FROM HER HOOD OF BONE: ADJUSTING TO SYLVIA PLATH

Books by Sylvia Plath: those marked * are published by **Faber & Faber**, London.
*The Colossus & Other Poems. New York: Knopf. 1962.
*Ariel. New York: Harper & Row. 1966.
*Crossing the Water. London: Faber & Faber. 1971.
*Winter Trees. New York: Harper & Row. 1972.
*The Bell Jar. New York: Harper & Row. 1971. (Novel.)

Critical studies:
Alvarez, A.: *The Savage God: A Study of Suicide*. New York: Random House. 1972. London: **Weidenfeld & Nicolson**, 1971.
Newman, Charles, ed.: *The Art of Sylvia Plath: A Symposium*. Bloomington, Ind.: Indiana University Press. 1970. London: **Faber & Faber**. 1970.

ANOTHER SIDE OF THIS LIFE: WOMEN AS POETS

Elizabeth Bishop: published by **Chatto & Windus**, London
The Complete Poems. New York: Farrar, Straus & Giroux. 1969.

Maxine Kumin:
Halfway. New York: Holt, Rinehart & Winston. 1961.
The Privilege. New York: Harper & Row. 1965.
The Nightmare Factory. New York: Harper & Row. 1970.
Up Country: Poems of New England, New and Selected. New York: Harper & Row. 1972.

Sylvia Plath: published by **Faber & Faber**, London.
Ariel. New York: Harper & Row. 1966.

Anne Sexton: those marked * are published by **Oxford University Press**, London.
To Bedlam and Part Way Back. Boston: Houghton Mifflin. 1960.
All My Pretty Ones. Boston: Houghton Mifflin. 1961.
*Live or Die. Boston: Houghton Mifflin. 1966.
*Love Poems. Boston: Houghton Mifflin. 1969.

Transformations. Boston: Houghton Mifflin. 1971.
The Book of Folly. Boston: Houghton Mifflin. 1972.

Mona Van Duyn:
Valentines to the Wide World. Iowa City: Cummington Press. 1958.
To See, To Take. New York: Atheneum. 1970.

JAMES TATE AND SIDNEY GOLDFARB AND THE INEXHAUSTIBLE
NATURE OF THE MURMUR

Books by James Tate:
The Lost Pilot. New Haven: Yale University Press. 1967.
The Oblivion Ha-Ha. Boston: Atlantic Monthly Press. 1970.
Absences. Boston: Atlantic Monthly Press. 1972.

Books by Sidney Goldfarb:
Speech, For Instance. New York: Farrar, Straus & Giroux. 1969.
Messages. New York: Farrar, Straus & Giroux. 1971.

A CONVERSATION WITH MARK STRAND

Books by Mark Strand:
Sleeping With One Eye Open. Iowa City: The Stone Wall Press. 1964.
Reasons for Moving. New York: Atheneum. 1968.
Darker. New York: Atheneum. 1970.
18 Poems from the Quechua. Translations. Halty Ferguson. 1972.

Contributors' Notes

JAMES ATLAS recently completed his studies as a Rhodes Scholar at New College, Oxford. He has edited an anthology, *Ten American Poets*, for Carcanet Press. His poems and reviews have appeared in *Poetry* and other magazines.

HAROLD BLOOM is a Professor of English at Yale. His many studies of the Romantic tradition include *Blake's Apocalypse*, *Yeats*, *The Ringers in the Tower*, and, most recently, *The Anxiety of Influence: A Theory of Poetry*.

FRANCES FERGUSON is an Assistant Professor of English at the Johns Hopkins University. She attended Yale Graduate School where she wrote a dissertation on Wordsworth. A somewhat revised version of her essay in this book will appear in *Partisan Review*.

ALBERT GELPI's books are *Emily Dickinson: The Mind of the Poet* and *The Poet in America: 1650 to the Present*, an anthology with notes and introductions. He is writing a critical study of American poetry, tracing strands of tradition through a detailed consideration of fifteen poets. He teaches American literature at Stanford University.

SUSAN HOLAHAN has been teaching English at Yale (mostly contemporary literature and writing) on and off since 1966.

J. D. MCCLATCHY teaches English at La Salle College, Philadelphia. His poems, stories, translations, articles and reviews have appeared in many journals. Currently he is completing his doctoral dissertation at Yale on contemporary confessional poetry.

EDWARD MENDELSON was co-author of the new edition of *W. H. Auden: A Bibliography* and made the selection for *Forewords and Afterwords*, a volume of Auden's critical pieces. He is now writing a critical study, *Auden's Landscape*, and essays on Thomas Pynchon and other novelists. He teaches twentieth century literature at Yale.

MICHAEL MESIC, who studied at the University of Chicago, remains in that city as Assistant Editor of *Poetry*. *New Arrival*, a small collection of poems, was published in 1971 by the Bergman Gallery of the U. of C. in a limited edition of 100 copies.

PEGGY RIZZA was Poetry Editor of the *Harvard Advocate* for two years and studied writing with Robert Lowell and Elizabeth Bishop. Her poems have appeared in *Poetry Miscellany*, *Chicago Review* and elsewhere. She is now a student at Harvard Divinity School.

R. D. ROSEN was a Poetry Editor of the *Harvard Advocate*. He now writes and edits for the Boston *Phoenix*, a weekly. His collection of essays on post-modern culture, *Me and My Friends, We No Longer Profess Any Graces*, appeared in 1971. He is writing a novel.

ROBERT B. SHAW has published two booklets of poems, *In Witness* (Anvil Press Poetry) and *Curious Questions* (Carcanet Press). He studied writing at Harvard with Robert Fitzgerald and Robert Lowell. He is now a doctoral candidate at Yale.

ALAN WILLIAMSON teaches at the University of Virginia. His poems have appeared in *The Yale Review*, *Poetry*, *The New Yorker*, and other magazines. He was recently awarded a grant by the National Endowment for the Arts. His study of the political poetry of Robert Lowell is now seeking a publisher.

Index